A Great Big VISUAL HUG

Andrés J. Colmenares

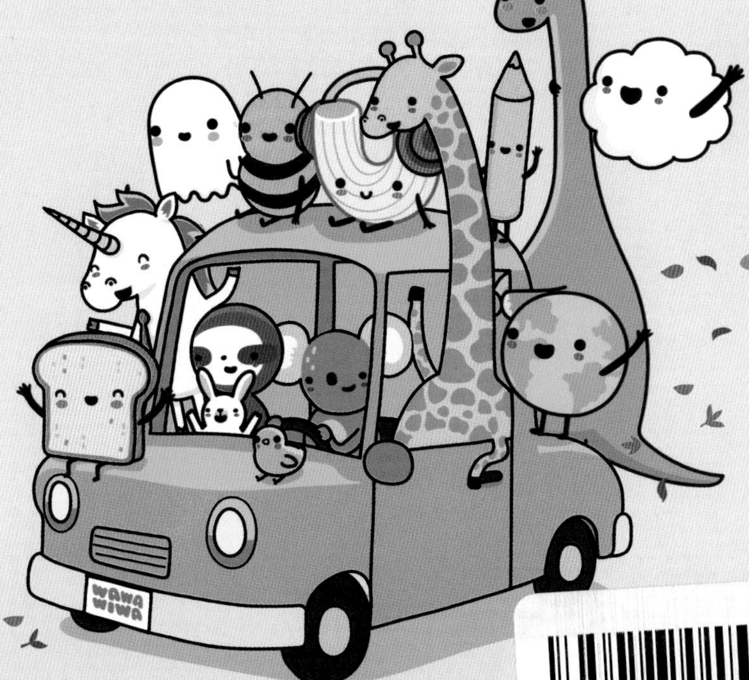
WAWA
WIWA

Andrews McMeel
PUBLISHING®

Andrews McMeel Publishing
a division of Andrews McMeel Universal
1130 Walnut Street, Kansas City, Missouri 64106

24 25 26 27 28 RLP 10 9 8 7 6 5 4 3 2 1

ISBN: 978-1-5248-9388-0

Library of Congress Control Number: 2024931866

www.andrewsmcmeel.com

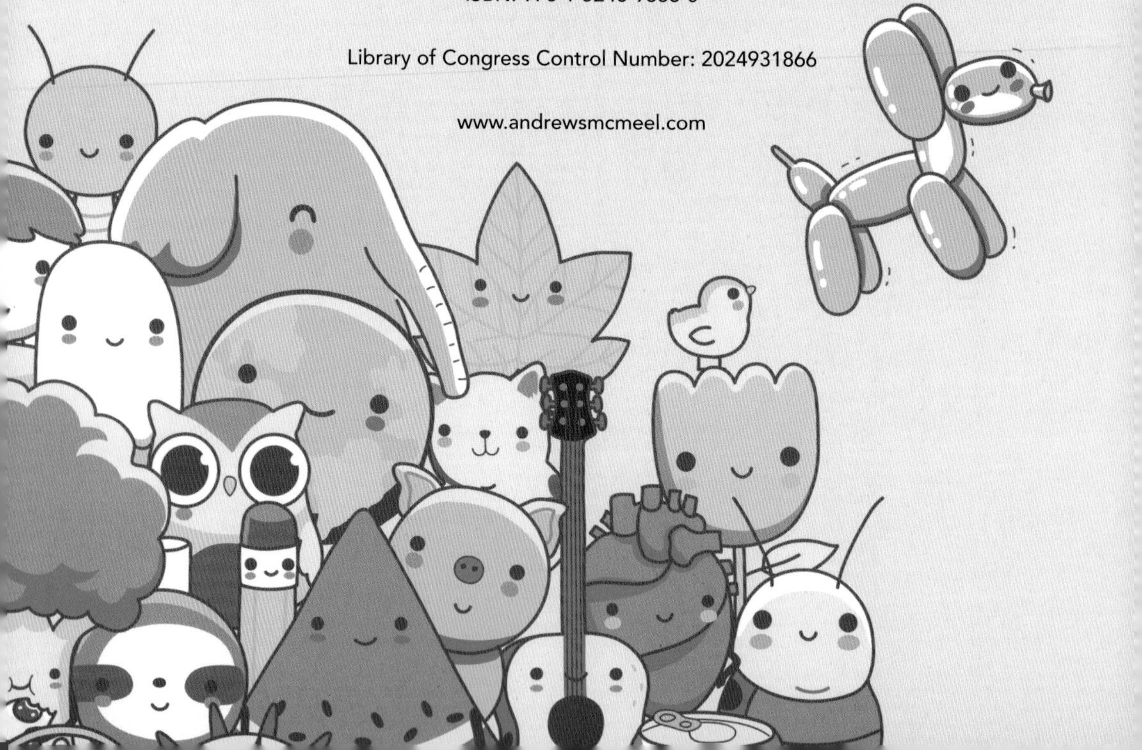

Hey, friends! The following compilation of comics has been a labor of love since 2009, when this journey began as a mere hobby. A time when the ancient art of blending humor and illustration were like hidden treasures waiting to be unearthed. There were no online courses, no easy shortcuts. All I had was passion, a tremendous admiration for other comic creators, and likes from my mom and a few friends. Hours upon hours were devoted to sketching in my spare moments.

As the years rolled by, this innocent project transformed into something truly special. It became a brand, and each comic meant a few seconds of delight for those in search of lighthearted moments in a busy world. Then, in 2016, something magical happened. Viviana, a fellow enthusiast of all things funny and wholesome, entered my life and the project. With her business knowledge, creative flair, and boundless energy (she's always dancing), she became an integral part of Wawawiwa. Together, we forged a partnership that started a family and fueled the growth of the brand, adding new layers of humor and heart to every comic strip created.

So, dear readers, it is safe now to unbuckle your seat belts and sail through pages full of our favorite comics, your most-liked ones, plus many new panels! These comics are a testament to the power of passion, dedication, and the joy that can be found in the simple act of sharing a smile. We truly hope that these comics warm your heart and, most importantly, make you feel hugged.

Enjoy!
-Andrés

Read me before sleep.

Other books by Andrés J. Colmenares

When Sharks Attack with Kindness
Peculiar Woods: The Ancient Underwater City
Peculiar Woods: The Mystery of the Intelligents

GOODBYE, MY FRIEND.

YOU CALL THAT A
HUG?

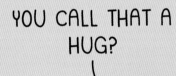

1

LIFE CYCLE OF PASTA

HE TOLD ME I HAD
BAD BREATH
AND GAVE ME MENTOS.

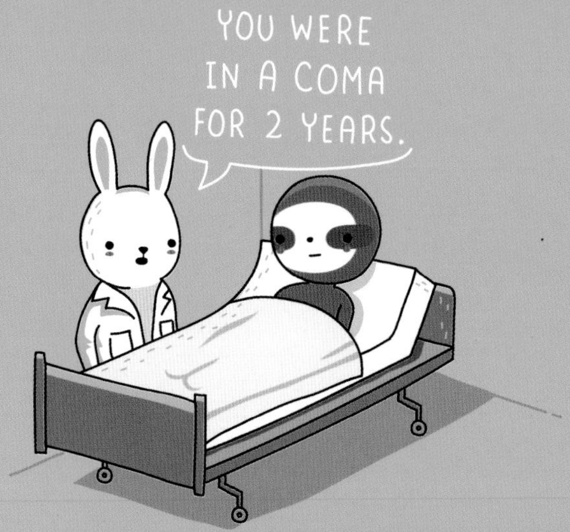
YOU WERE IN A COMA FOR 2 YEARS.

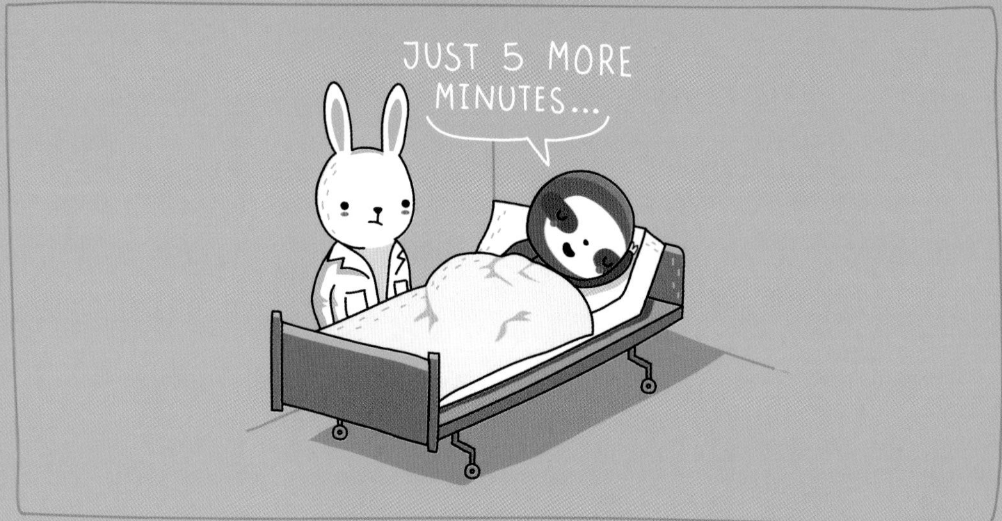
JUST 5 MORE MINUTES...

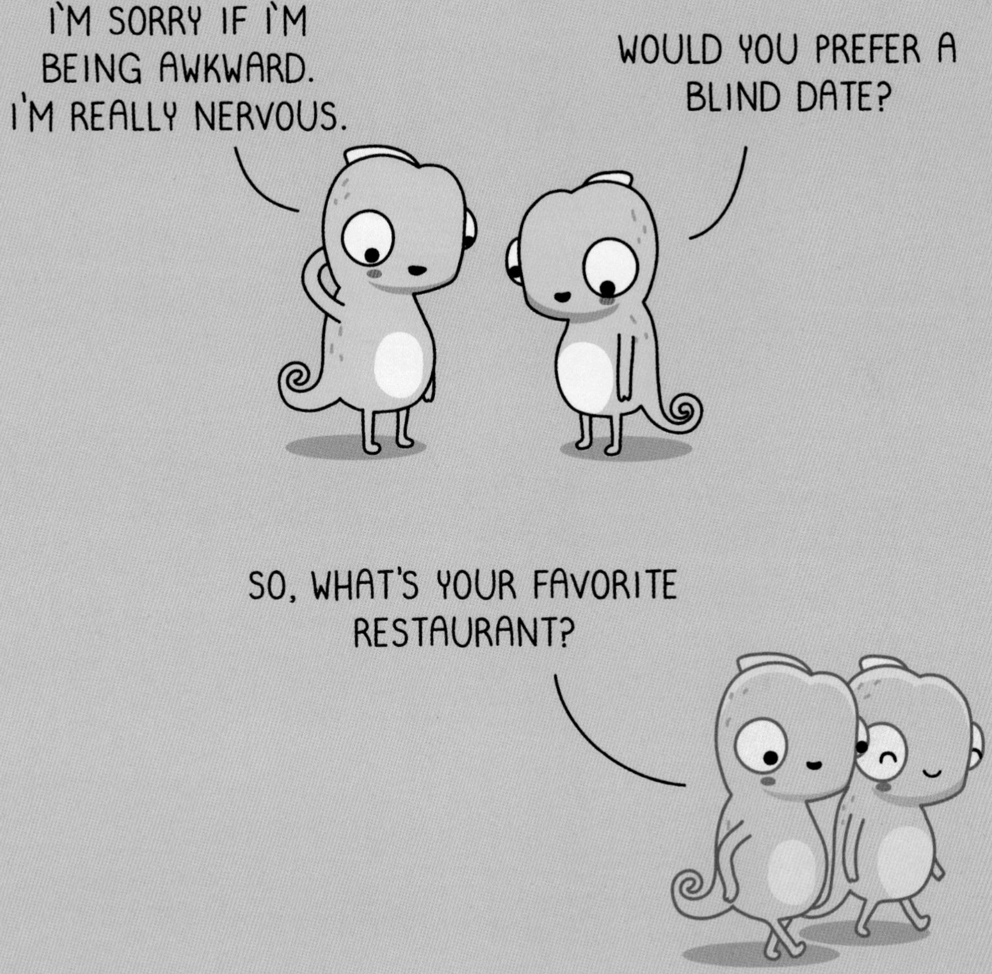
I'M SORRY IF I'M BEING AWKWARD. I'M REALLY NERVOUS.
WOULD YOU PREFER A BLIND DATE?
SO, WHAT'S YOUR FAVORITE RESTAURANT?

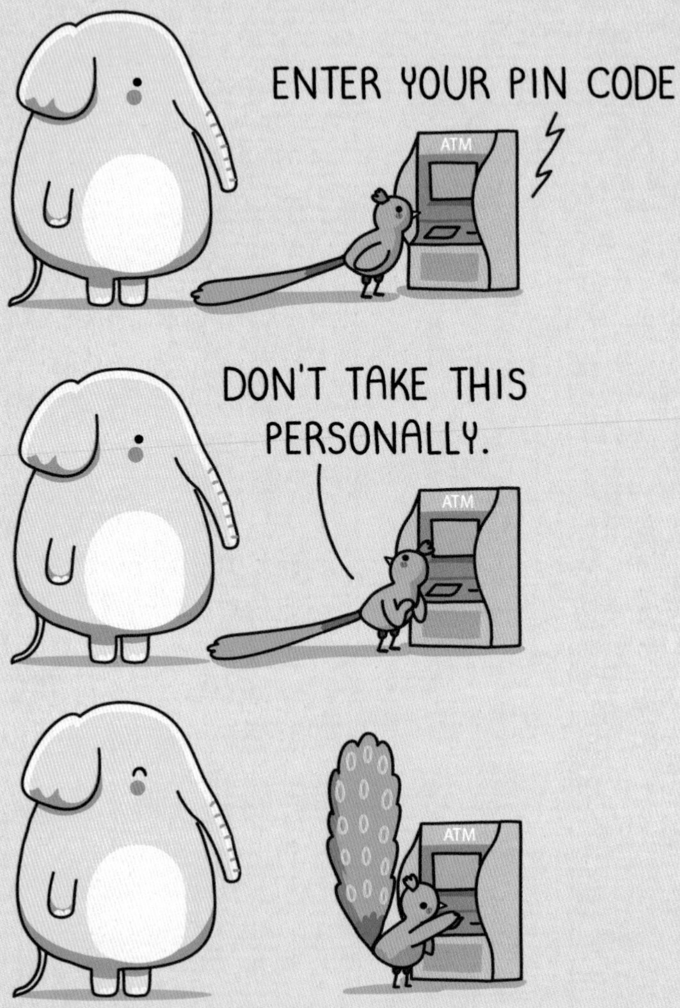
ENTER YOUR PIN CODE
ATM
DON'T TAKE THIS PERSONALLY.
ATM
ATM

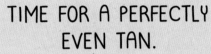
TIME FOR A PERFECTLY
EVEN TAN.

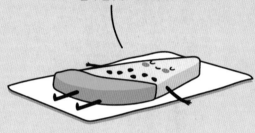

I DIDN'T TAKE
MY SHORTS OFF!

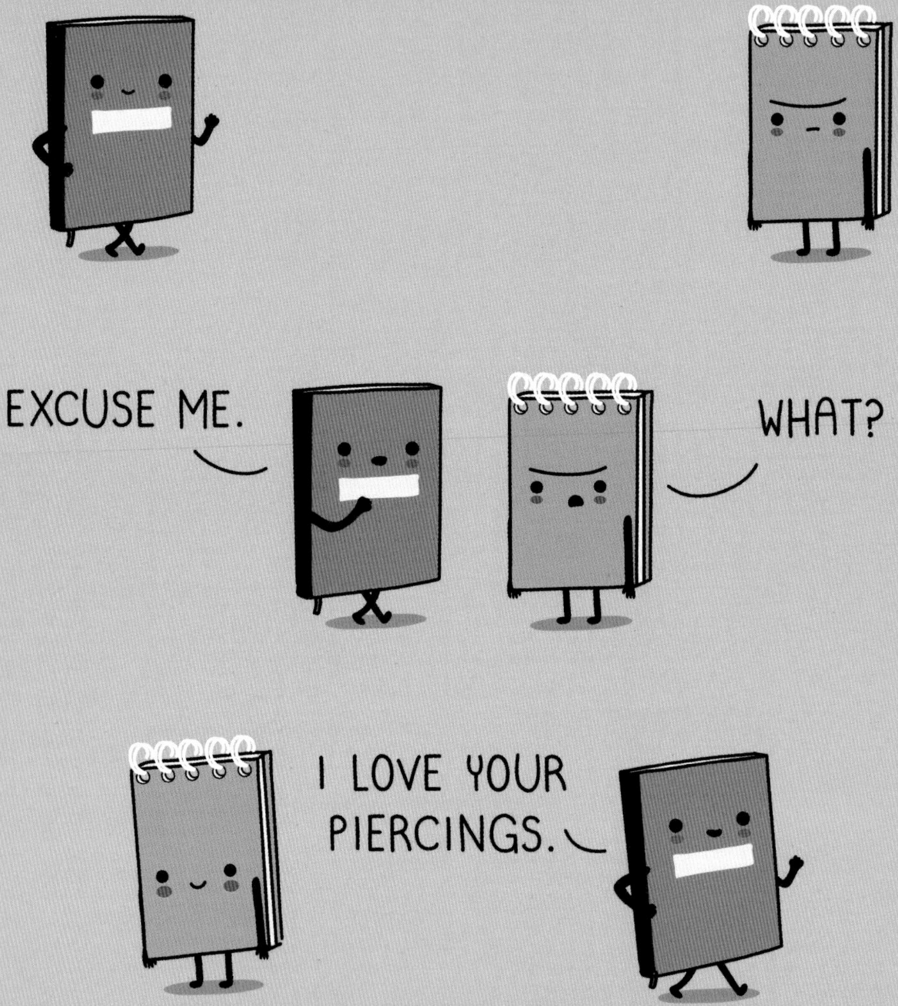
EXCUSE ME.
WHAT?
I LOVE YOUR PIERCINGS.

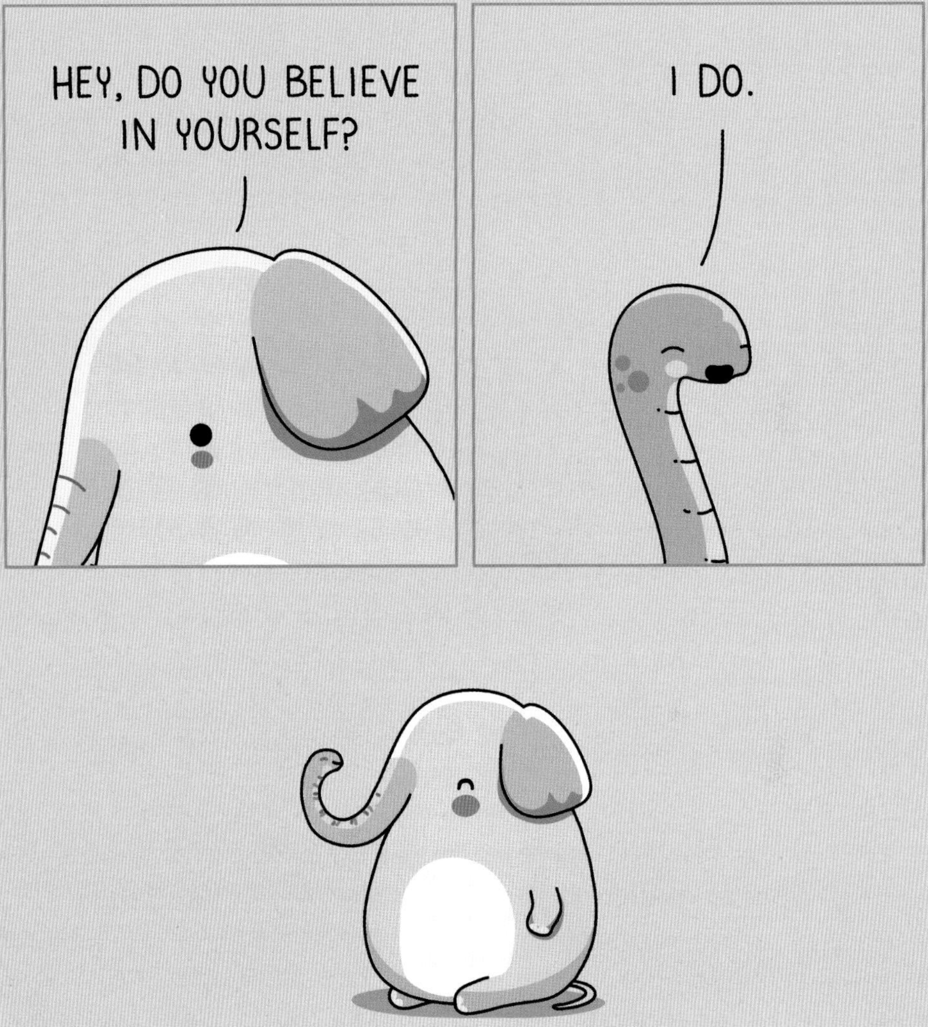
HEY, DO YOU BELIEVE IN YOURSELF?
I DO.

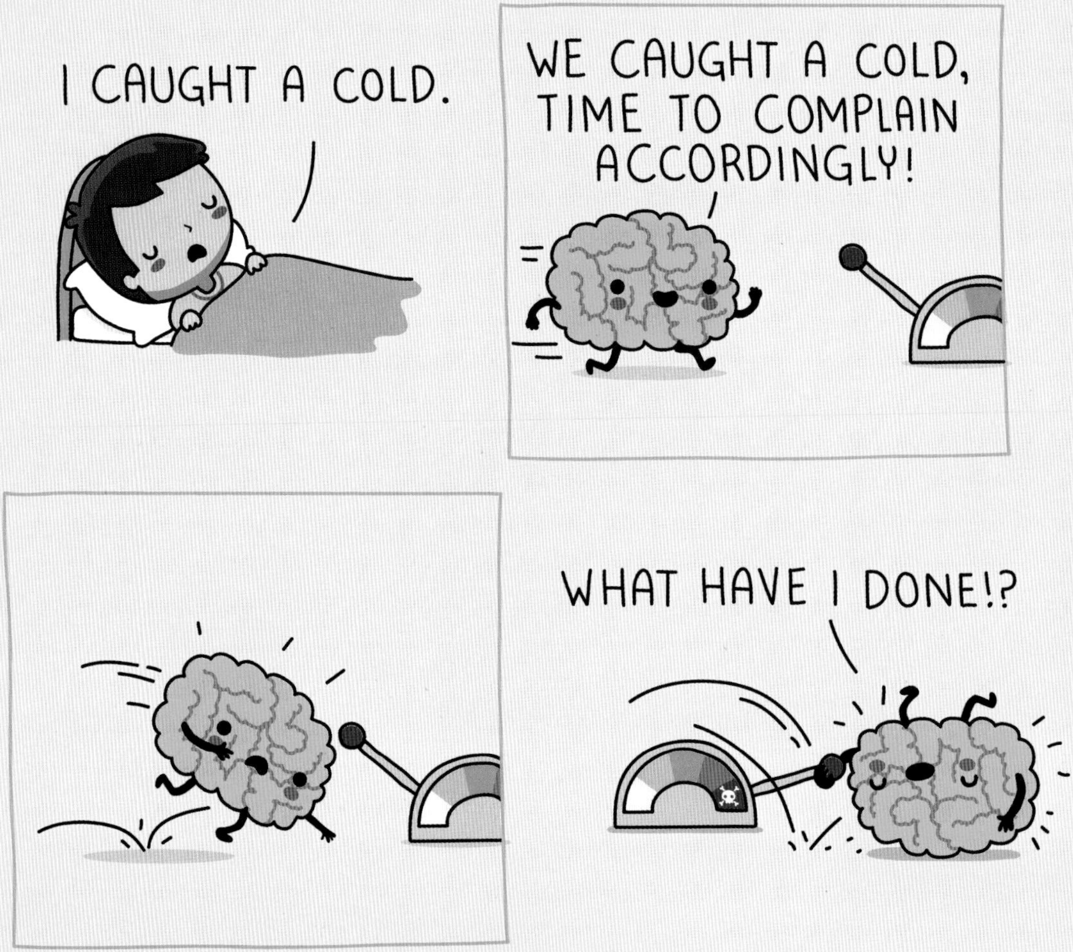
I CAUGHT A COLD.
WE CAUGHT A COLD, TIME TO COMPLAIN ACCORDINGLY!
WHAT HAVE I DONE!?

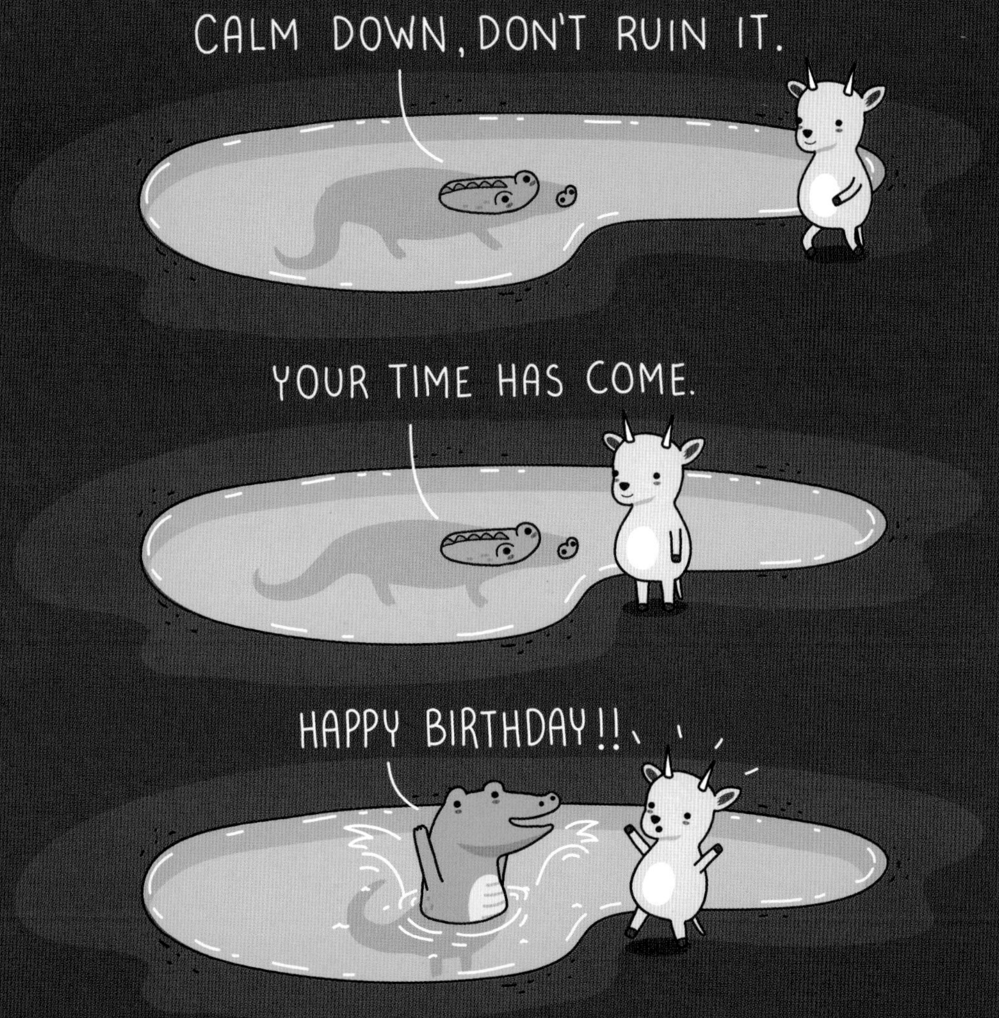
CALM DOWN, DON'T RUIN IT.
YOUR TIME HAS COME.
HAPPY BIRTHDAY!!

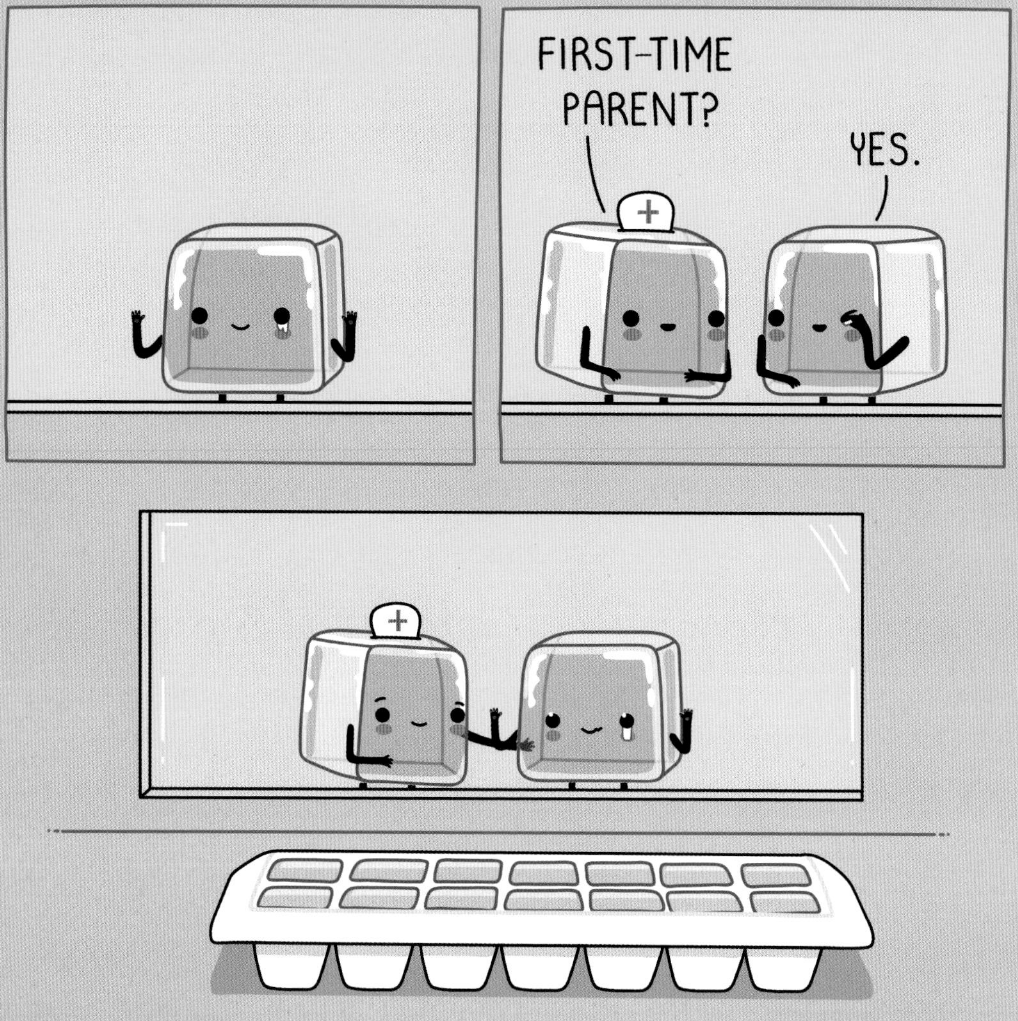
FIRST-TIME PARENT?
YES.

I BET DAD IS GONNA TELL THE SAME JOKE HE TELLS EVERY YEAR.

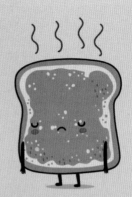

IT'S MY FAVORITE.

WHO'S READY FOR THE NEW YEAR'S TOAST!?

13

WE WELCOME THE NEW BABY! THERE'S
ENOUGH ROOM IN HERE FOR ALL OF US.

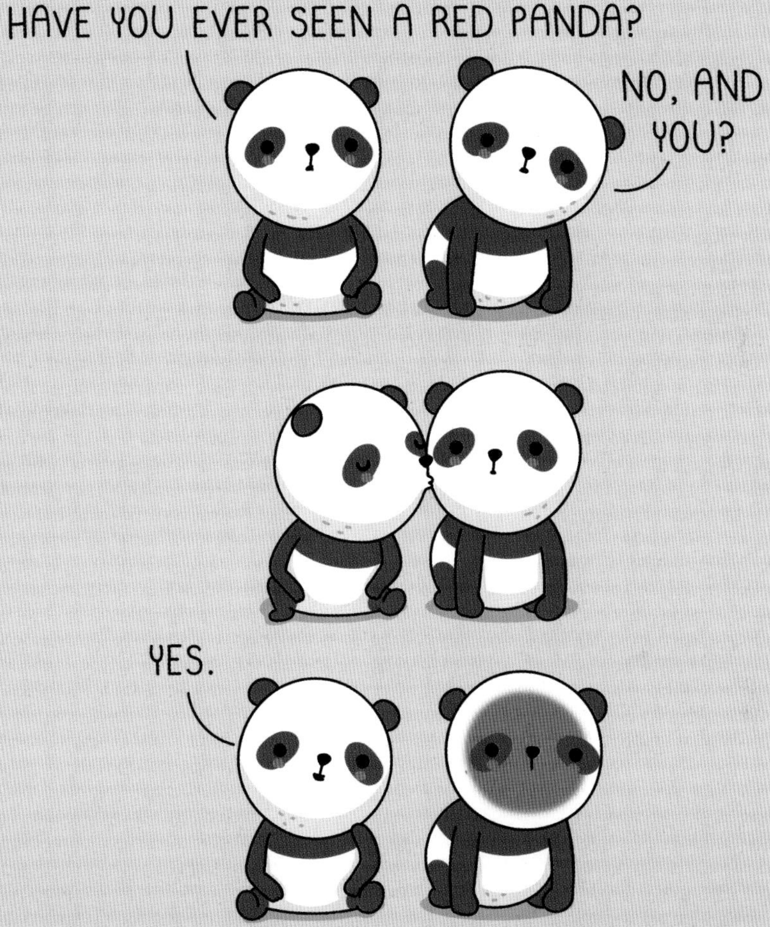
HAVE YOU EVER SEEN A RED PANDA?
NO, AND YOU?
YES.

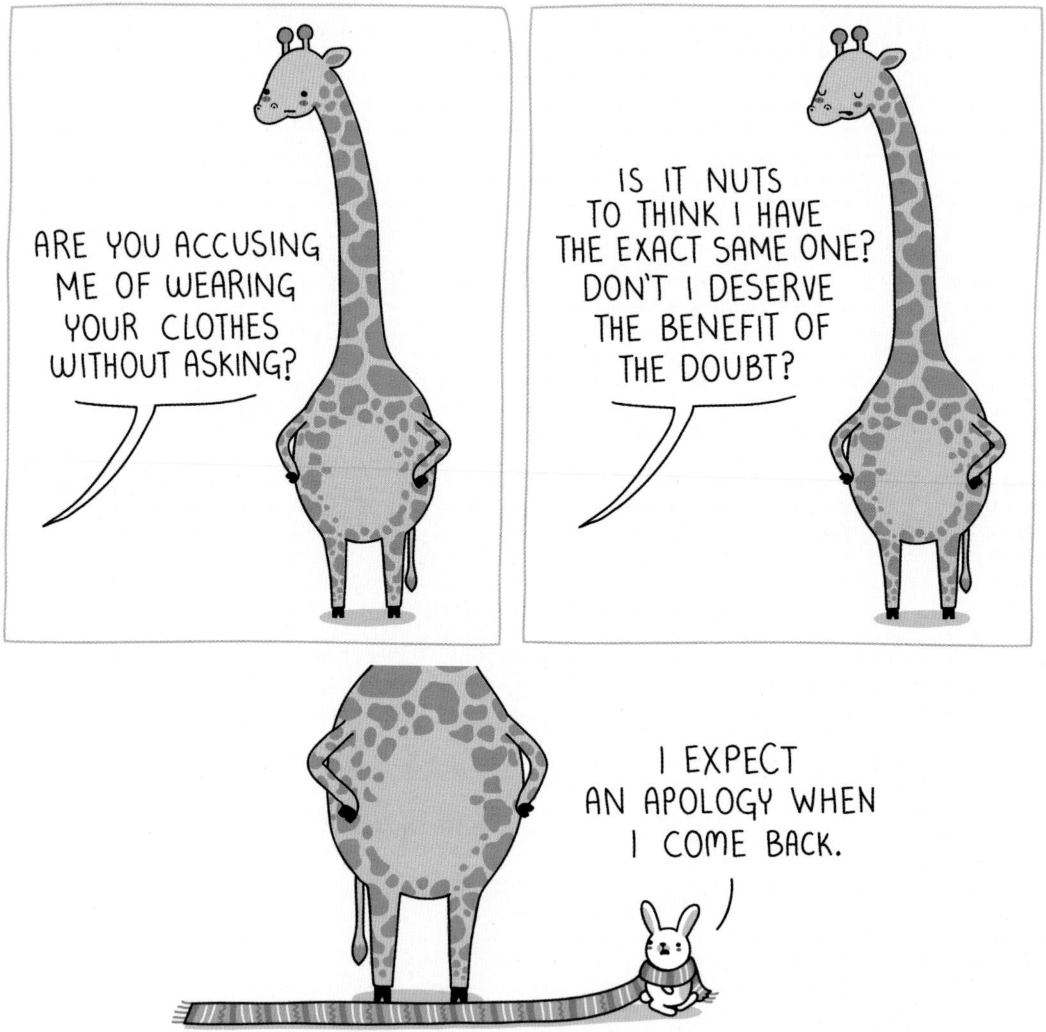
ARE YOU ACCUSING ME OF WEARING YOUR CLOTHES WITHOUT ASKING?
IS IT NUTS TO THINK I HAVE THE EXACT SAME ONE? DON'T I DESERVE THE BENEFIT OF THE DOUBT?
I EXPECT AN APOLOGY WHEN I COME BACK.

WHAT ARE YOU DOING?
THIS IS HOW I WATCH HORROR MOVIES.

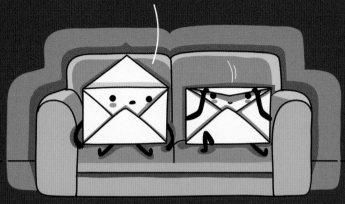

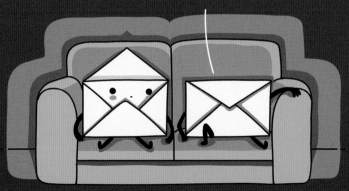

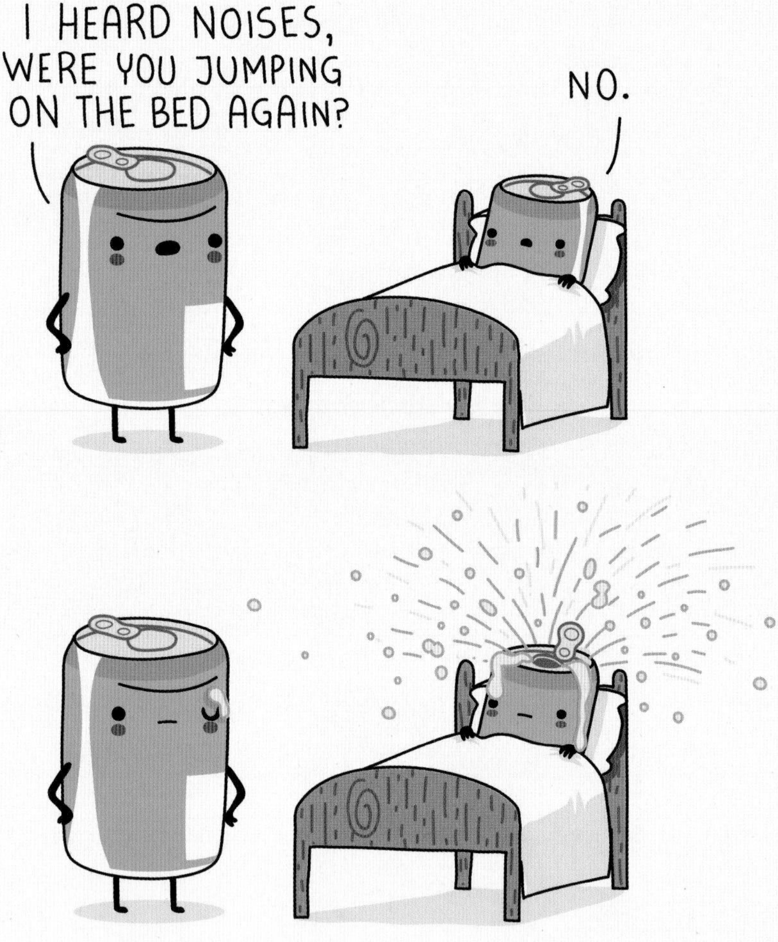
I HEARD NOISES, WERE YOU JUMPING ON THE BED AGAIN?
NO.

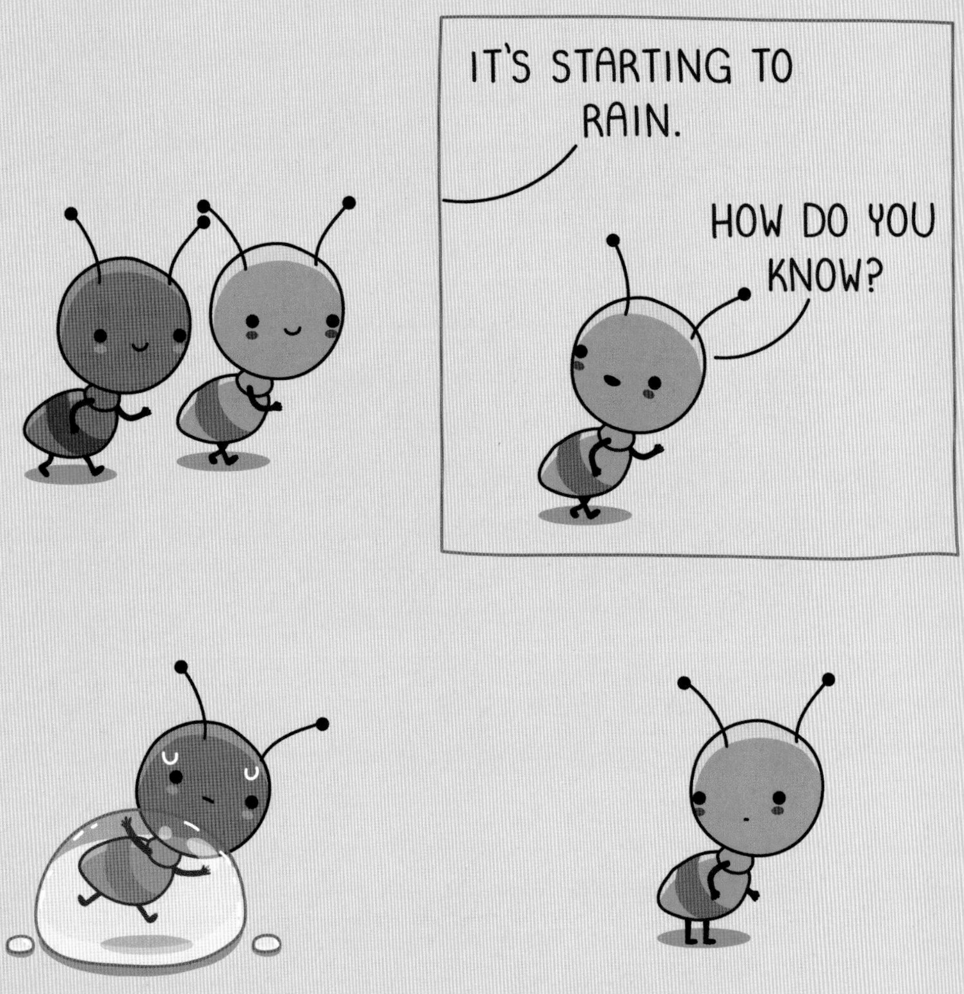
IT'S STARTING TO RAIN.
HOW DO YOU KNOW?

MOM, DAD!
I GOT A TATTOO.
DO YOU LIKE IT?

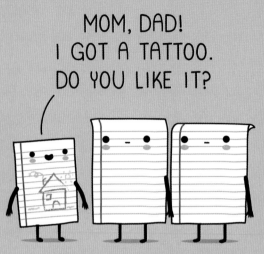

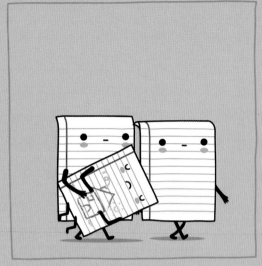

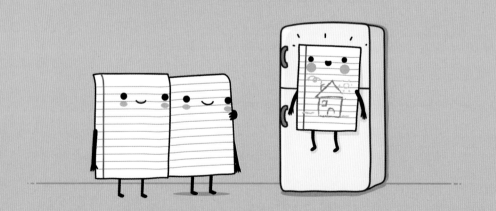

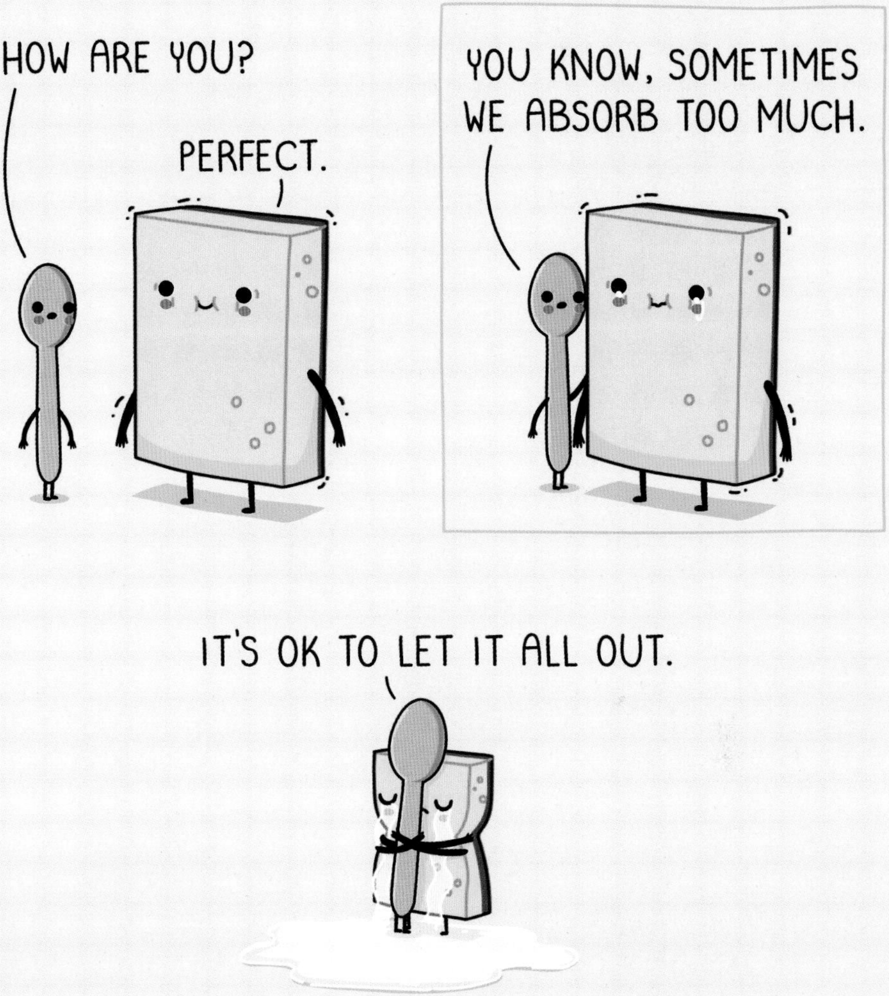
HOW ARE YOU?
PERFECT.
YOU KNOW, SOMETIMES WE ABSORB TOO MUCH.
IT'S OK TO LET IT ALL OUT.

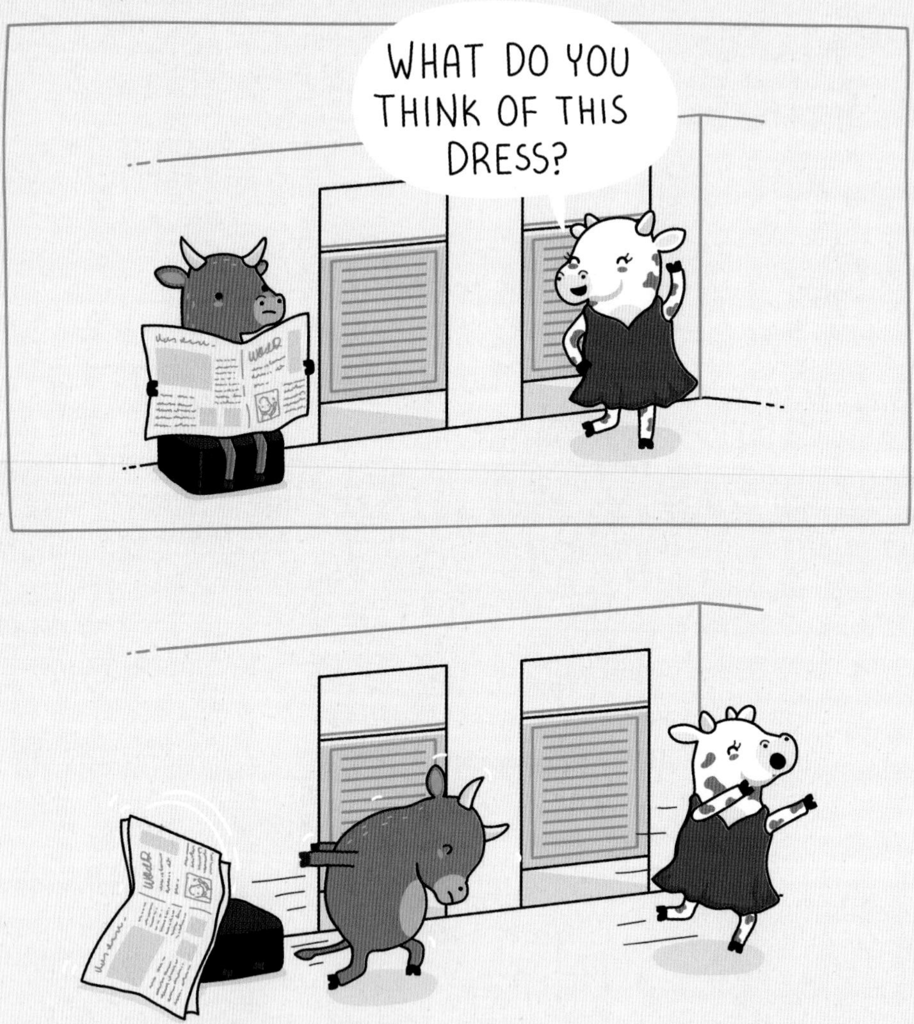
WHAT DO YOU THINK OF THIS DRESS?

IT MIGHT TAKE SOME TIME AND EFFORT.

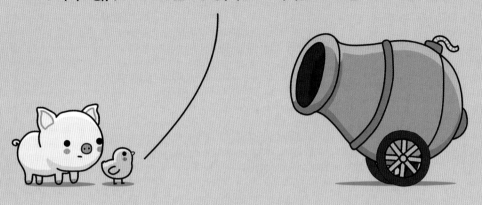

BUT THINGS
CAN CHANGE.

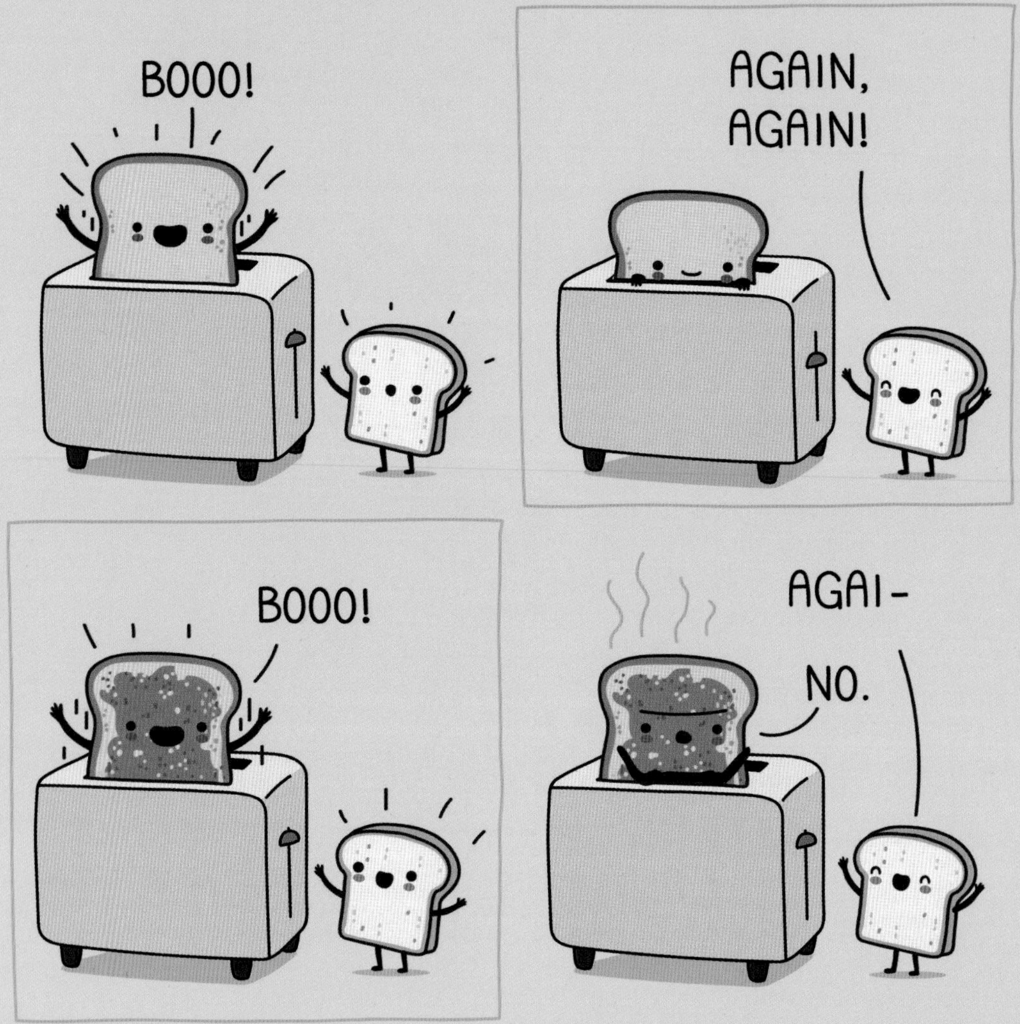
BOOO!
AGAIN, AGAIN!
BOOO!
AGAI-
NO.

TIPS TO KEEP YOUR DOG HAPPY

SHOW HIM YOUR LOVE

PLAY WITH HIM

INVITE HIM TO CLEAN THOSE HARD TO REACH SPOTS.

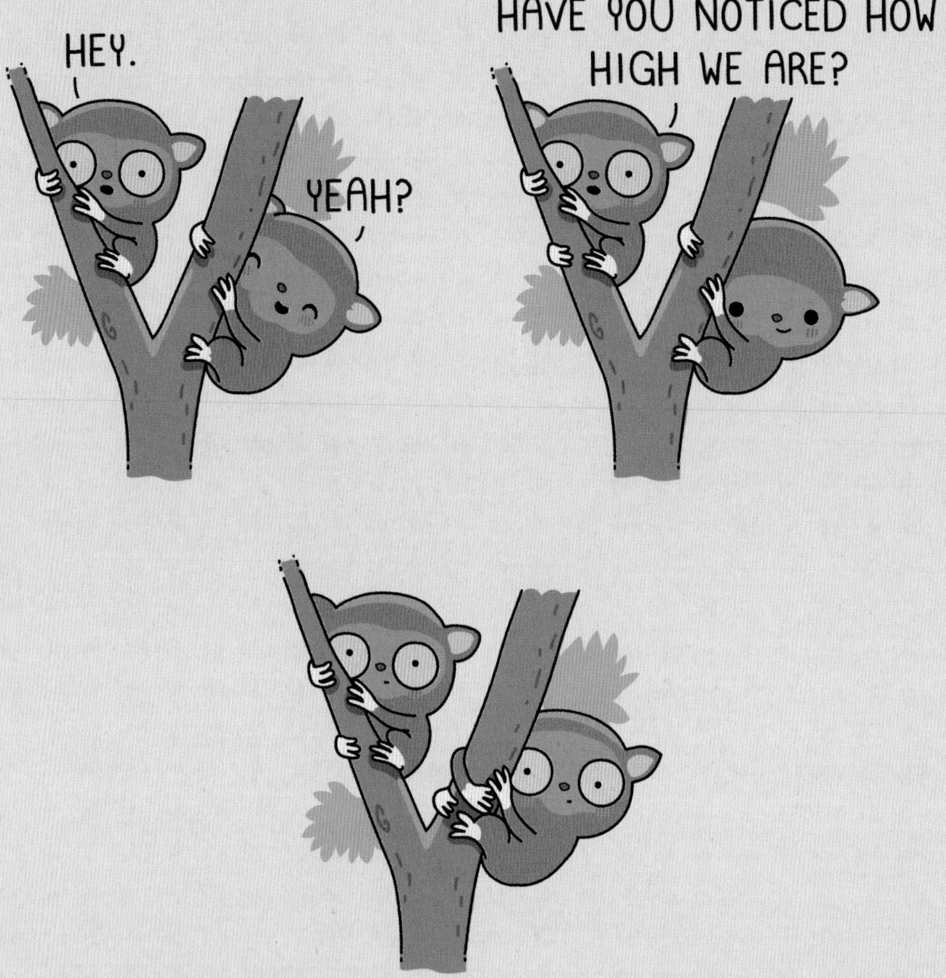
HEY.
YEAH?
HAVE YOU NOTICED HOW HIGH WE ARE?

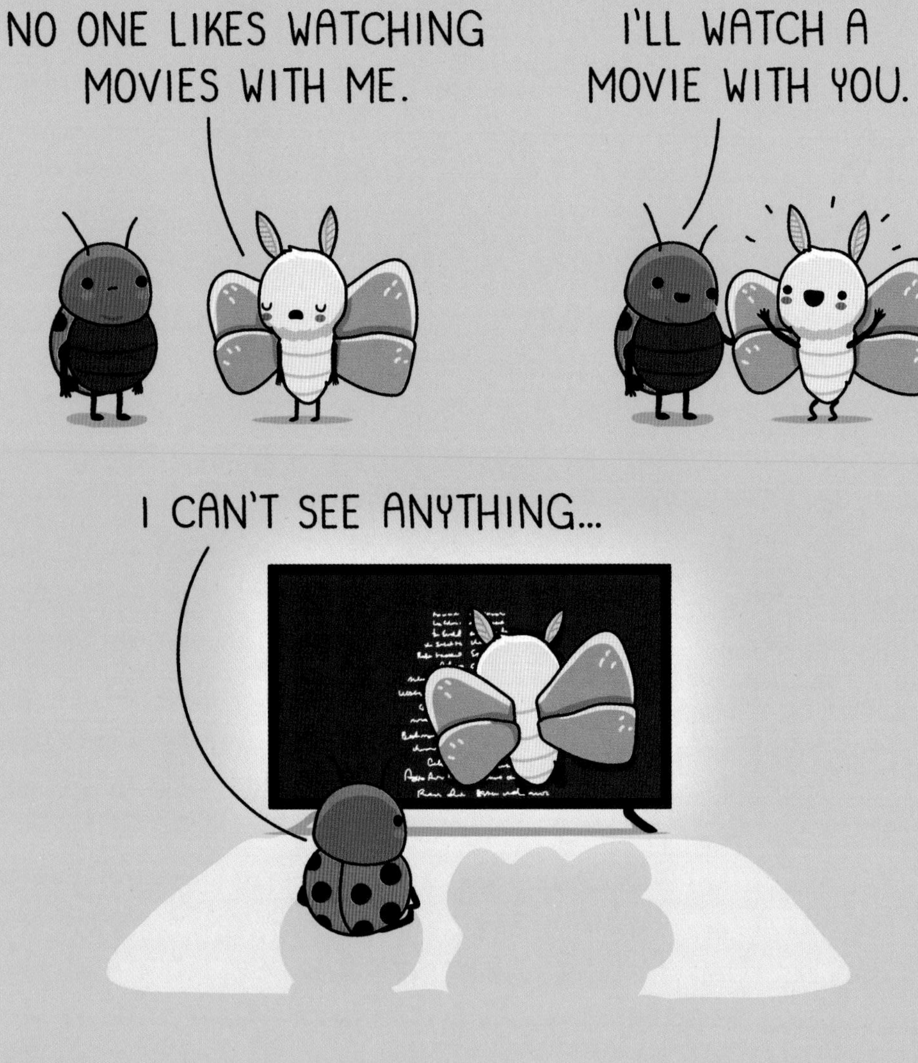
NO ONE LIKES WATCHING MOVIES WITH ME.
I'LL WATCH A MOVIE WITH YOU.
I CAN'T SEE ANYTHING...

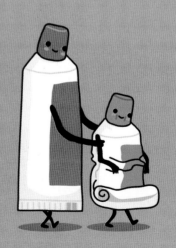

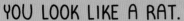

YOU LOOK LIKE A RAT.

WHAT'S A RAT?

Google RAT PHOTOS

OH MY...

I'M GORGEOUS!

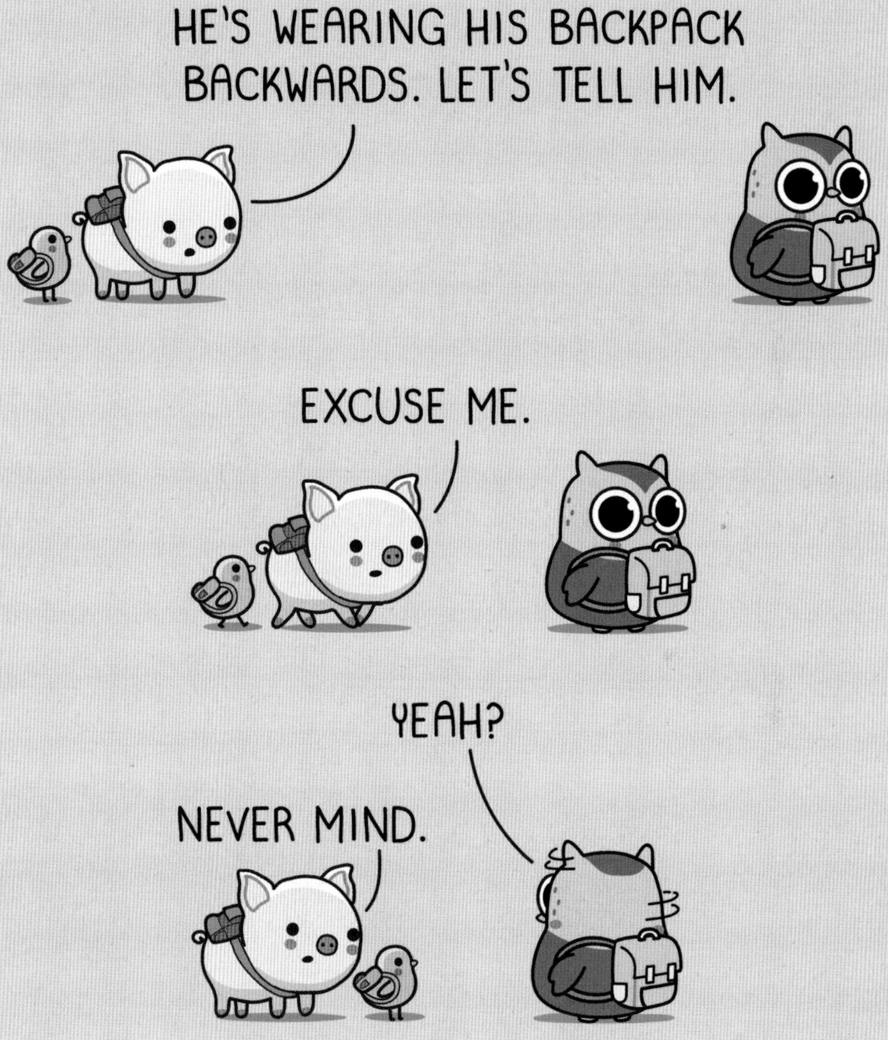
HE'S WEARING HIS BACKPACK BACKWARDS. LET'S TELL HIM.
EXCUSE ME.
YEAH?
NEVER MIND.

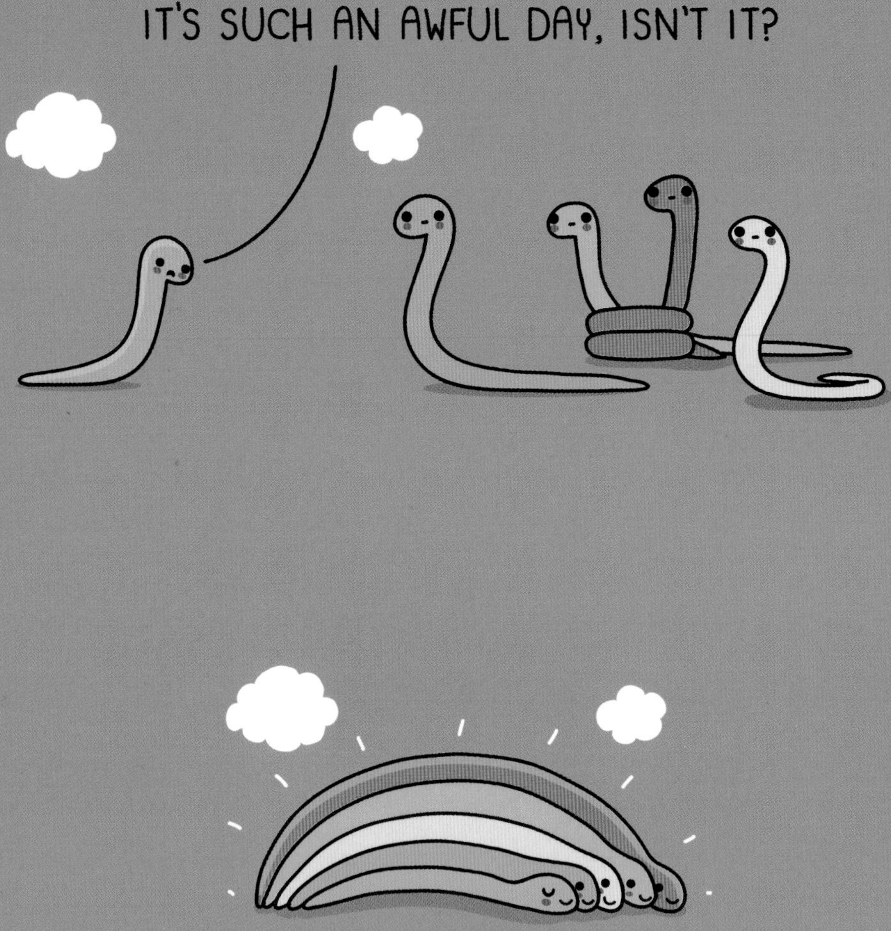
IT'S SUCH AN AWFUL DAY, ISN'T IT?

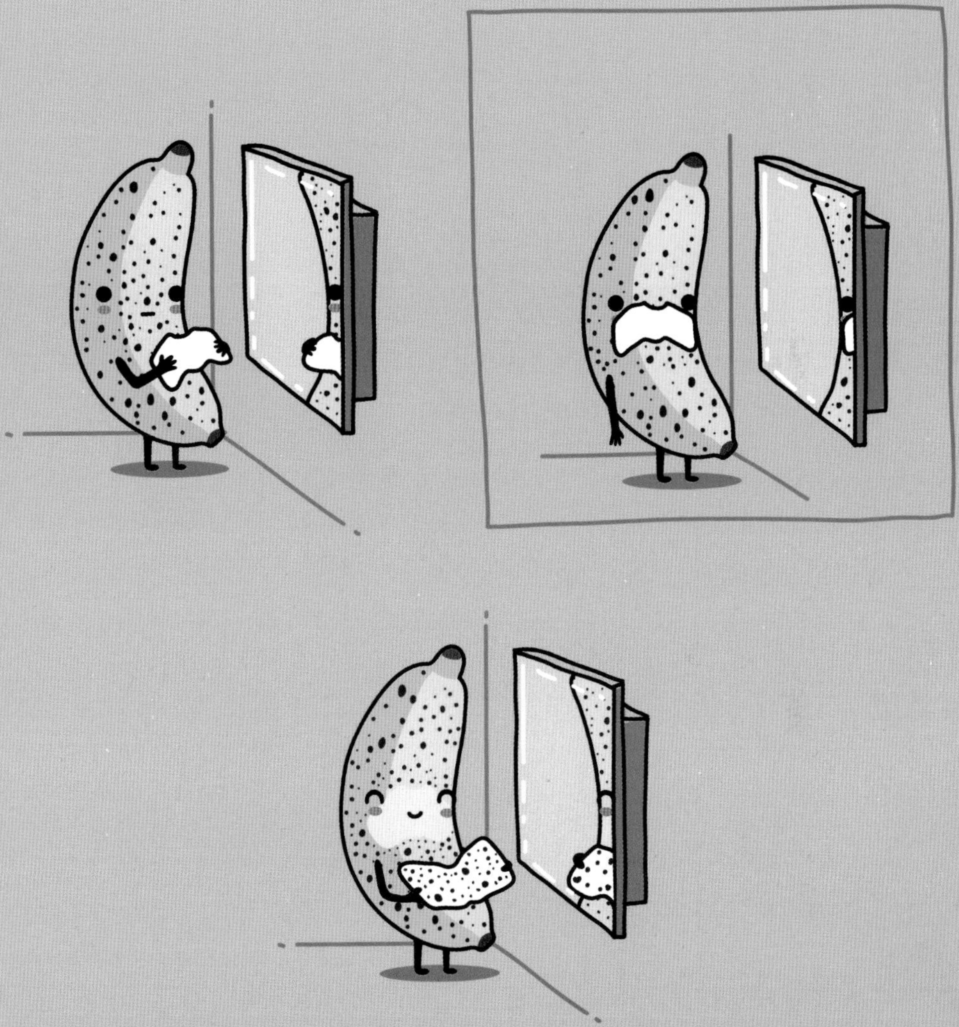

SEE? MY MOM HAS THE BIGGEST HEART IN THE WORLD.

IT'S COMING OUT THROUGH HER HEAD.

WHOA.

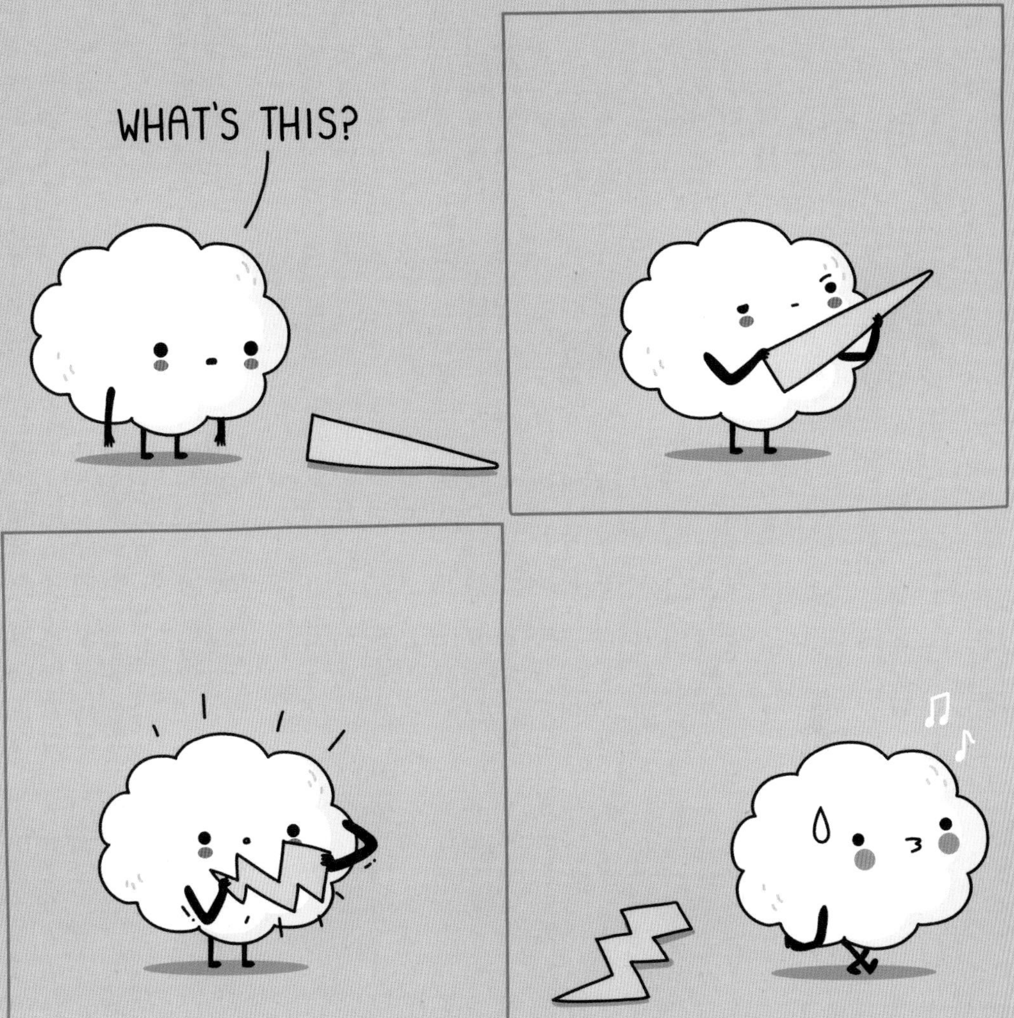
WHAT'S THIS?

HE'S FINALLY ASLEEP.
LET'S PUT HIM IN THE CRIB.

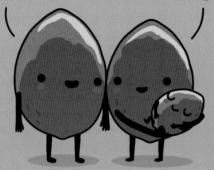

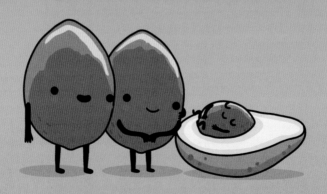

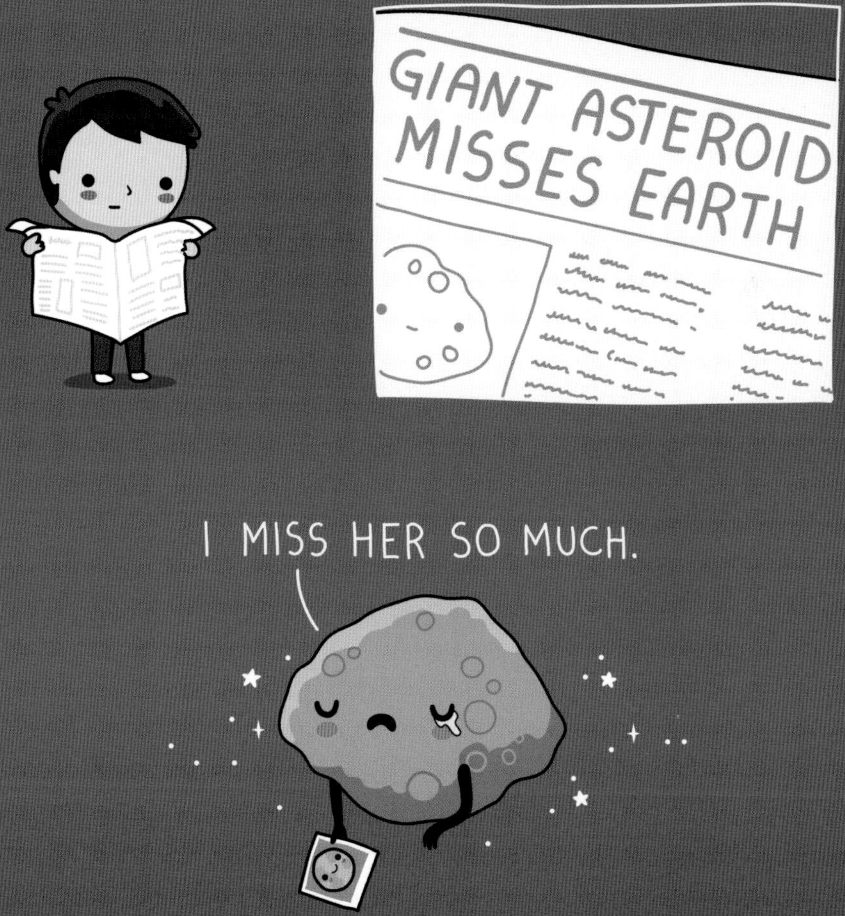
GIANT ASTEROID MISSES EARTH
I MISS HER SO MUCH.

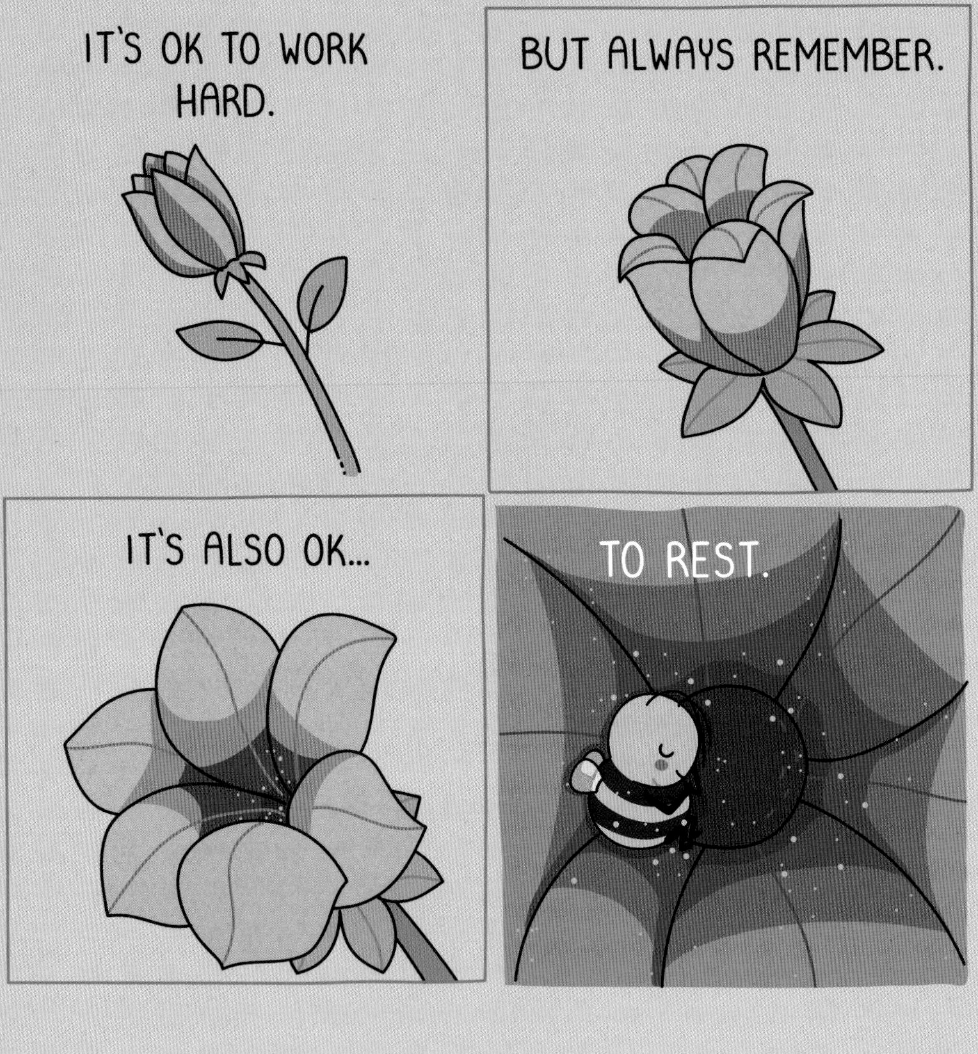
IT'S OK TO WORK HARD.
BUT ALWAYS REMEMBER.
IT'S ALSO OK...
TO REST.

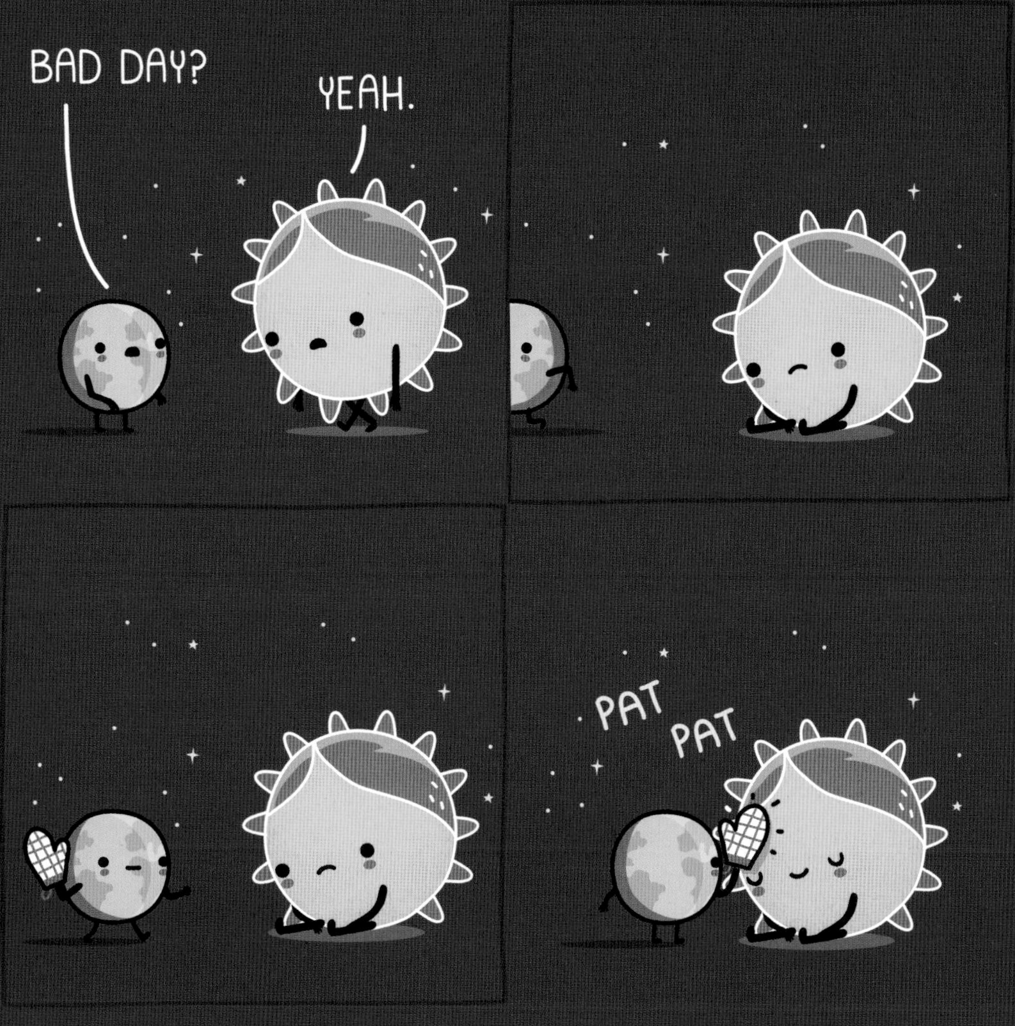
BAD DAY?
YEAH.
PAT
PAT

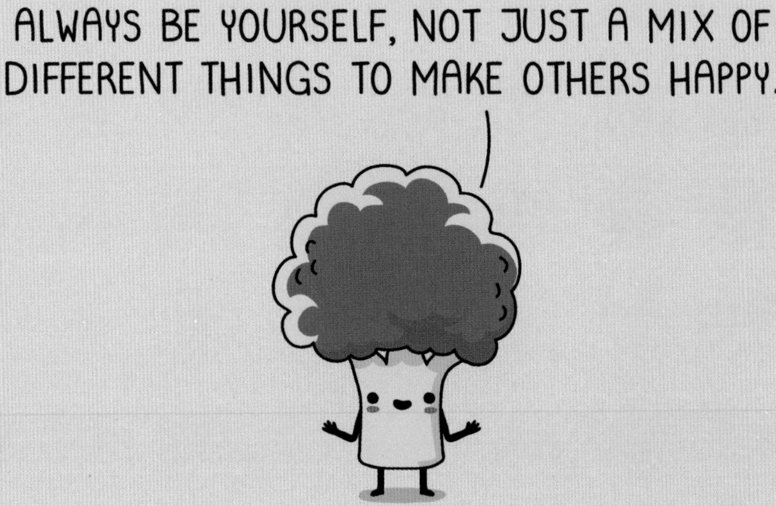
ALWAYS BE YOURSELF, NOT JUST A MIX OF DIFFERENT THINGS TO MAKE OTHERS HAPPY.

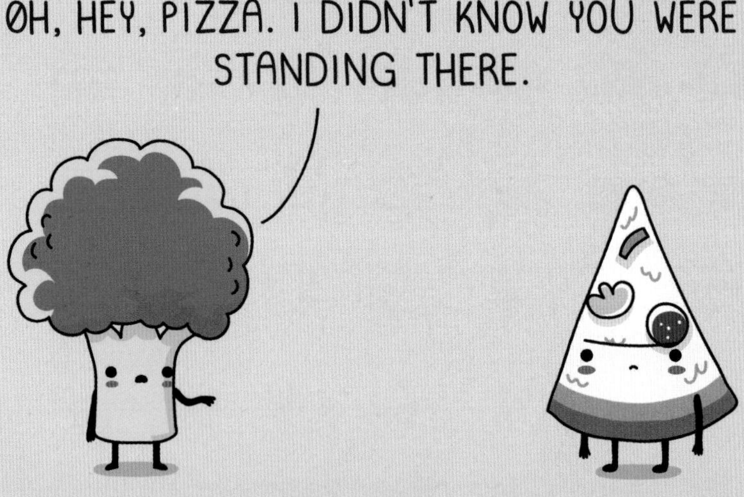
OH, HEY, PIZZA. I DIDN'T KNOW YOU WERE STANDING THERE.

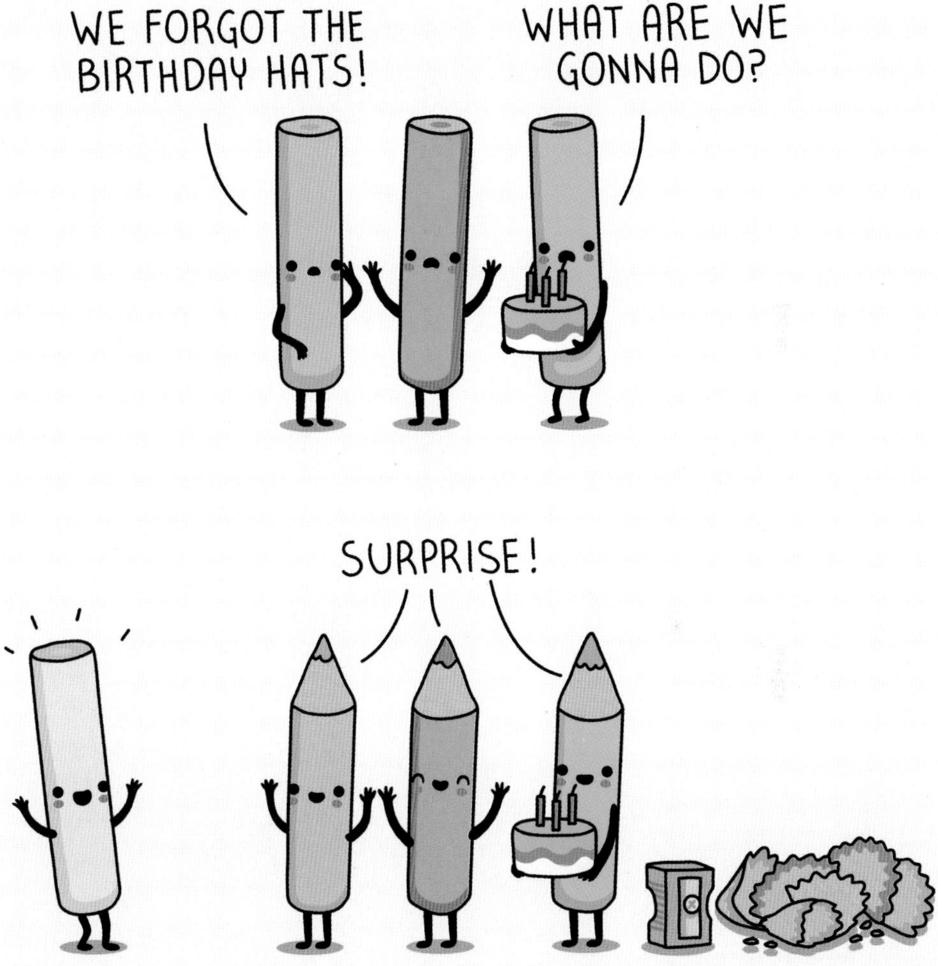
WE FORGOT THE BIRTHDAY HATS!
WHAT ARE WE GONNA DO?
SURPRISE!

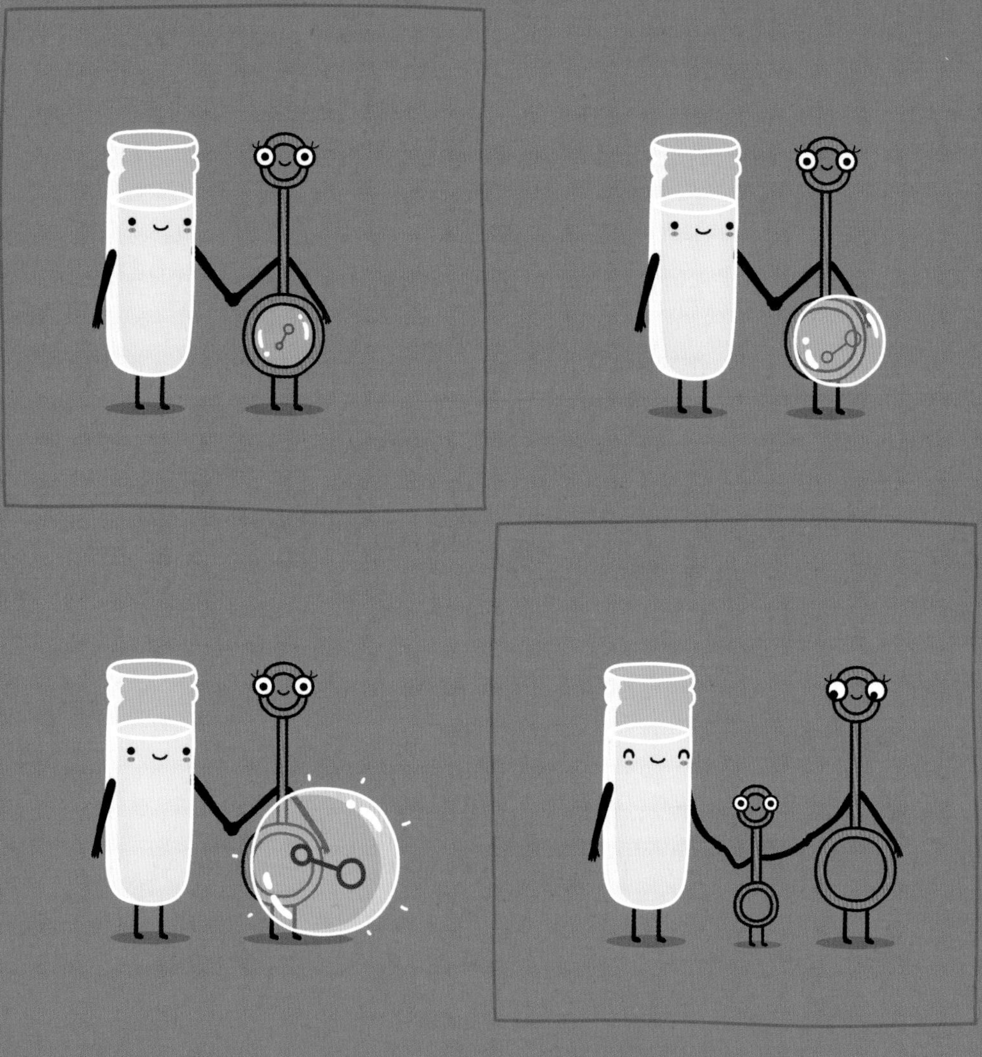

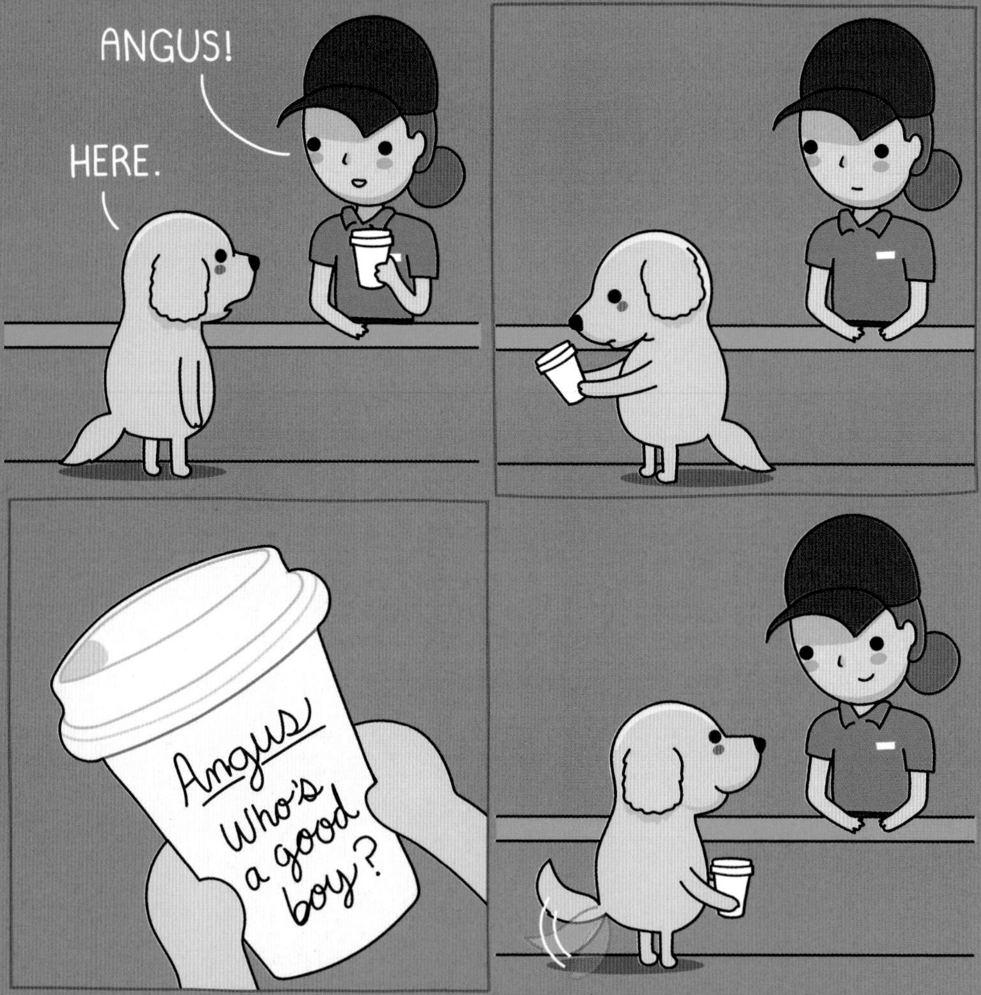
ANGUS!
HERE.
Angus
Who's a good boy?

THE ONE NEXT TO IT IS NAMED URSA MINOR,
WHICH MEANS LITTLE BEAR.

BEAUTIFUL.

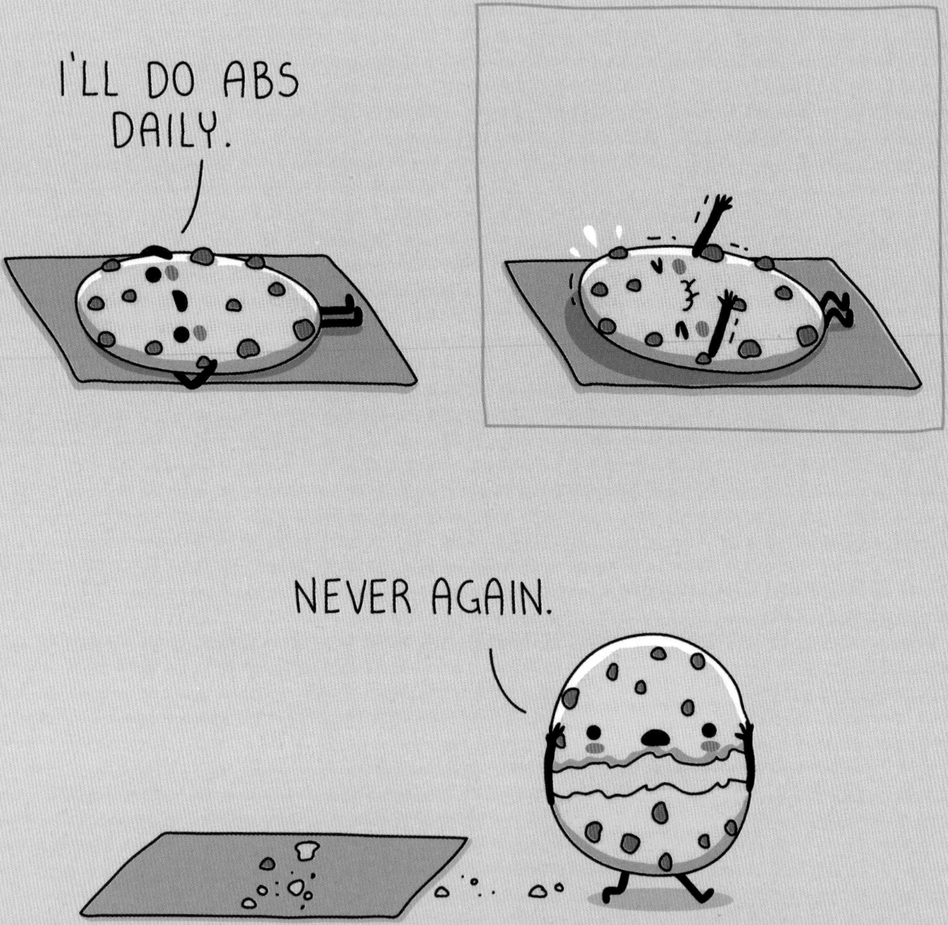
I'LL DO ABS DAILY.
NEVER AGAIN.

BINGE-WATCHING

BEFORE YOUR 20s

AFTER

CAN I JOIN YOU?

YOU'VE GOT THINGS TO DO.

GUILT

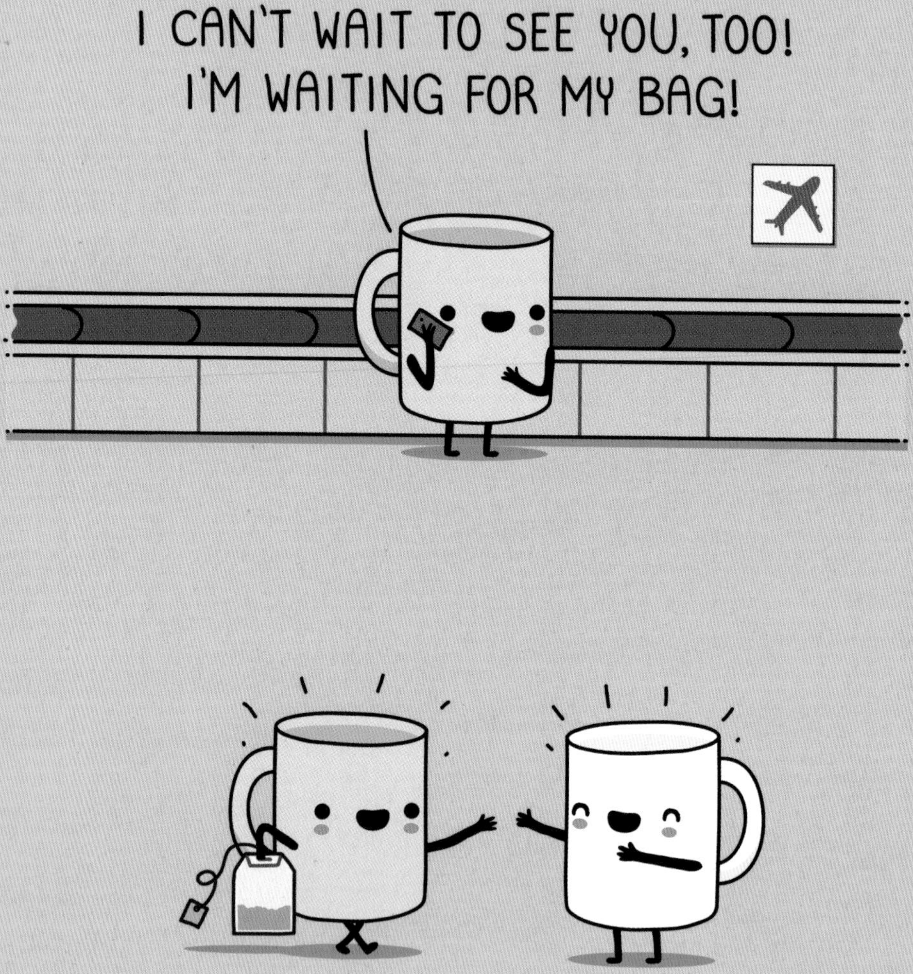
I CAN'T WAIT TO SEE YOU, TOO! I'M WAITING FOR MY BAG!

PEOPLE AT THE BEACH.

ME.

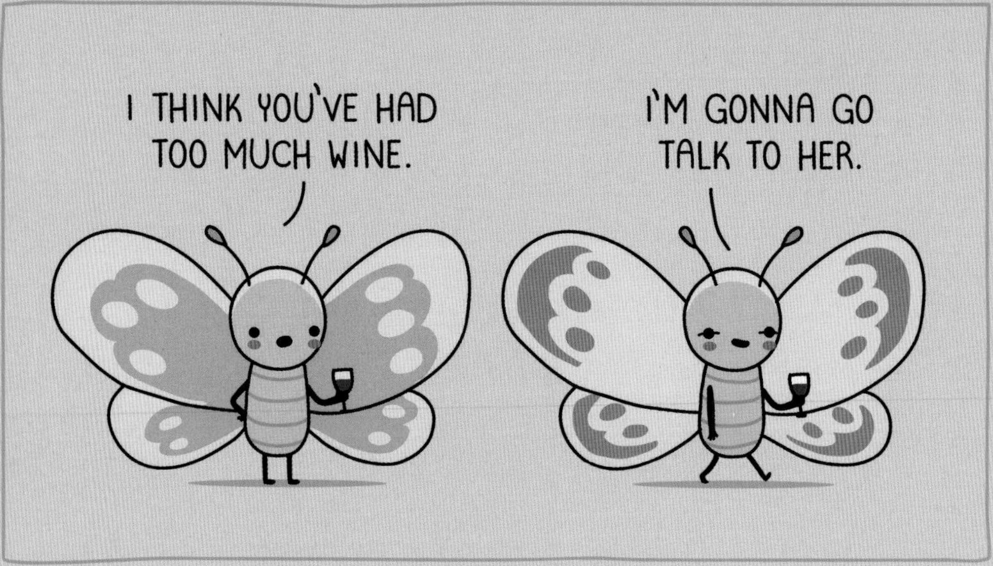
I THINK YOU'VE HAD
TOO MUCH WINE.
I'M GONNA GO
TALK TO HER.

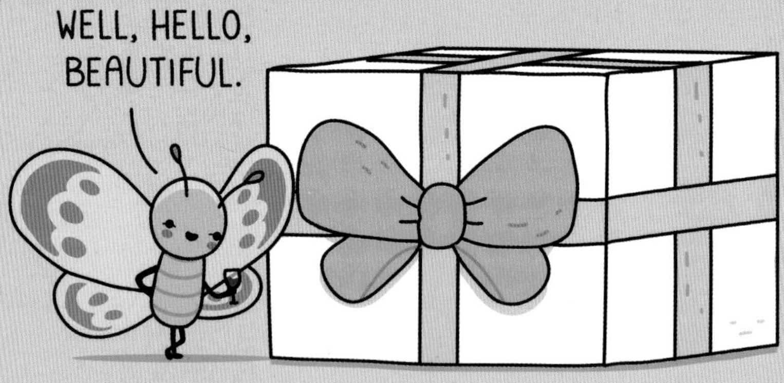
WELL, HELLO,
BEAUTIFUL.

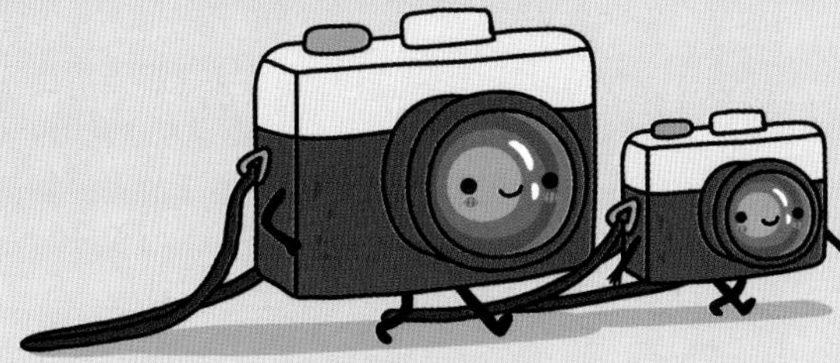

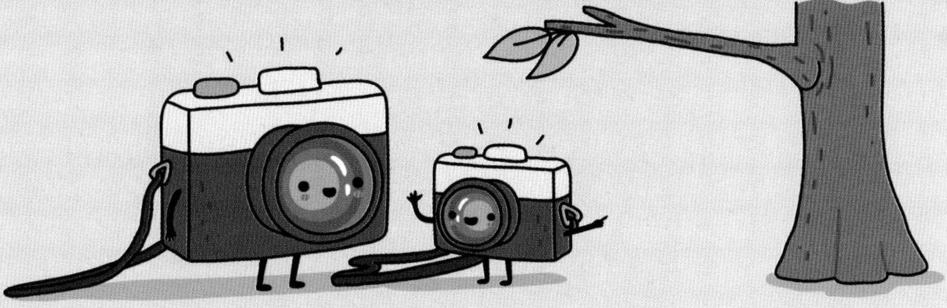

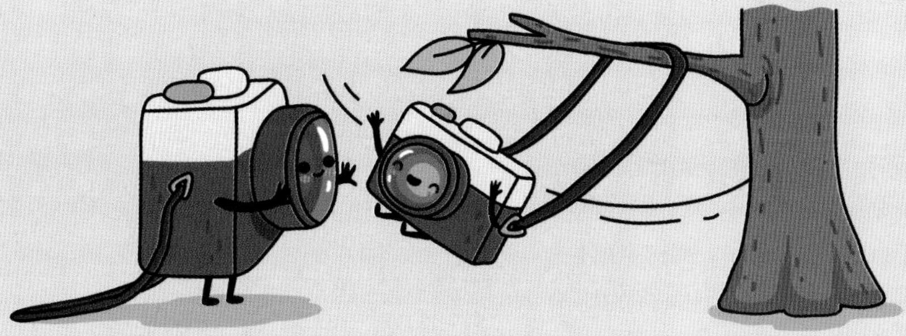

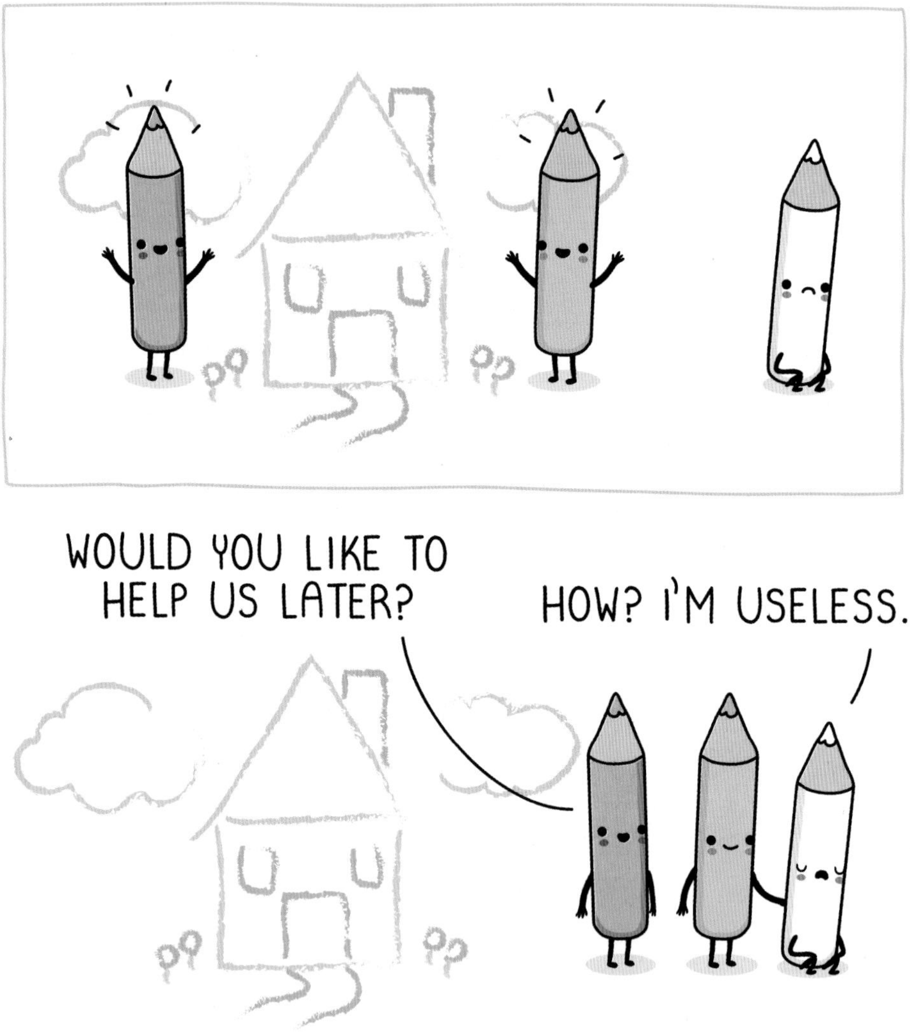
WOULD YOU LIKE TO HELP US LATER?
HOW? I'M USELESS.

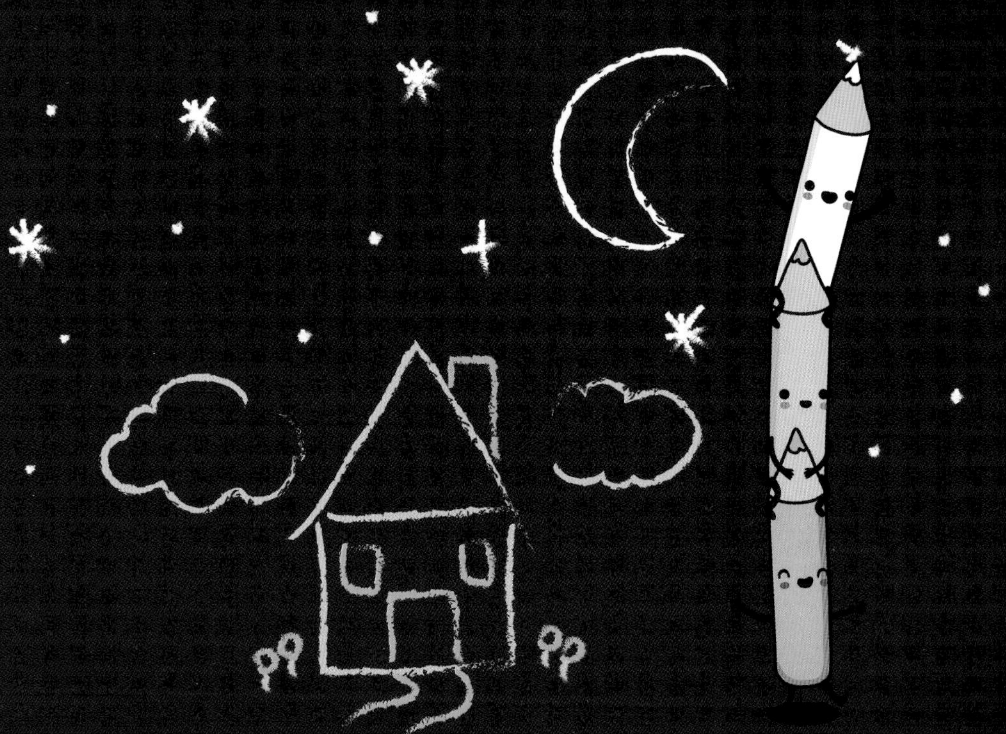

HERE COMES YOUR CRUSH, ACT NATURAL.

SUP.

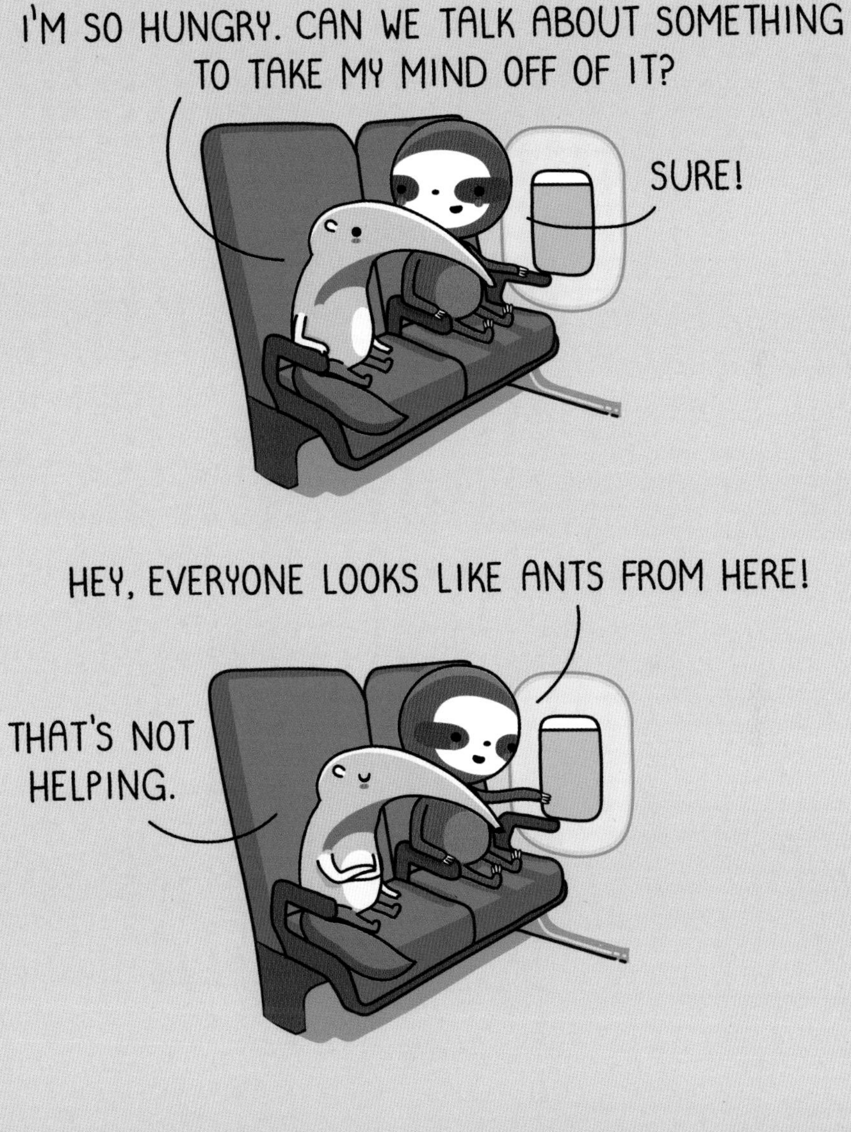
I'M SO HUNGRY. CAN WE TALK ABOUT SOMETHING TO TAKE MY MIND OFF OF IT?
SURE!
HEY, EVERYONE LOOKS LIKE ANTS FROM HERE!
THAT'S NOT HELPING.

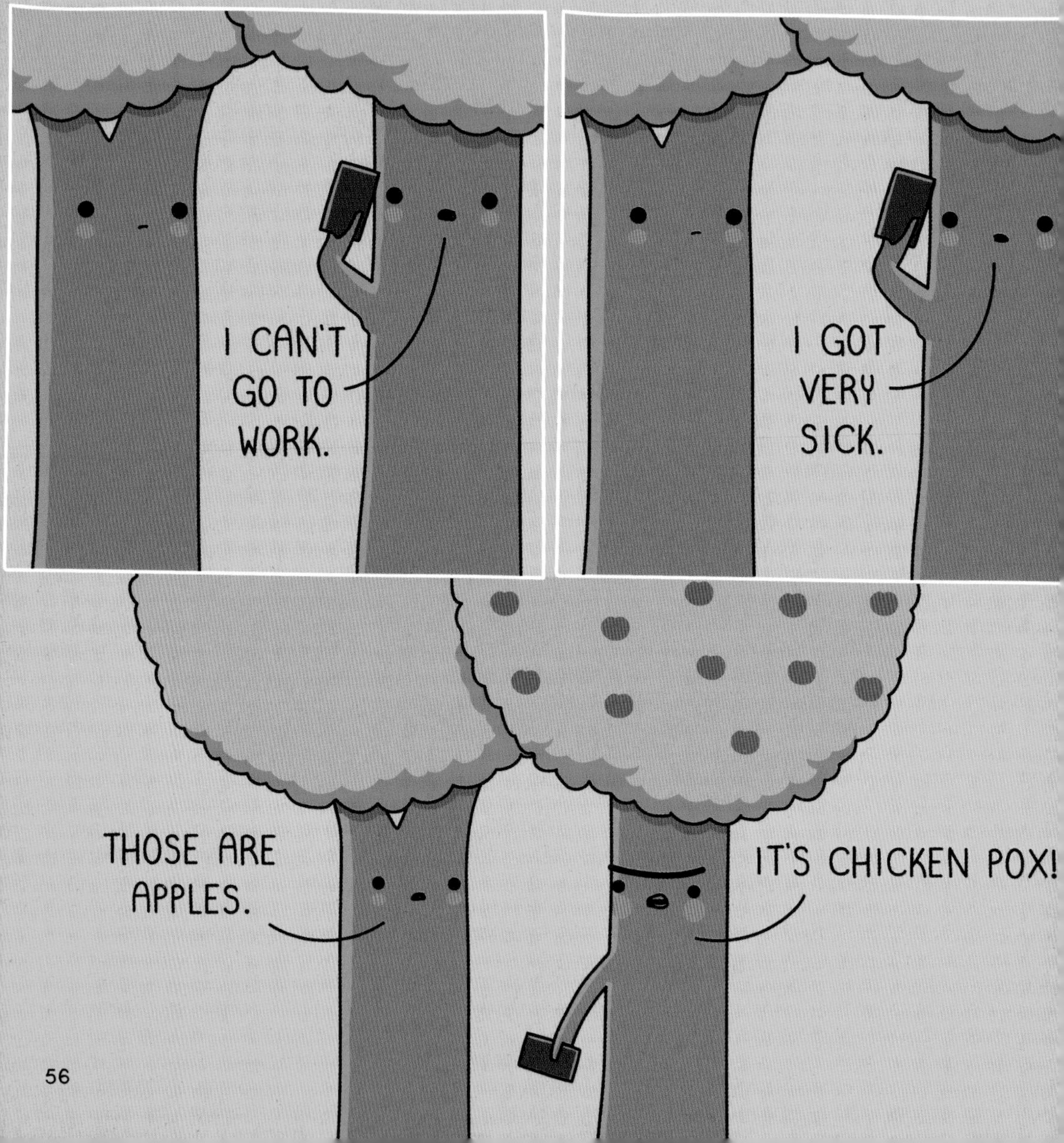
I CAN'T GO TO WORK.
I GOT VERY SICK.
THOSE ARE APPLES.
IT'S CHICKEN POX!

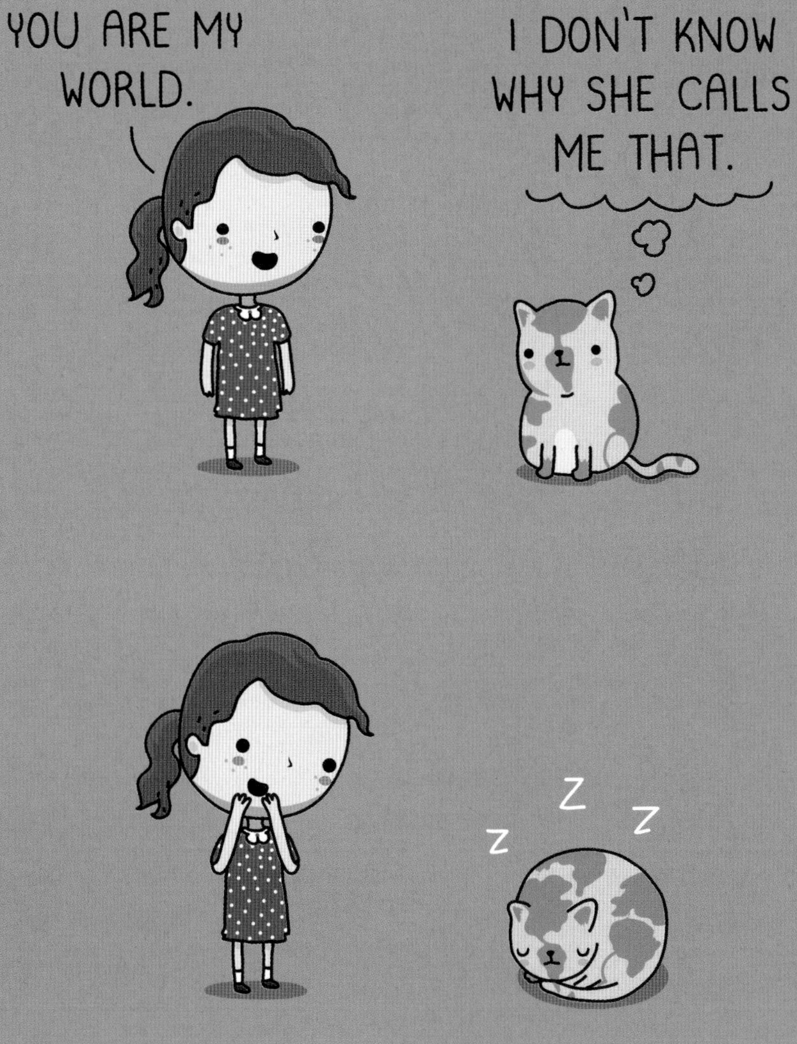
YOU ARE MY WORLD.
I DON'T KNOW WHY SHE CALLS ME THAT.
Z Z Z

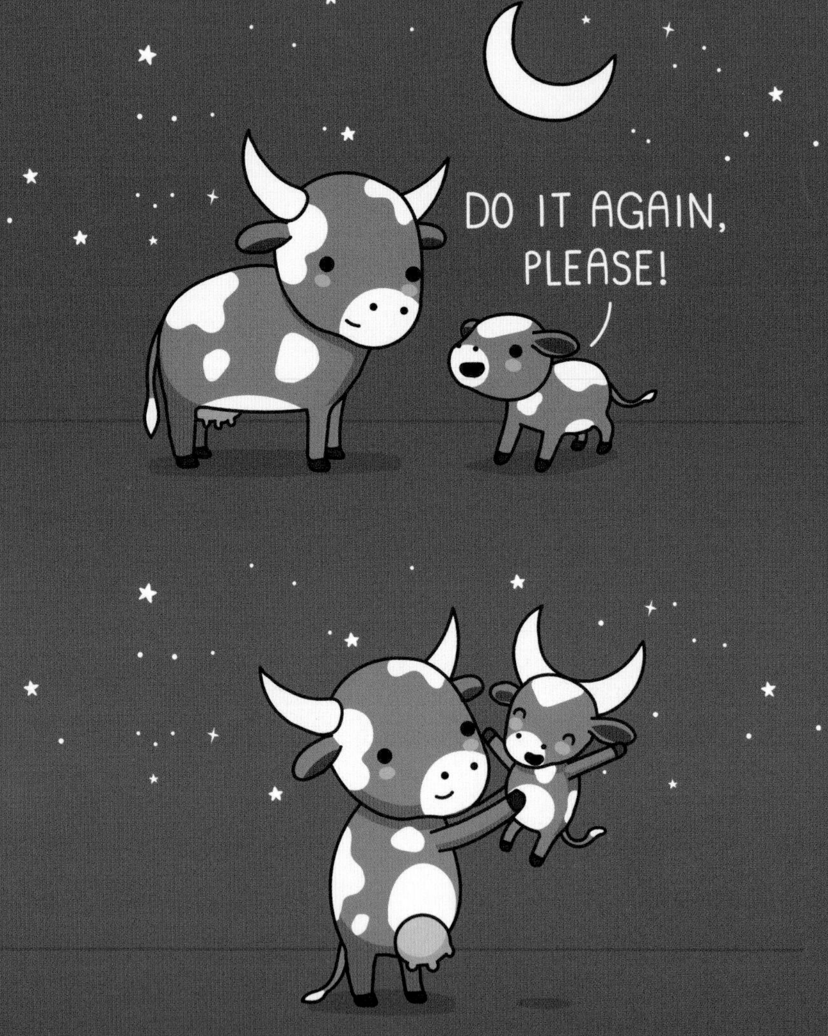
DO IT AGAIN, PLEASE!

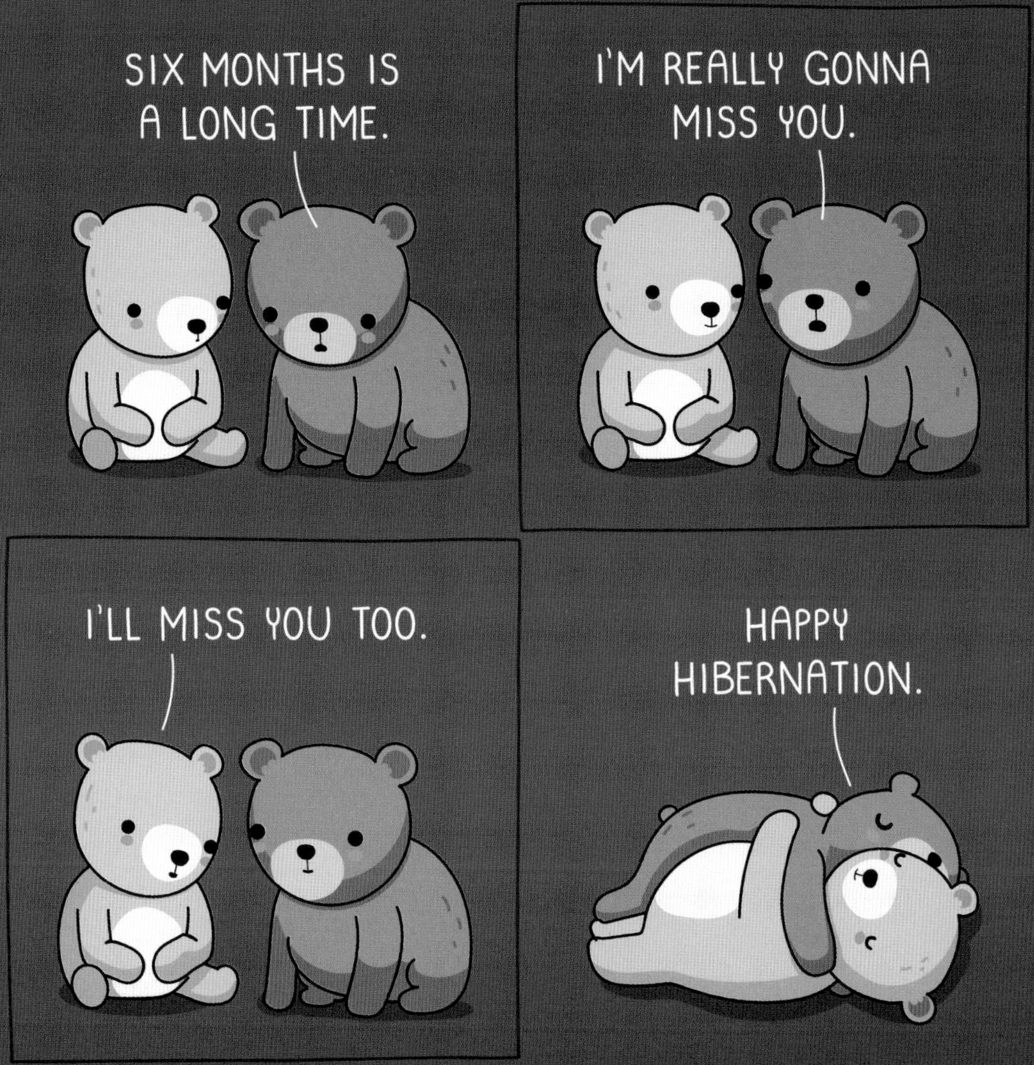
SIX MONTHS IS A LONG TIME.
I'M REALLY GONNA MISS YOU.
I'LL MISS YOU TOO.
HAPPY HIBERNATION.

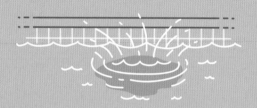

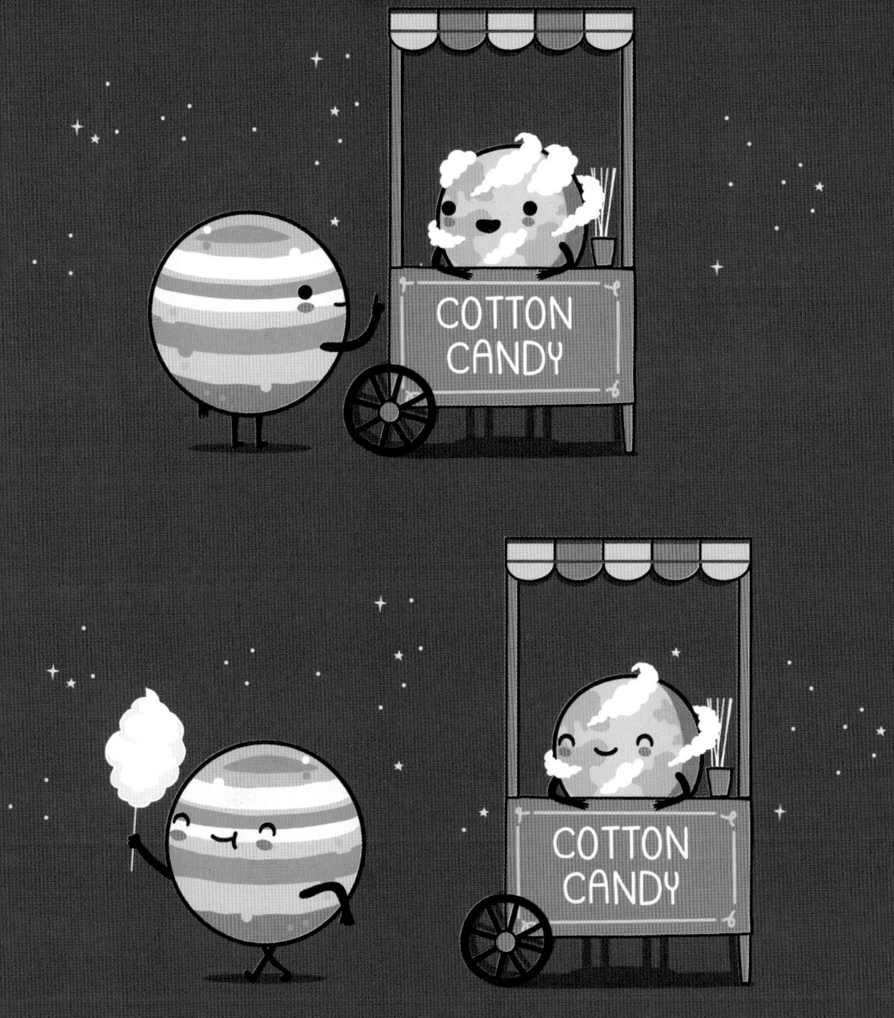
COTTON CANDY
COTTON CANDY

DOG WAITING FOR HIS HUMAN TO ARRIVE

HUMAN WAITING FOR A PACKAGE TO ARRIVE

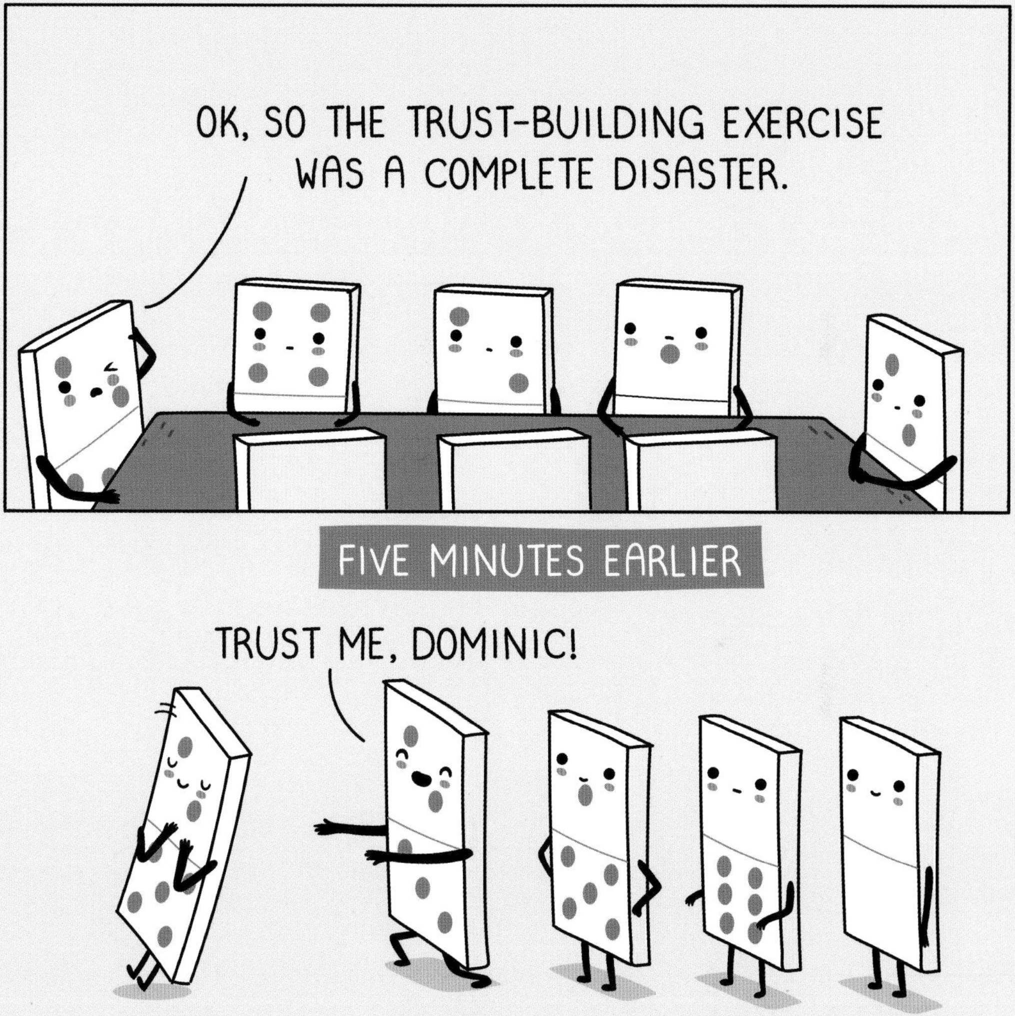
OK, SO THE TRUST-BUILDING EXERCISE WAS A COMPLETE DISASTER.
FIVE MINUTES EARLIER
TRUST ME, DOMINIC!

I REGRET NOTHING.

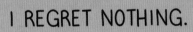

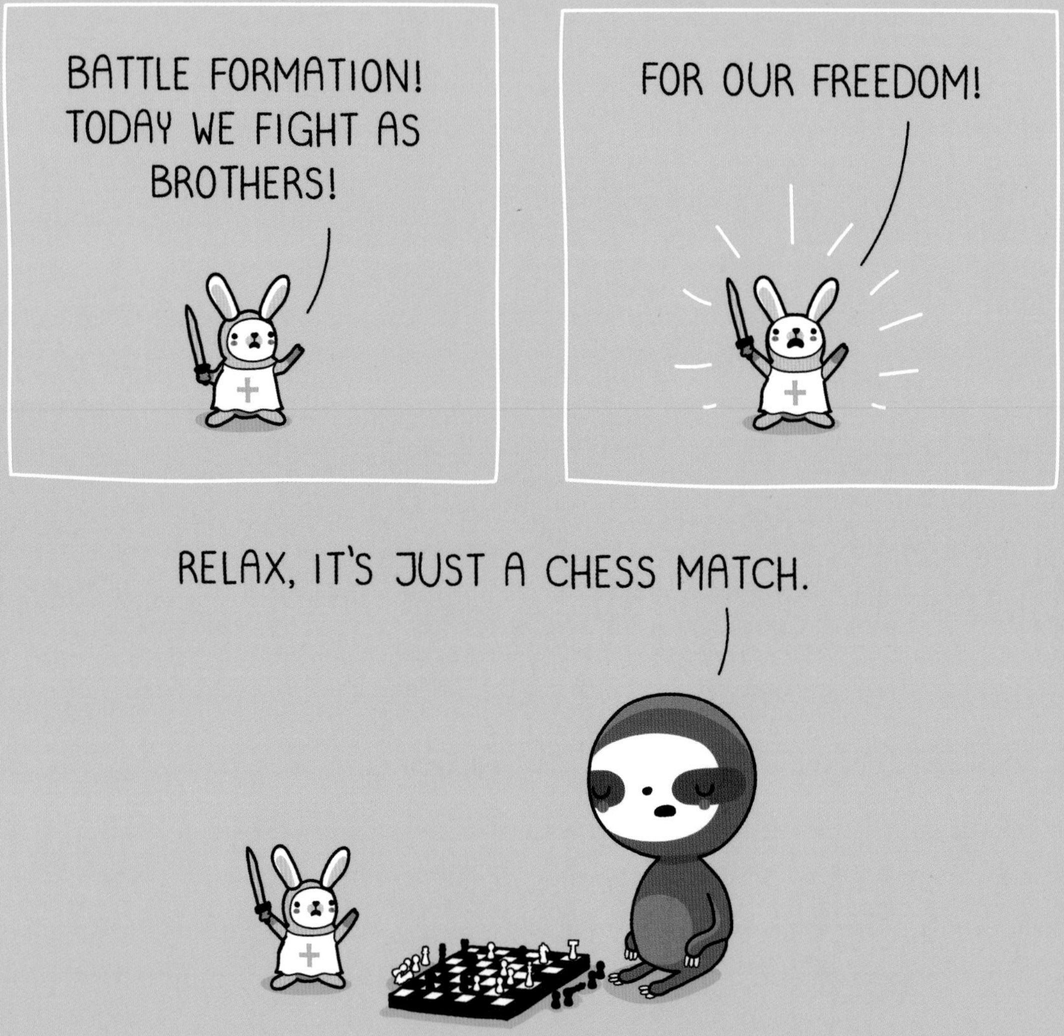
BATTLE FORMATION! TODAY WE FIGHT AS BROTHERS!
FOR OUR FREEDOM!
RELAX, IT'S JUST A CHESS MATCH.

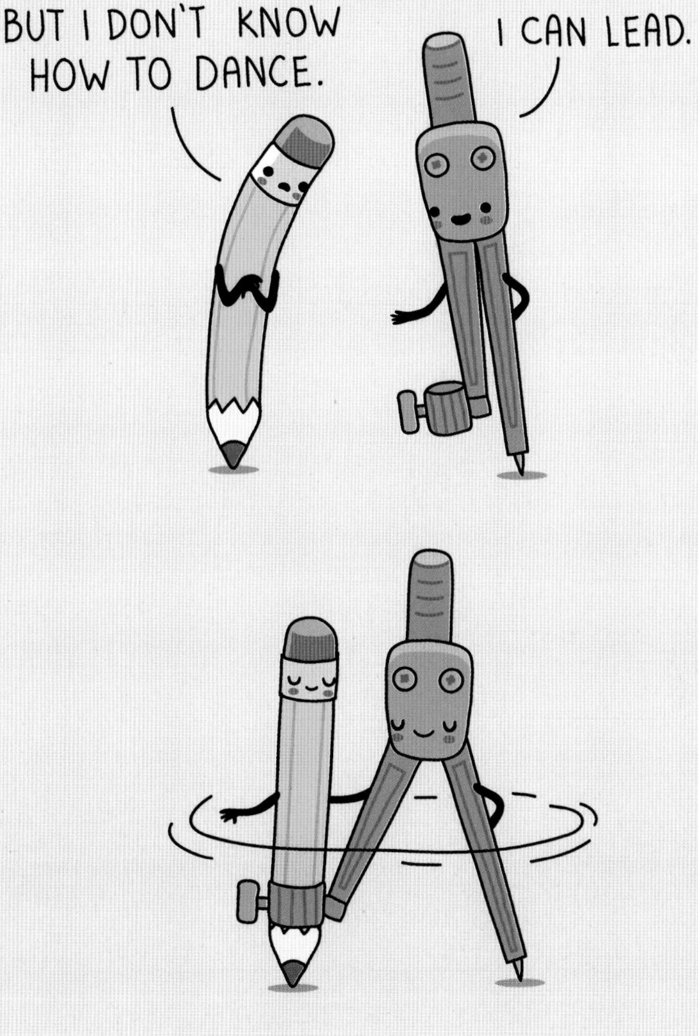
BUT I DON'T KNOW HOW TO DANCE.
I CAN LEAD.

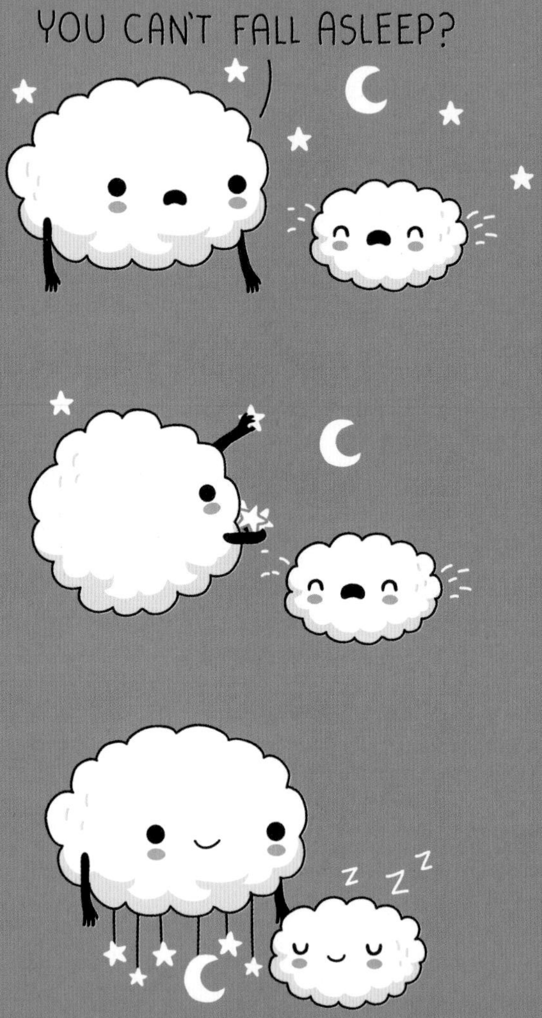
YOU CAN'T FALL ASLEEP?
Z Z Z

OK, DON'T MOVE.
DUDE...
I CAN'T STOP DOING IT!

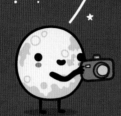

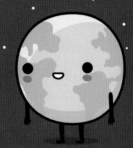

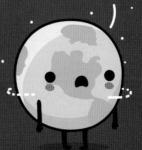

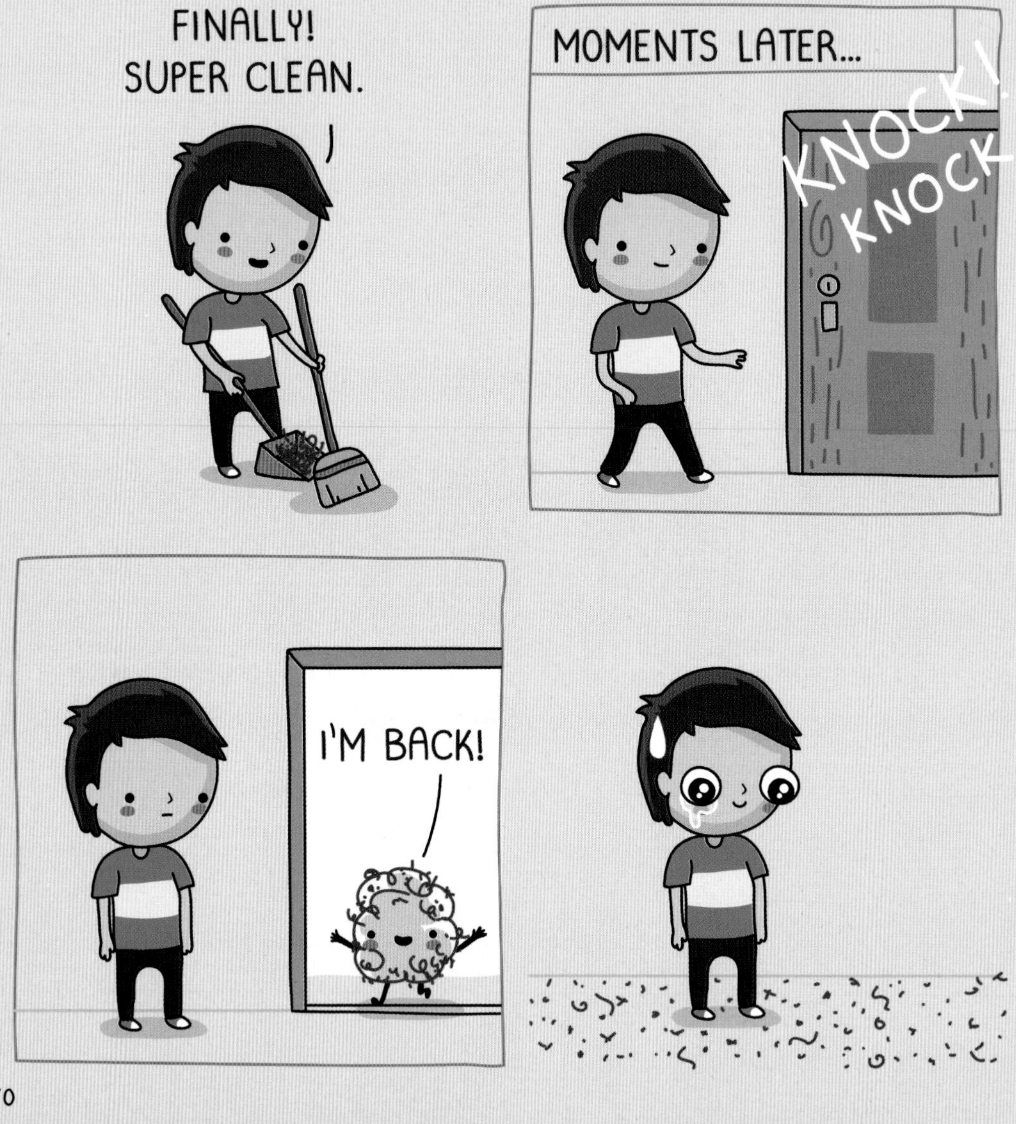
FINALLY! SUPER CLEAN.
MOMENTS LATER...
KNOCK! KNOCK
I'M BACK!

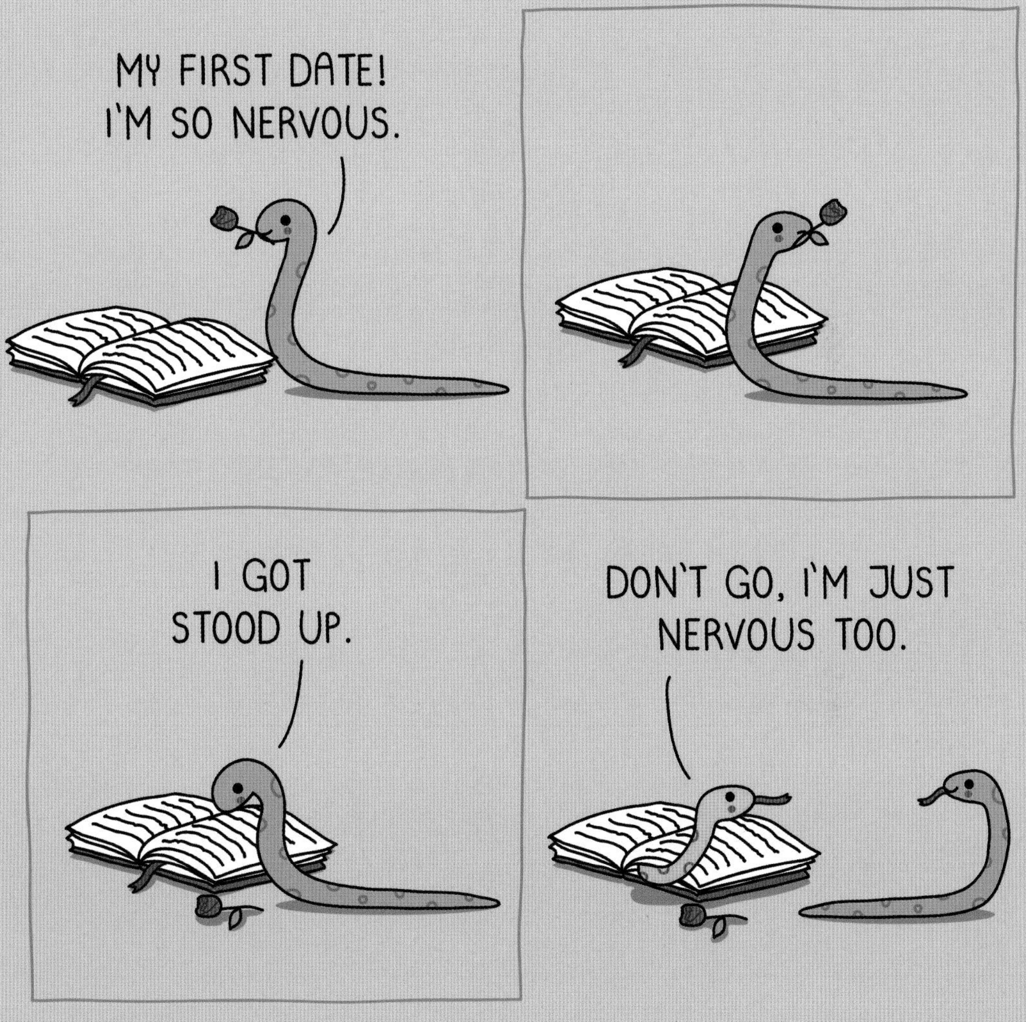
MY FIRST DATE! I'M SO NERVOUS.
I GOT STOOD UP.
DON'T GO, I'M JUST NERVOUS TOO.

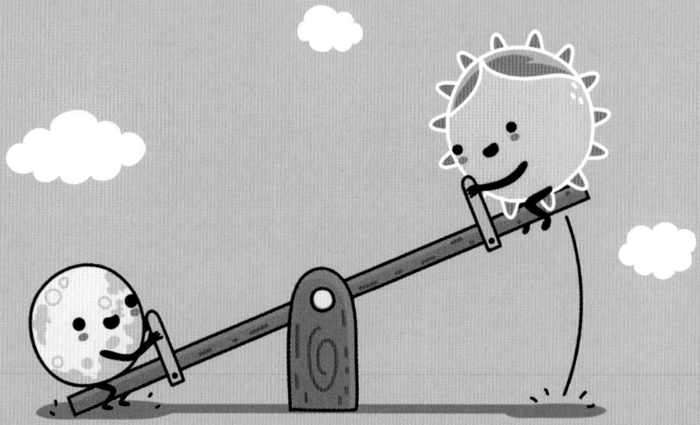

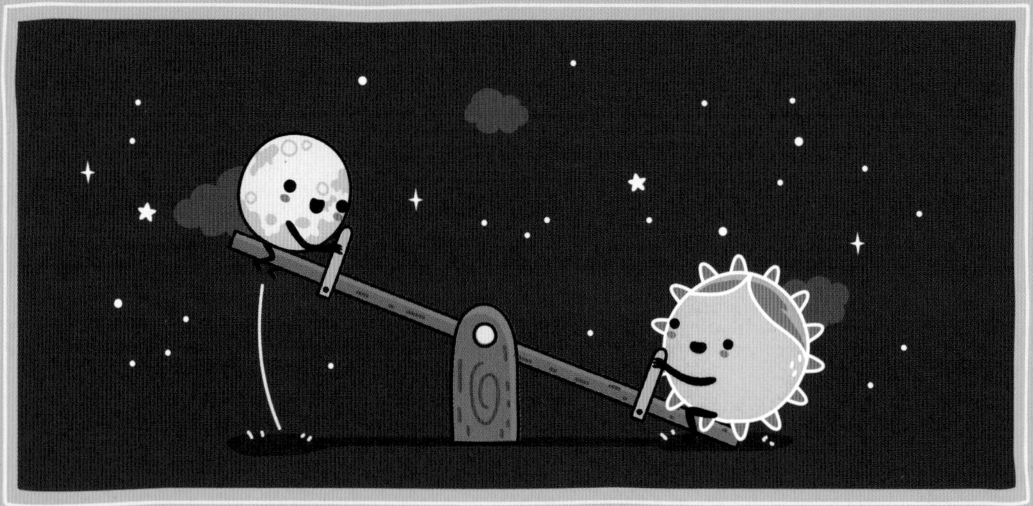

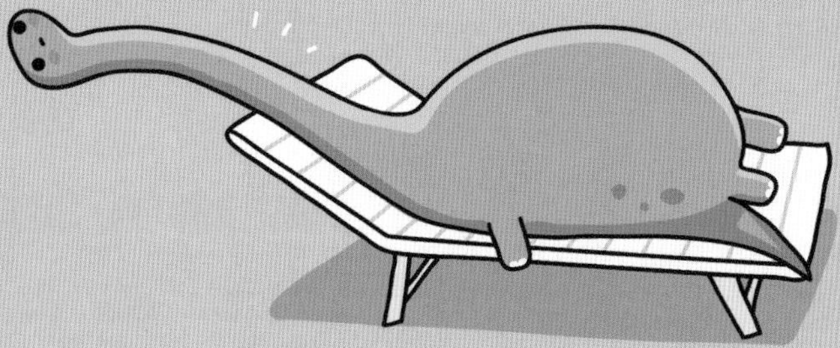

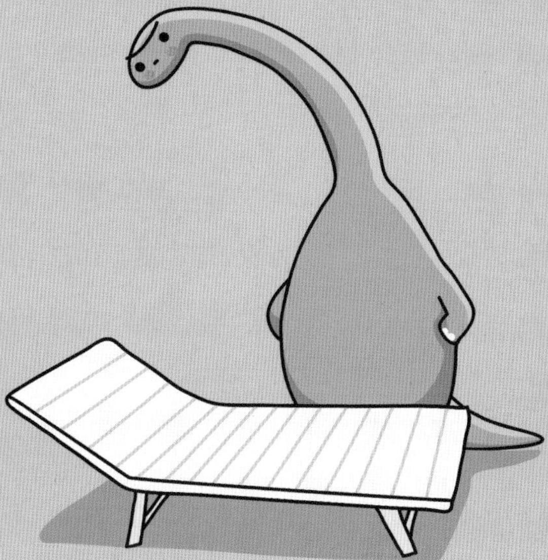

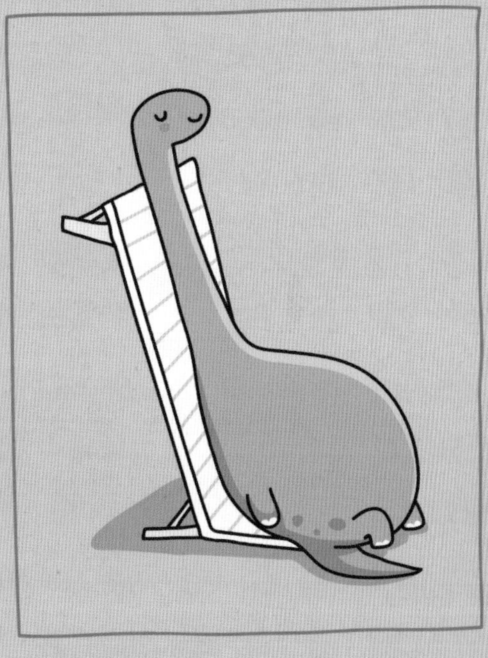

WE ARE GATHERED
HERE TODAY
TO JOIN THESE TWO...

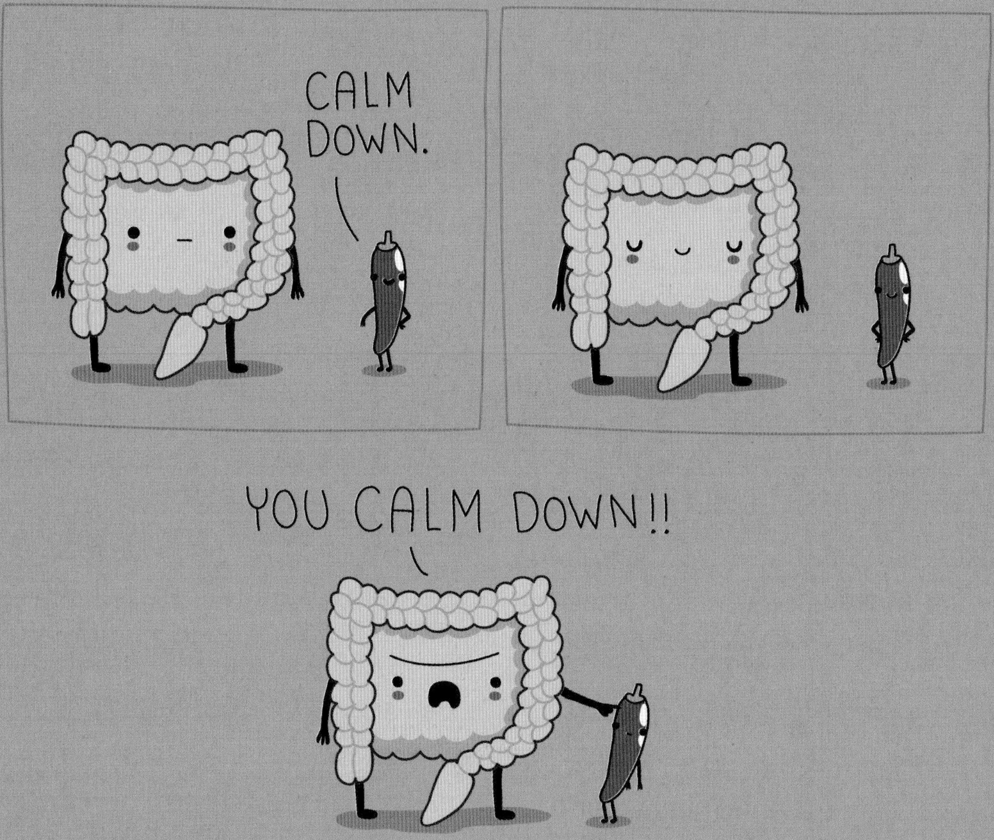
CALM DOWN.
YOU CALM DOWN!!

IRRITABLE BOWEL

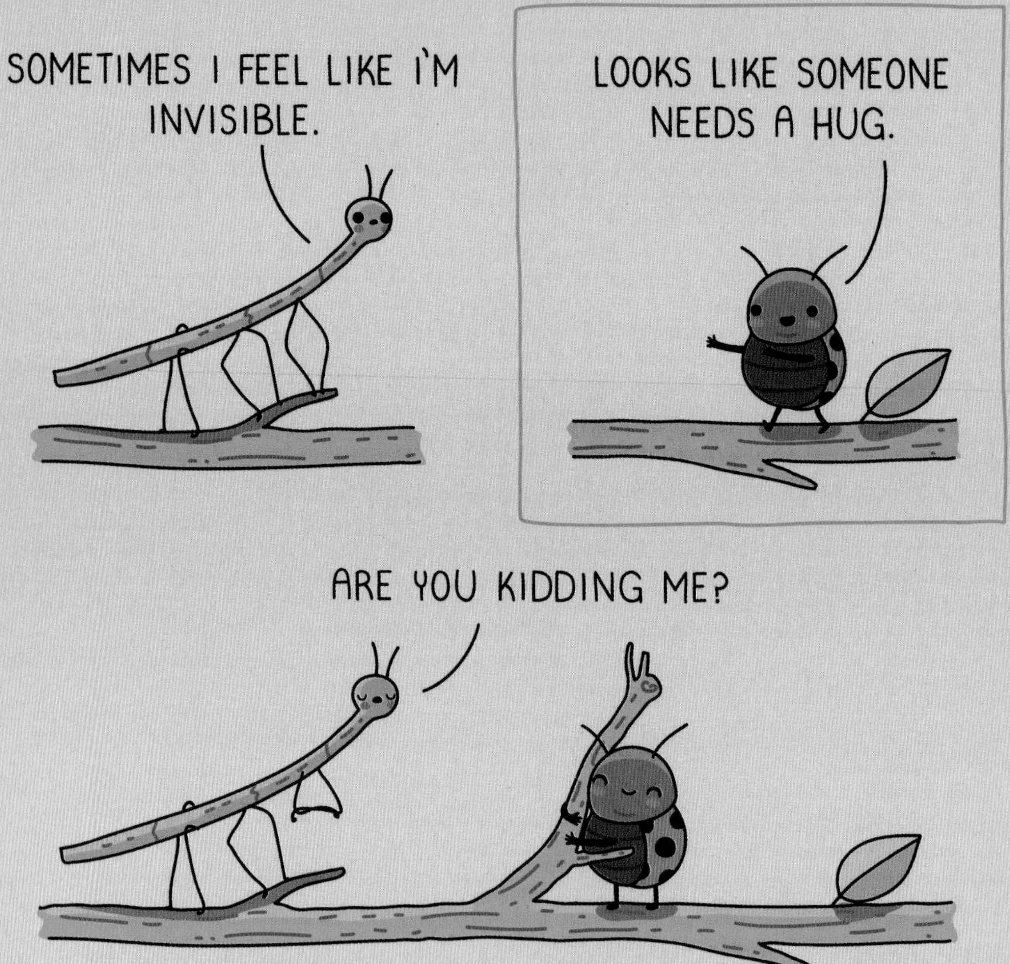
SOMETIMES I FEEL LIKE I'M INVISIBLE.
LOOKS LIKE SOMEONE NEEDS A HUG.
ARE YOU KIDDING ME?

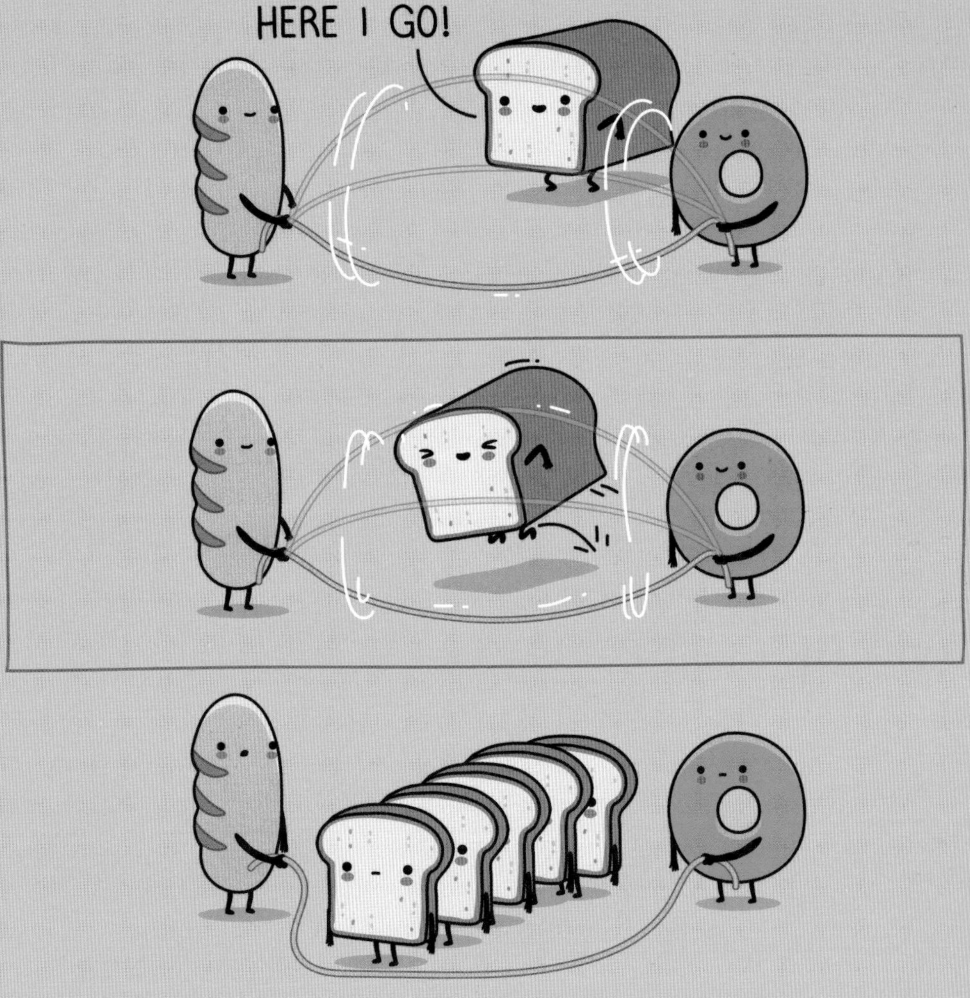
HERE I GO!

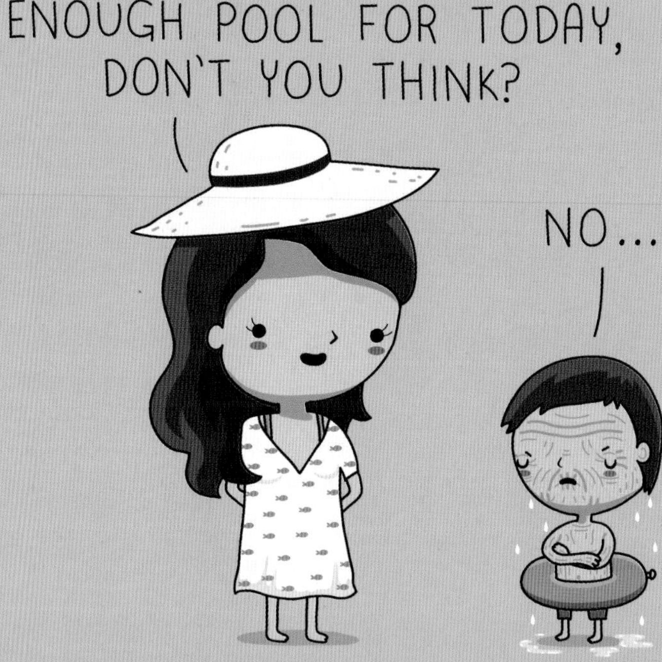
ENOUGH POOL FOR TODAY,
DON'T YOU THINK?
NO...

I'M GONNA RIDE MY BIKE!
WHAT DO I ALWAYS TELL YOU?
ALWAYS WEAR YOUR HELMET.

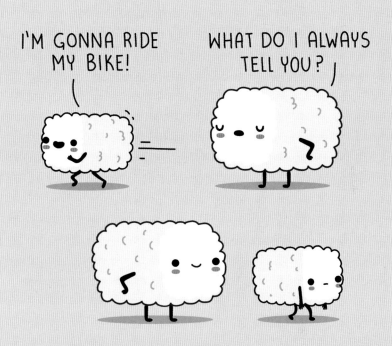

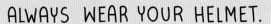

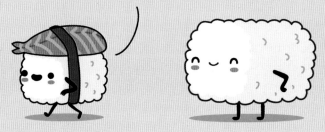

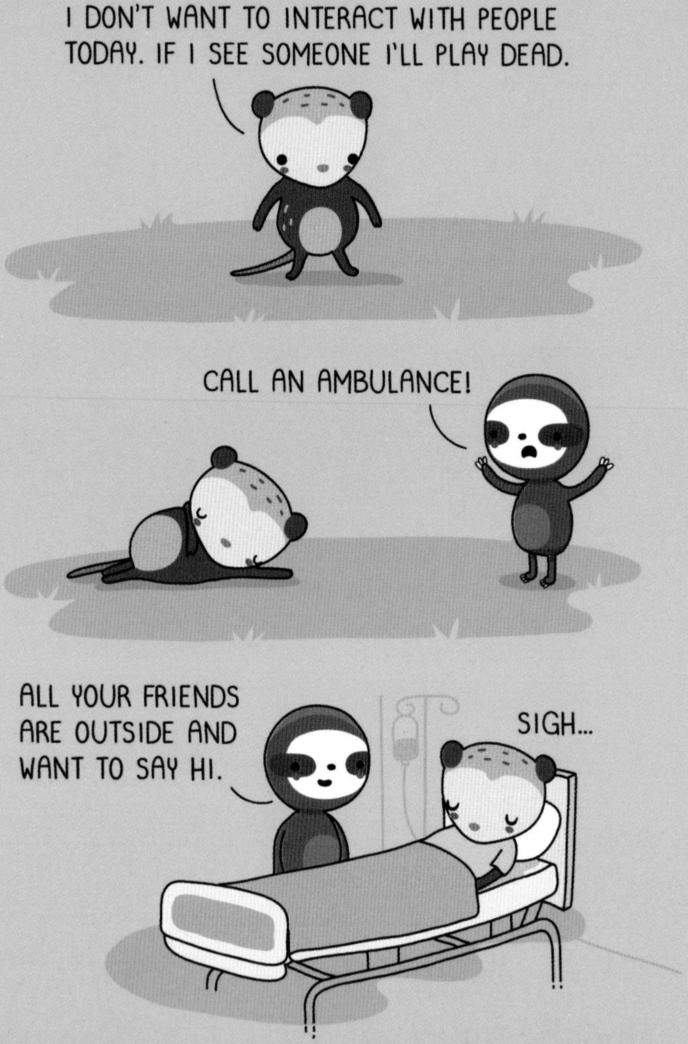
I DON'T WANT TO INTERACT WITH PEOPLE TODAY. IF I SEE SOMEONE I'LL PLAY DEAD.
CALL AN AMBULANCE!
ALL YOUR FRIENDS ARE OUTSIDE AND WANT TO SAY HI.
SIGH...

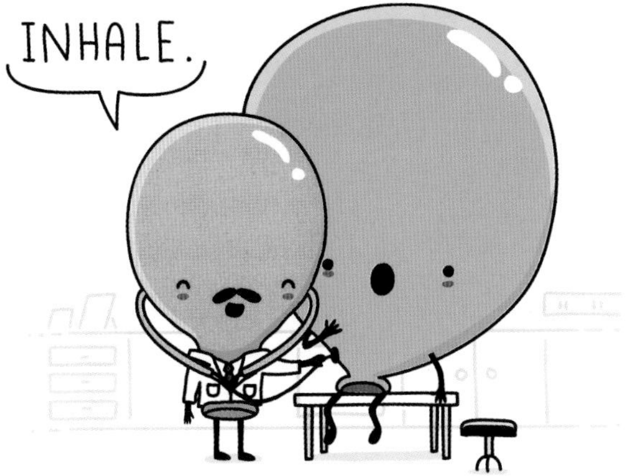
INHALE.

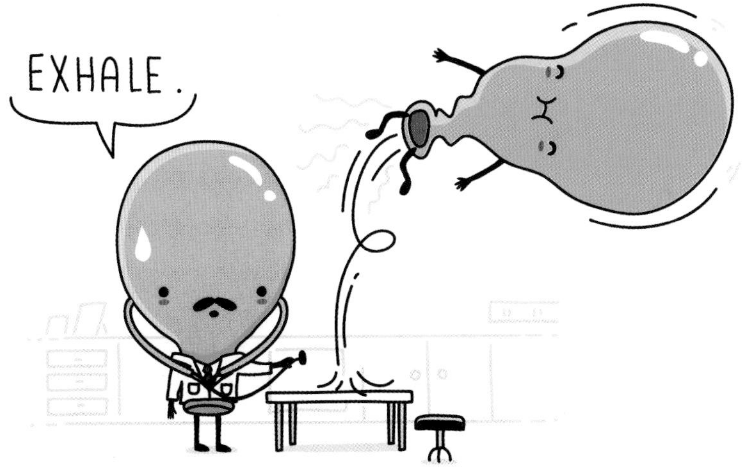
EXHALE.

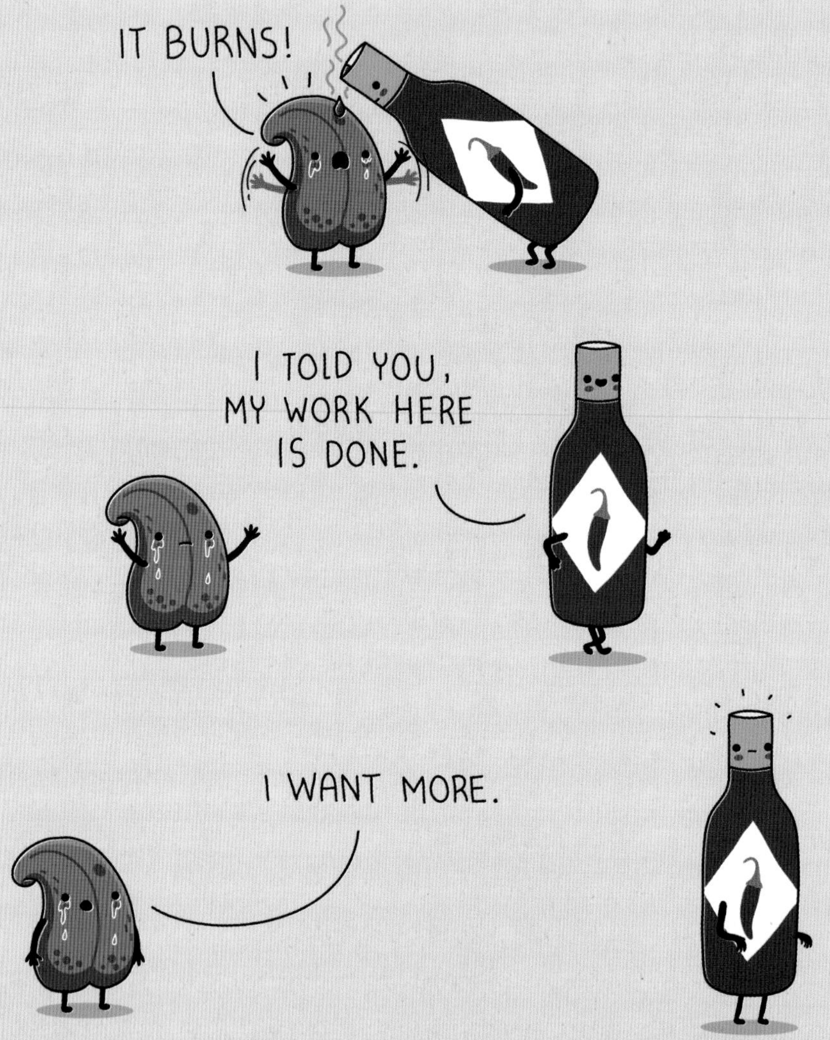
IT BURNS!
I TOLD YOU, MY WORK HERE IS DONE.
I WANT MORE.

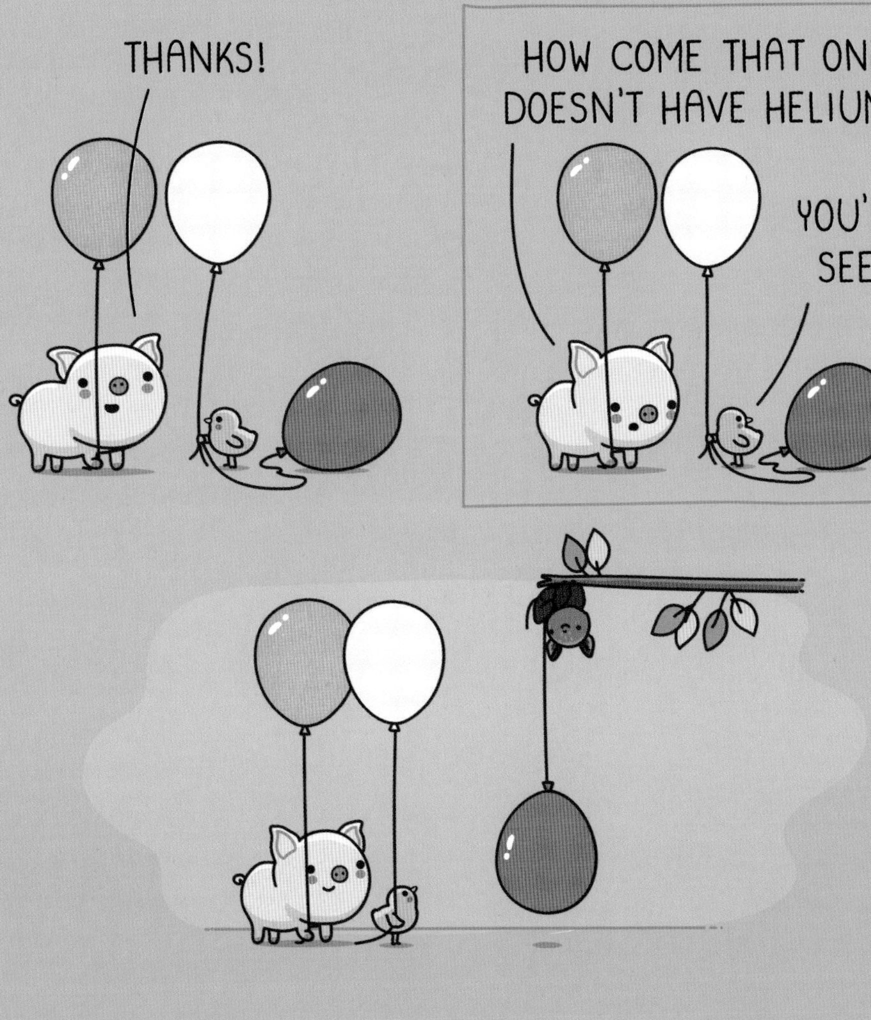
THANKS!
HOW COME THAT ONE DOESN'T HAVE HELIUM?
YOU'LL SEE.

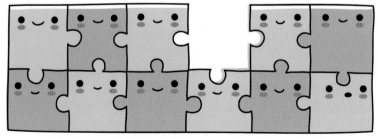

FITTING IN IS NOT ALWAYS
THE BEST THING.

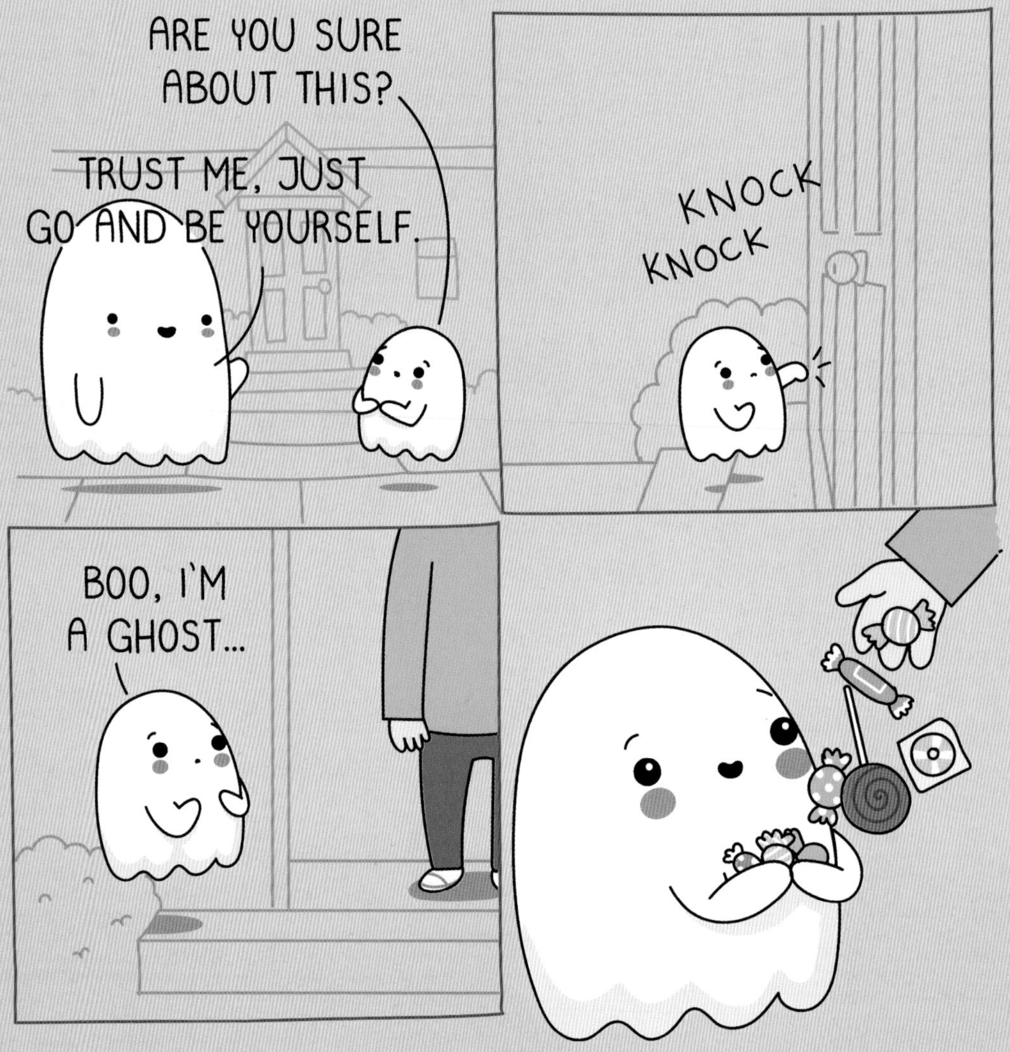
ARE YOU SURE ABOUT THIS?
TRUST ME, JUST GO AND BE YOURSELF.
KNOCK KNOCK
BOO, I'M A GHOST...

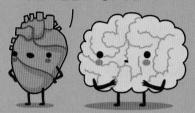

ANOTHER LOVE DISAPPOINTMENT. OUR HUMAN IS REALLY UPSET.

WHO'S RESPONSIBLE FOR LOVE HERE?

89

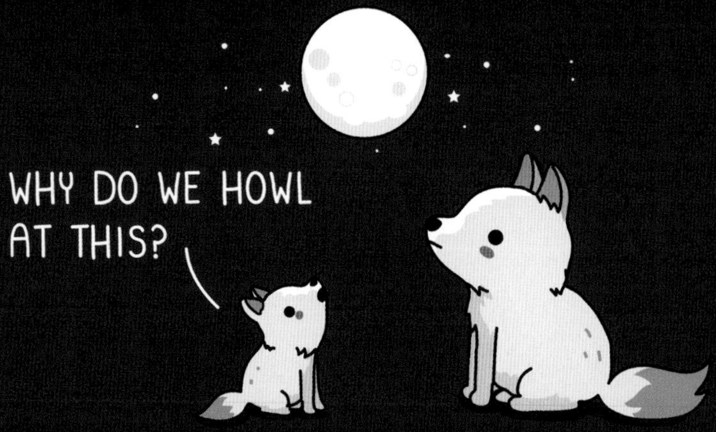
WHY DO WE HOWL
AT THIS?

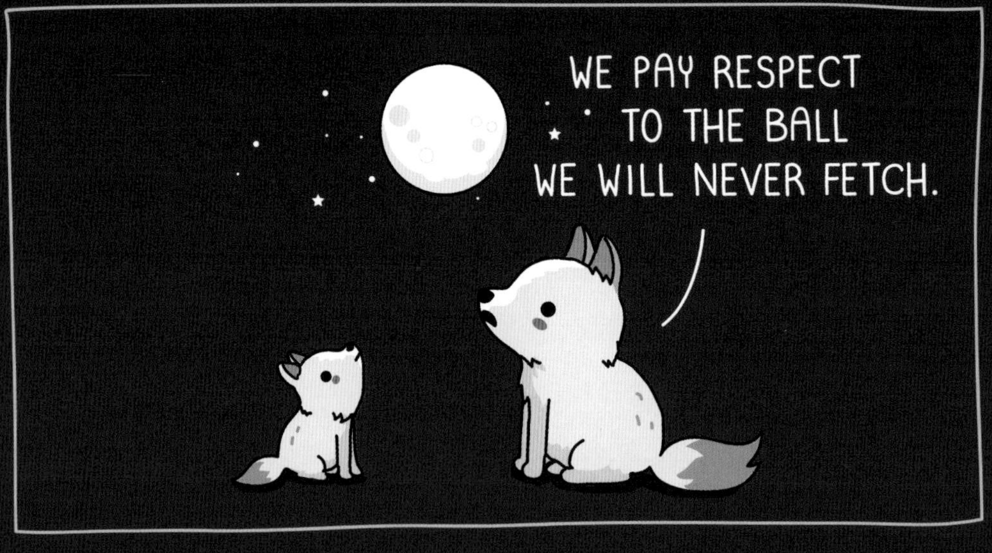
WE PAY RESPECT
TO THE BALL
WE WILL NEVER FETCH.

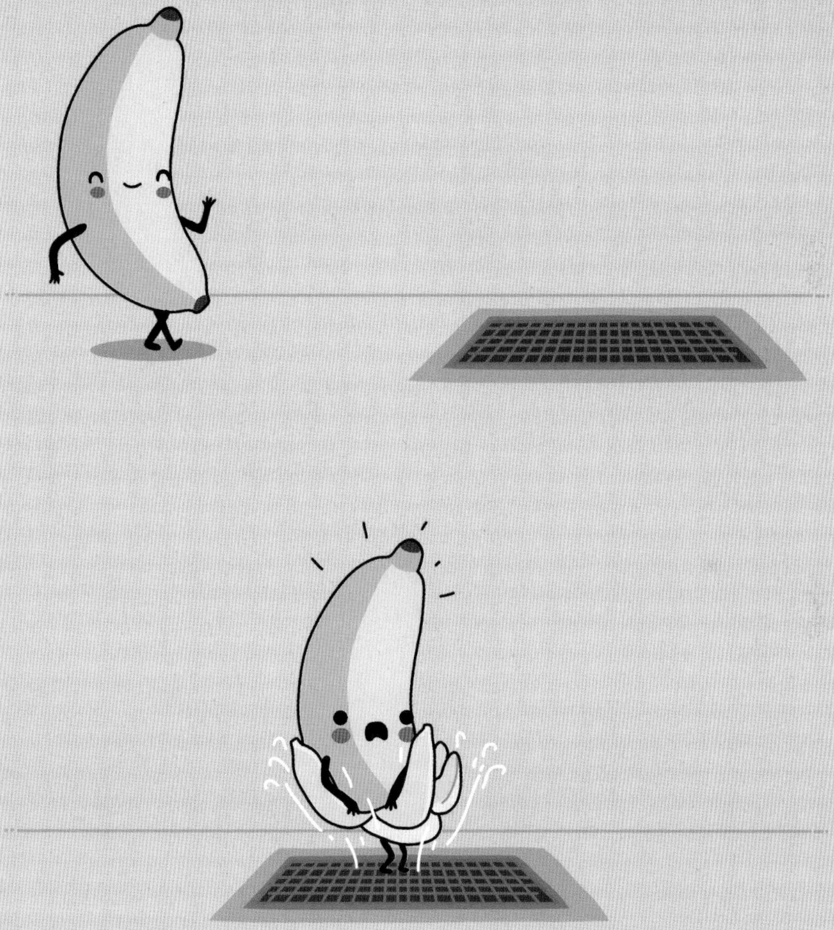

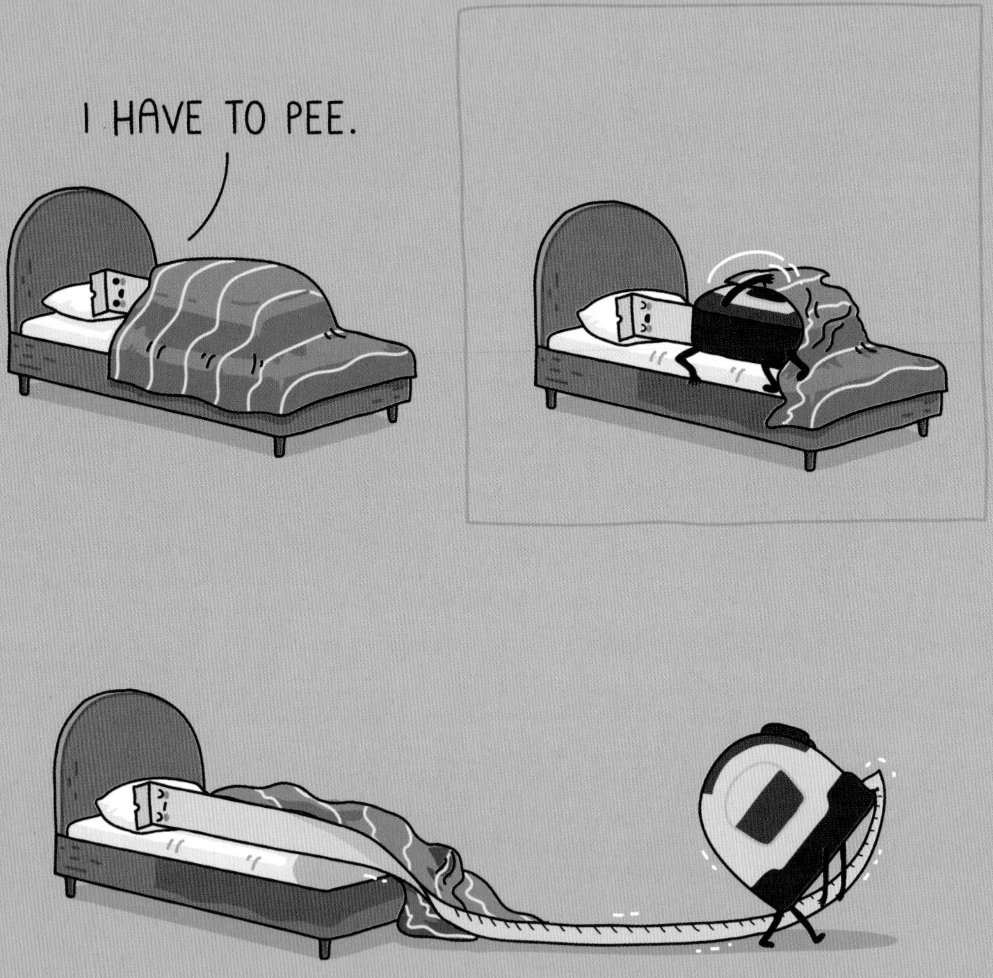
I HAVE TO PEE.

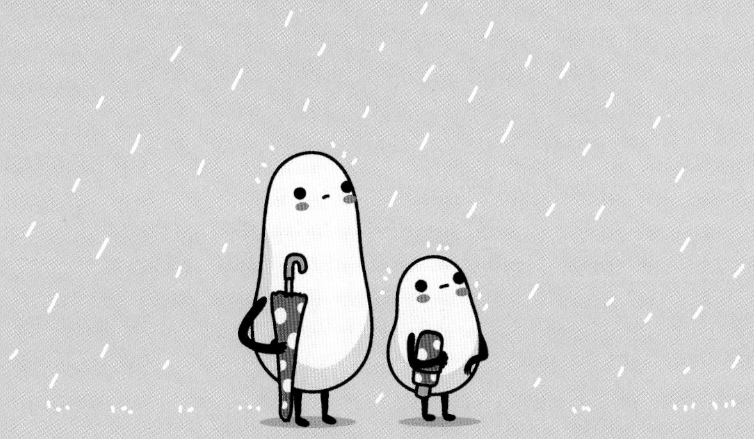

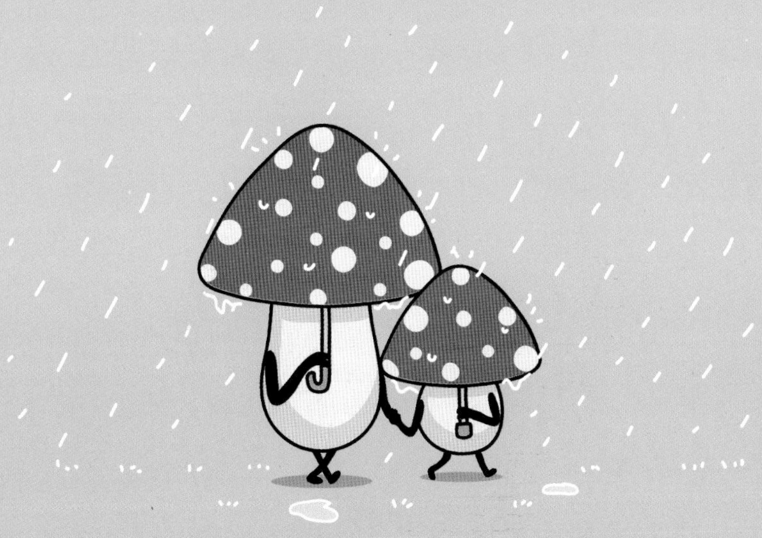

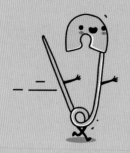

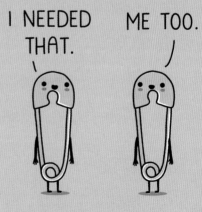

I NEEDED THAT.

ME TOO.

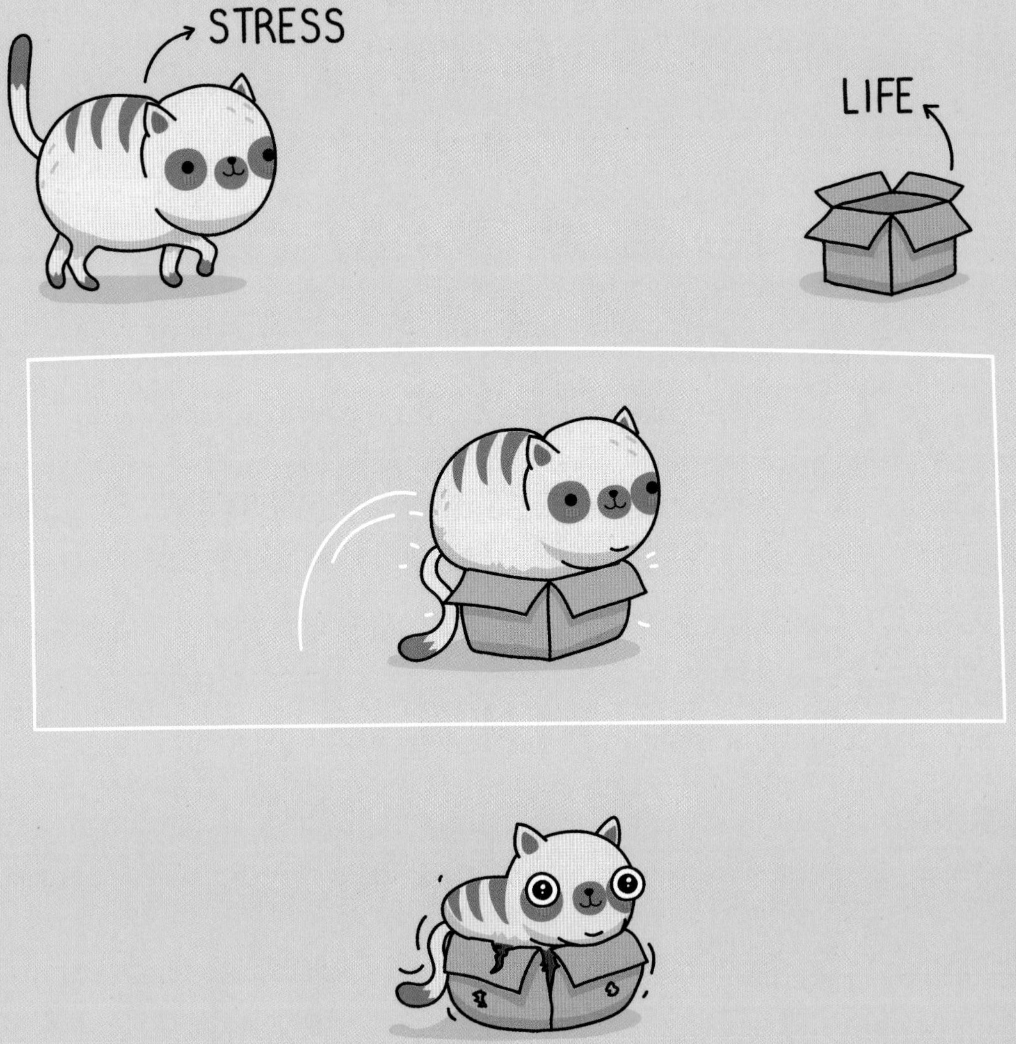
STRESS
LIFE

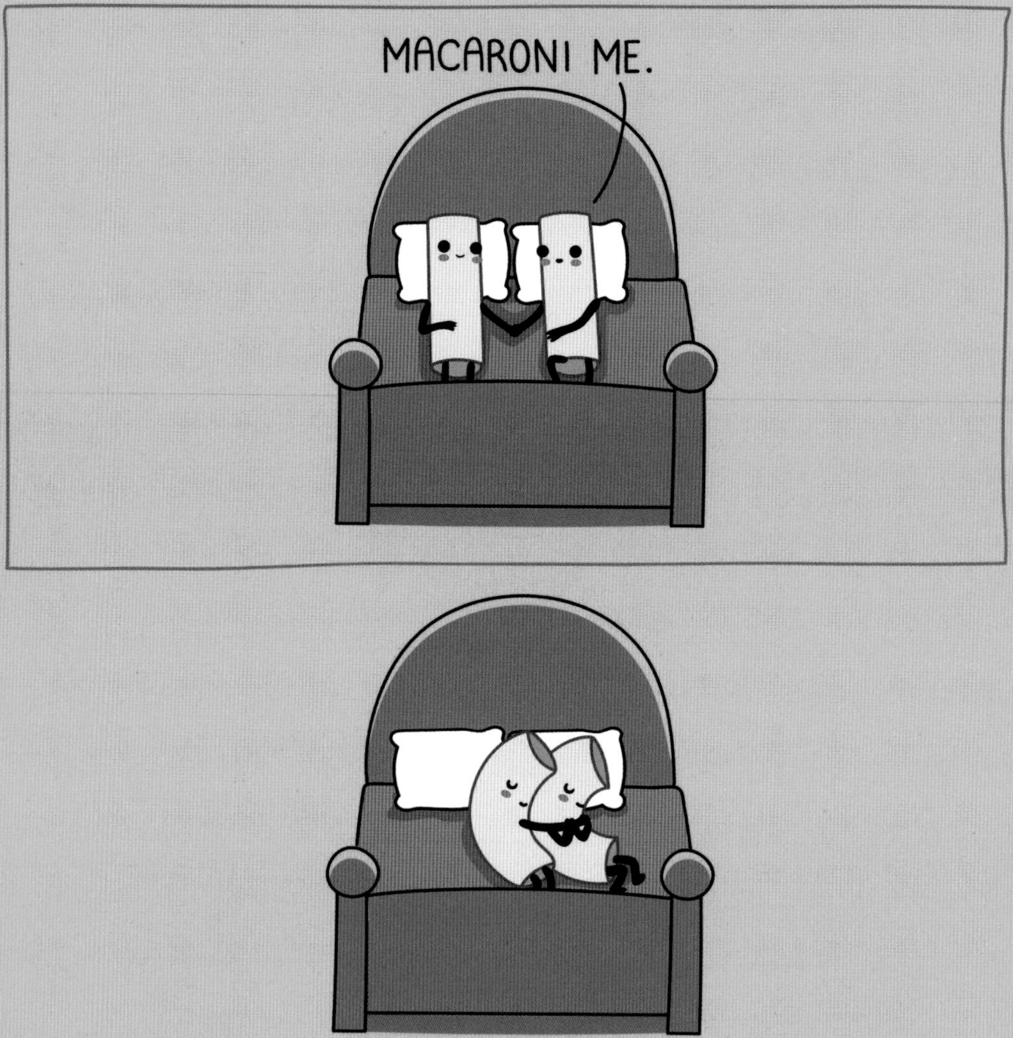
MACARONI ME.

PARANORMAL ACTIVITIES

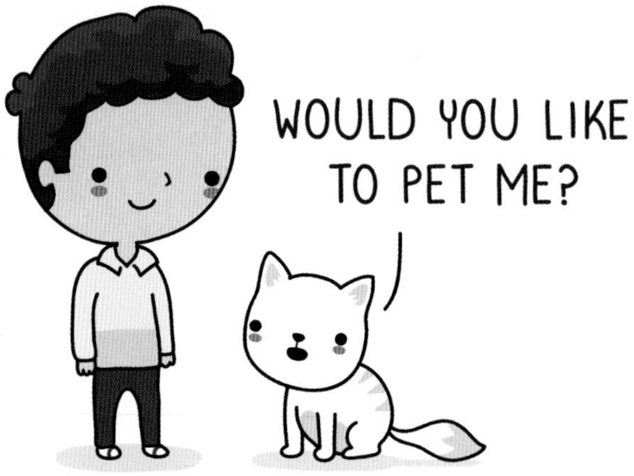
WOULD YOU LIKE TO PET ME?

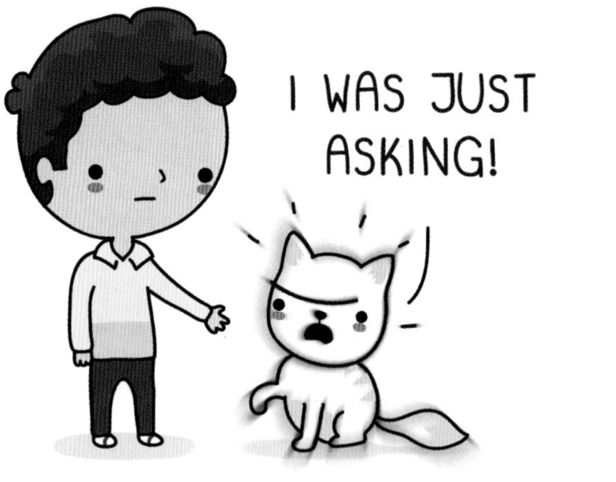
I WAS JUST ASKING!

REACTING TO CONFLICTS

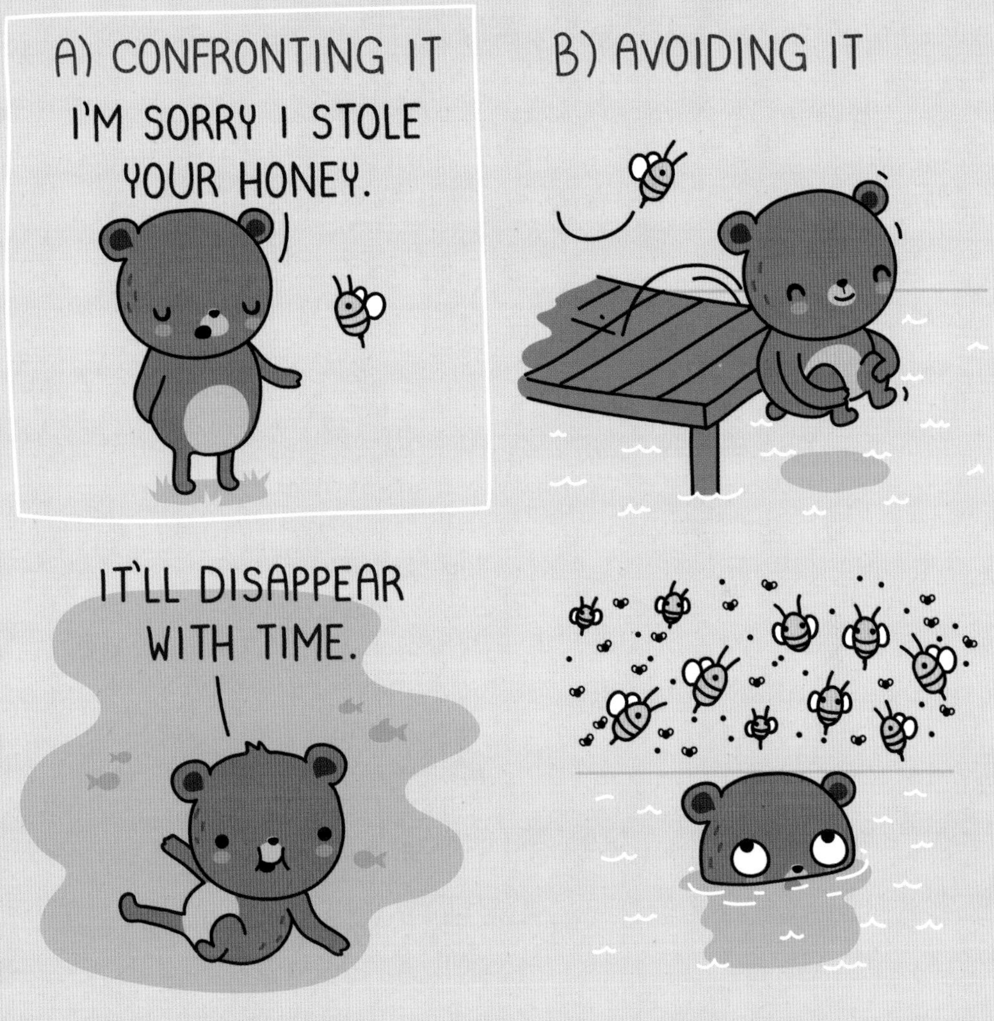
A) CONFRONTING IT
I'M SORRY I STOLE YOUR HONEY.
B) AVOIDING IT
IT'LL DISAPPEAR WITH TIME.

YOU DON'T NEED TO HOLD MY SEAT.

BUT IT'LL FOLD BACK UP.

I SEE BETTER FROM HERE.

ME IN MY PROFILE PIC.

ME IN REAL LIFE.

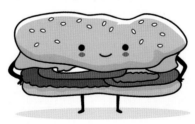

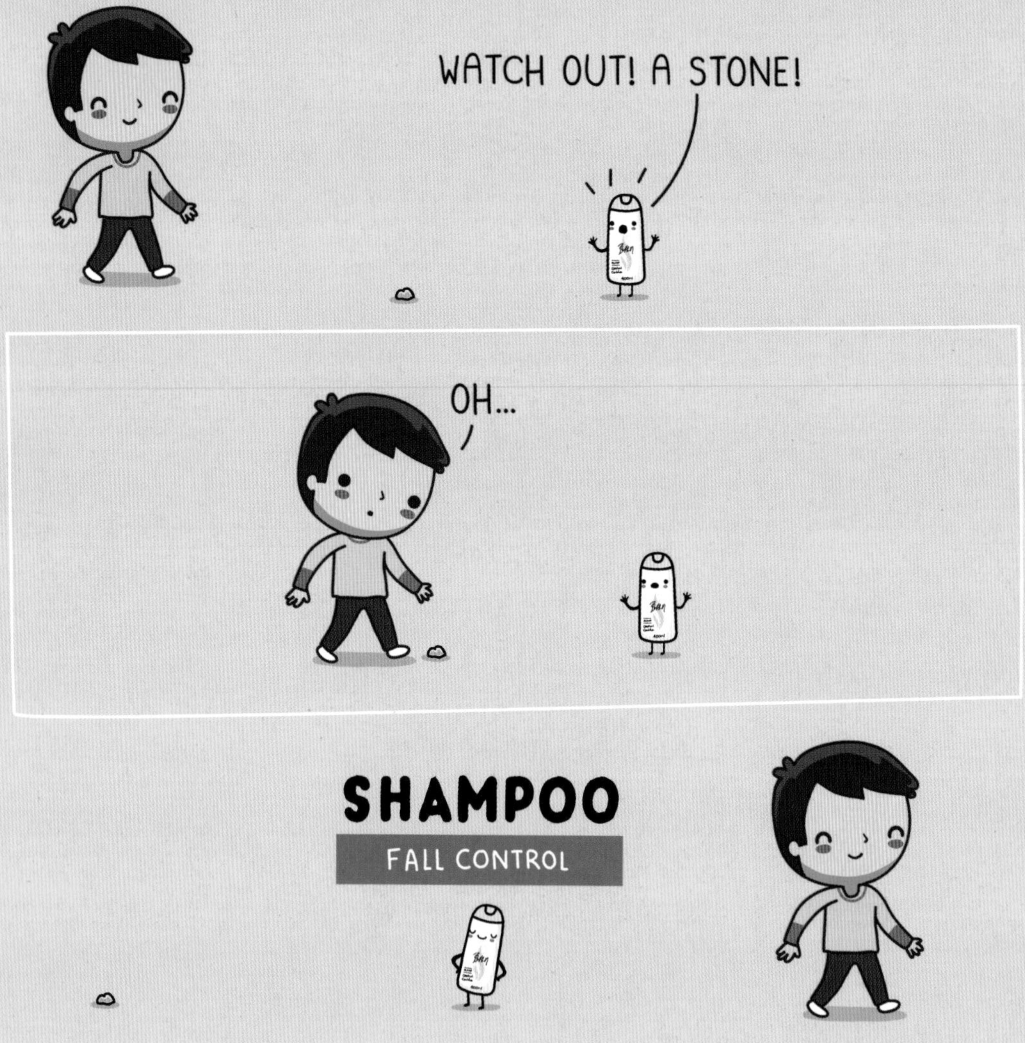
WATCH OUT! A STONE!
OH...
SHAMPOO
FALL CONTROL

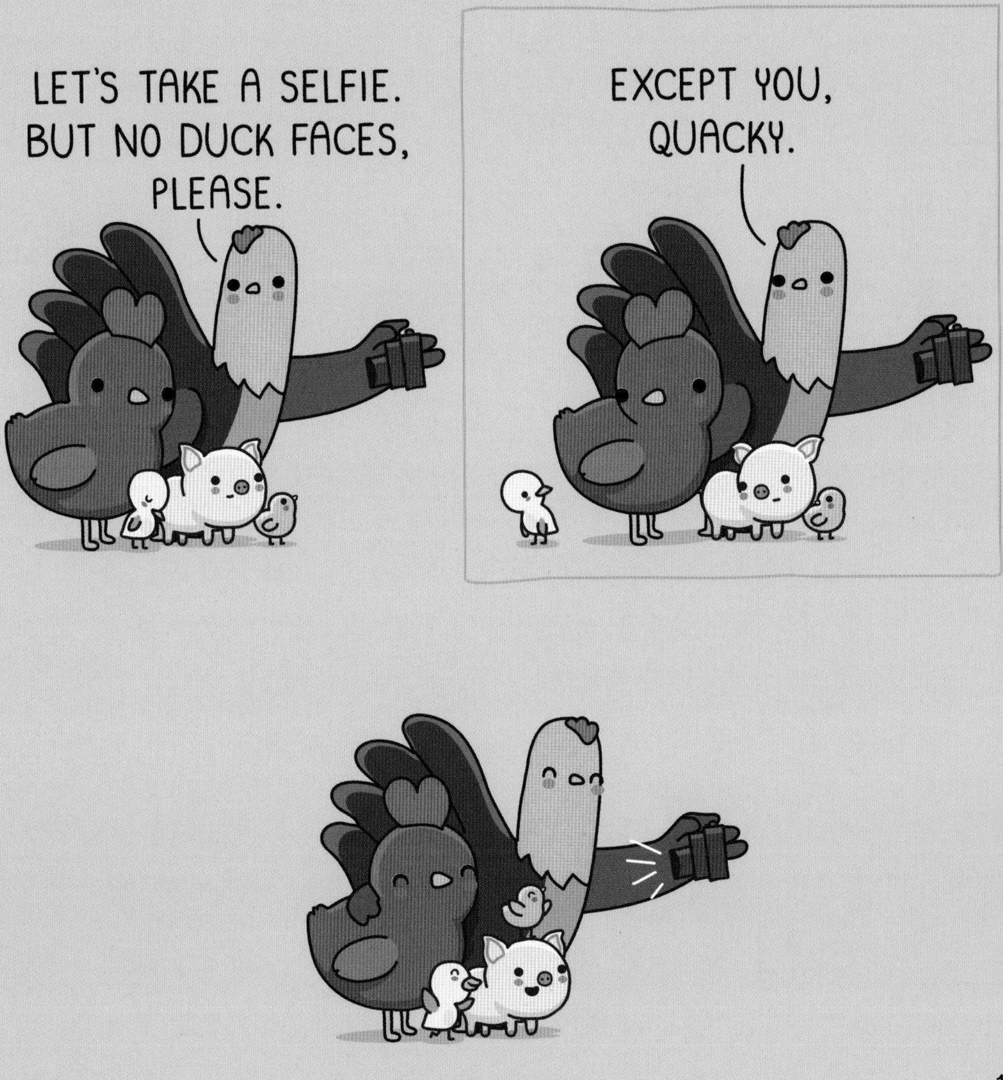
LET'S TAKE A SELFIE. BUT NO DUCK FACES, PLEASE.
EXCEPT YOU, QUACKY.

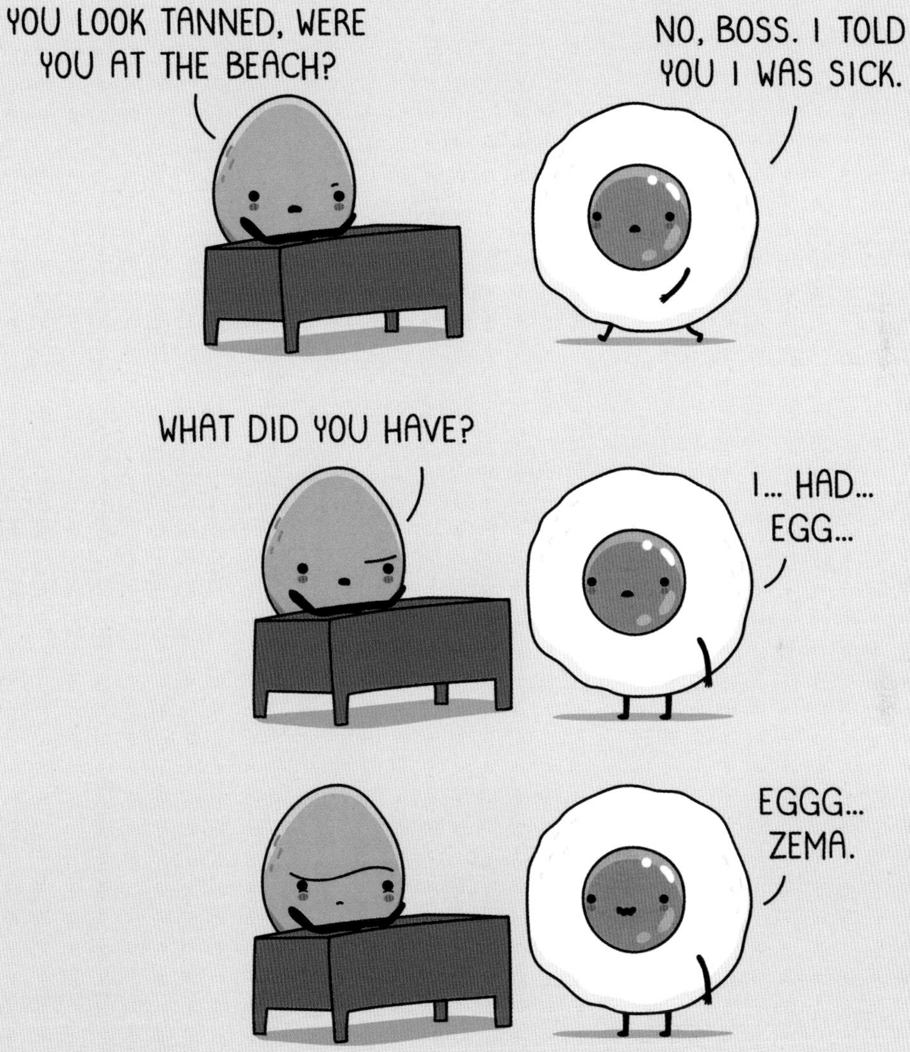
YOU LOOK TANNED, WERE YOU AT THE BEACH?
NO, BOSS. I TOLD YOU I WAS SICK.
WHAT DID YOU HAVE?
I... HAD... EGG...
EGGG... ZEMA.

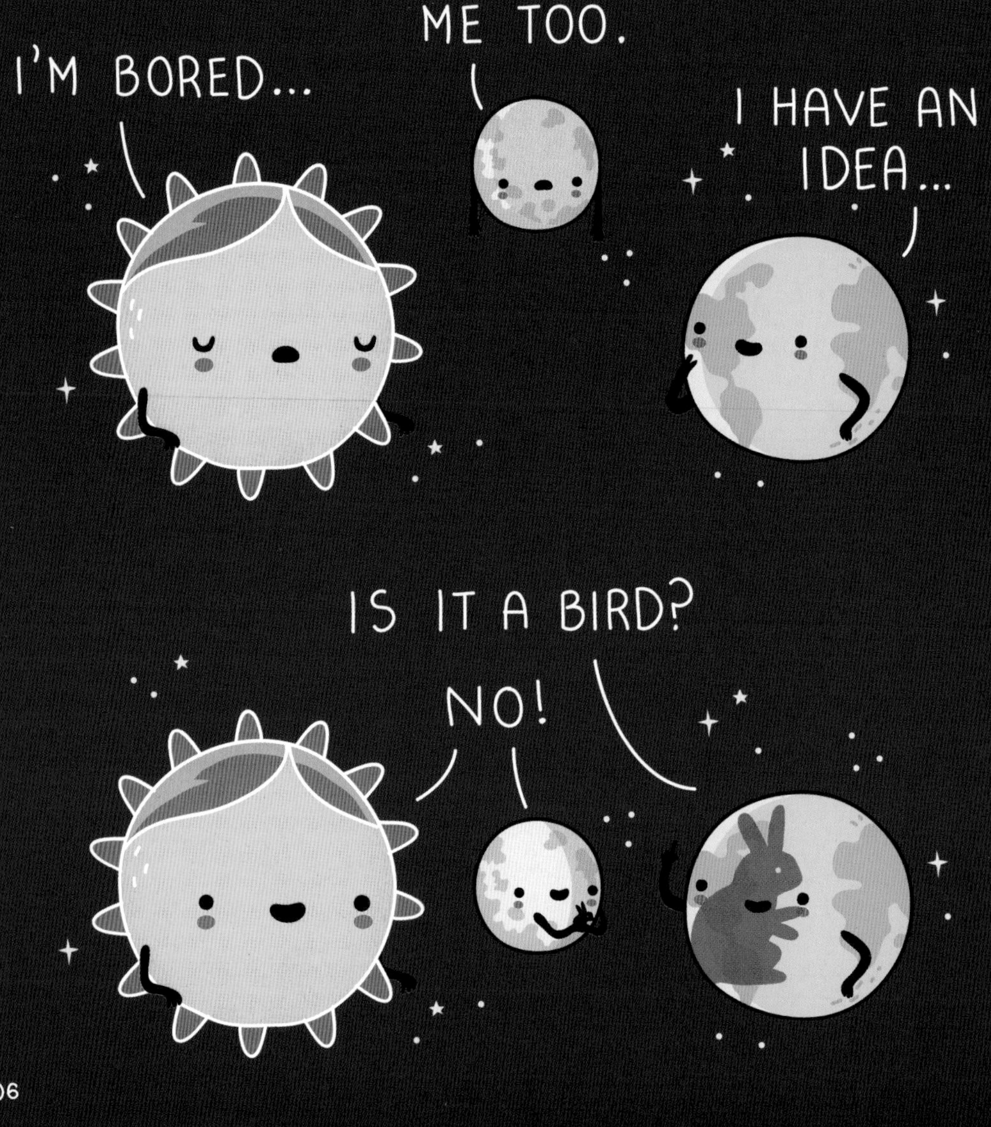
I'M BORED...
ME TOO.
I HAVE AN IDEA...
IS IT A BIRD?
NO!
NO!

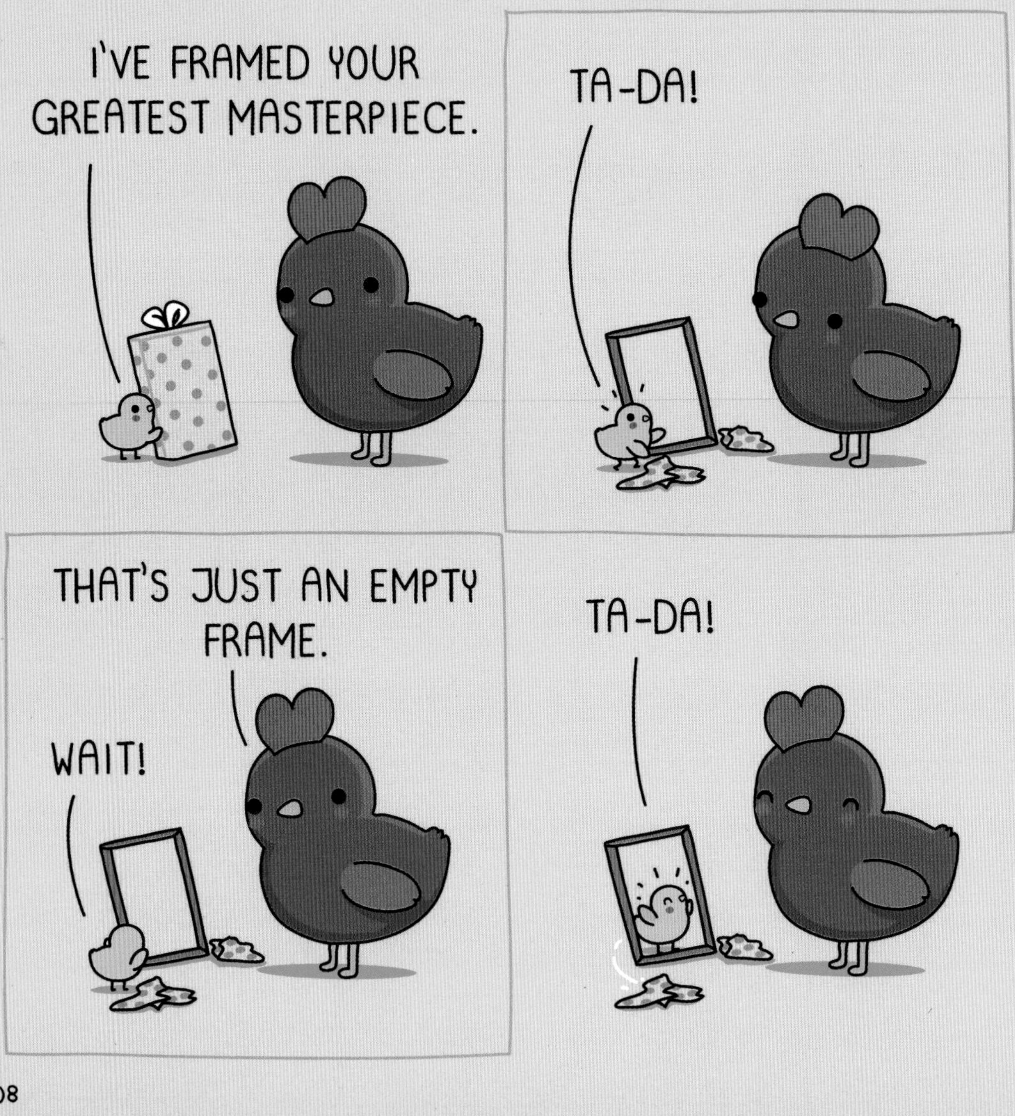
I'VE FRAMED YOUR GREATEST MASTERPIECE.
TA-DA!
THAT'S JUST AN EMPTY FRAME.
WAIT!
TA-DA!

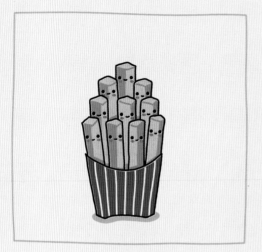

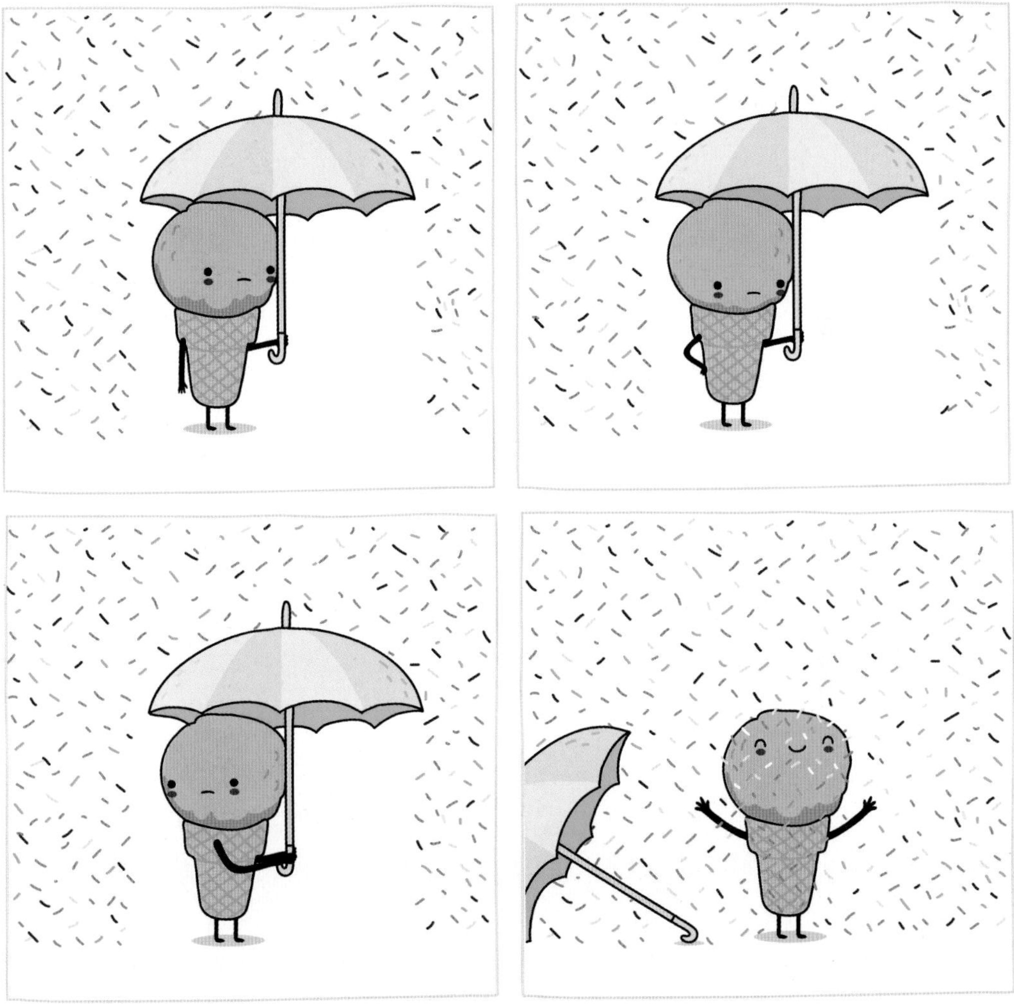

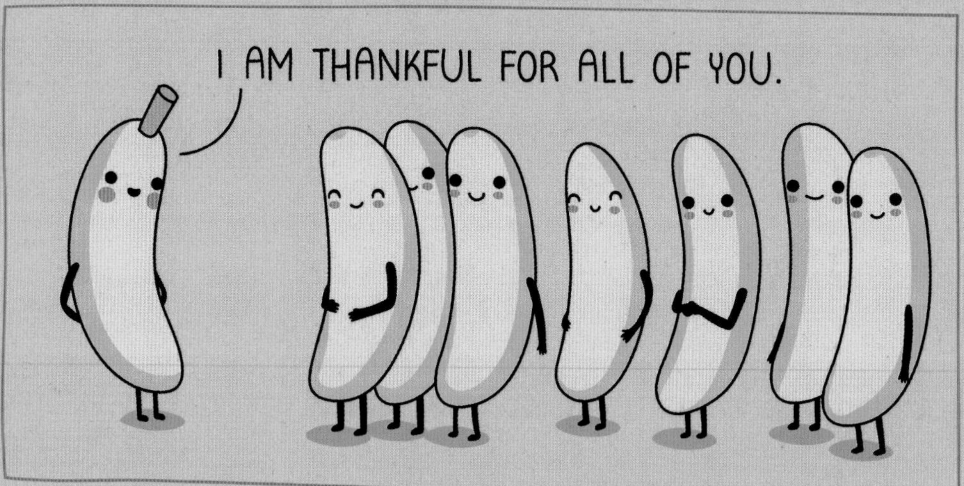
I AM THANKFUL FOR ALL OF YOU.

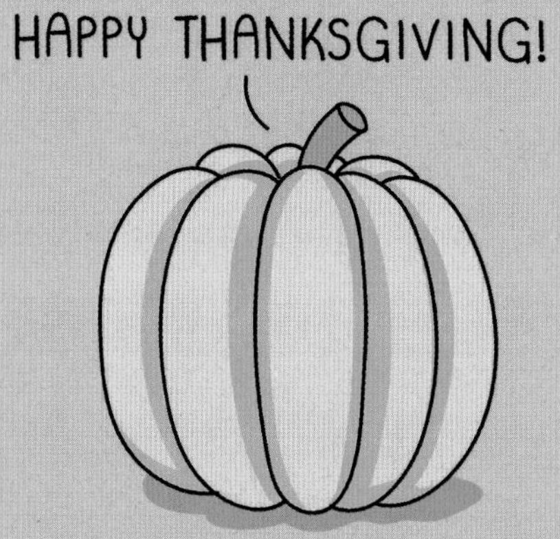
HAPPY THANKSGIVING!

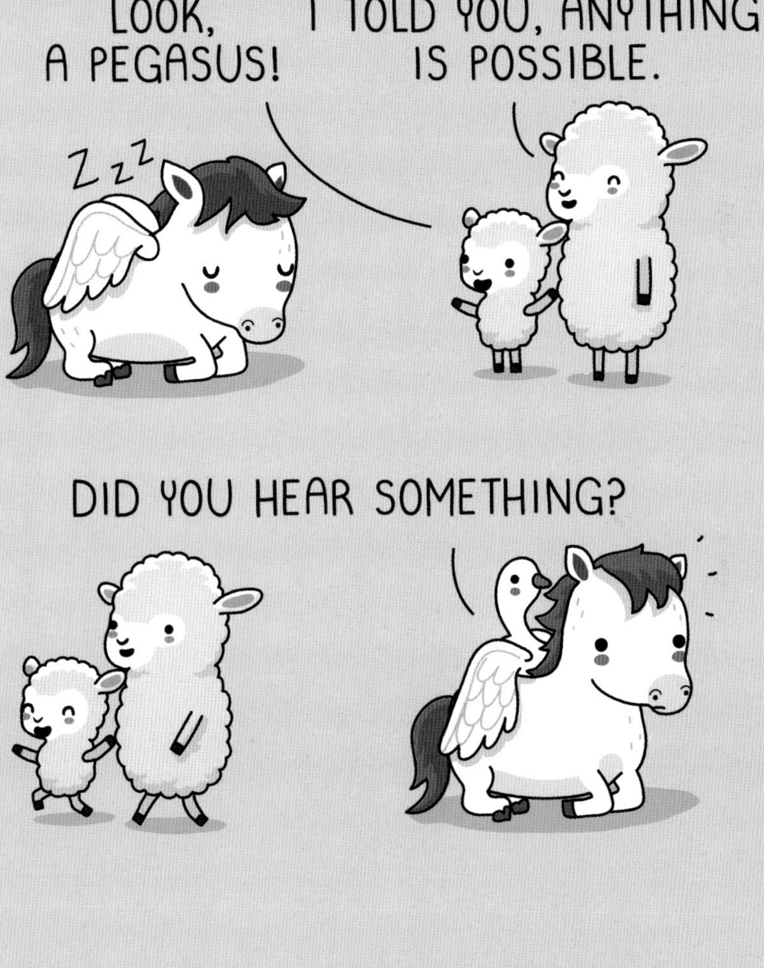
LOOK, A PEGASUS!
I TOLD YOU, ANYTHING IS POSSIBLE.
Z z z
DID YOU HEAR SOMETHING?

IT'S TIME TO WAKE UP. COME ON, WAKE UP.
I CAN'T KEEP MY EYES OPEN.

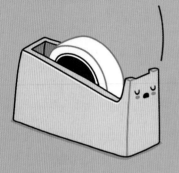

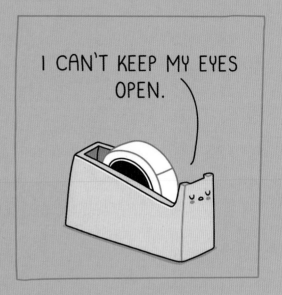

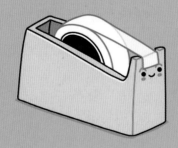

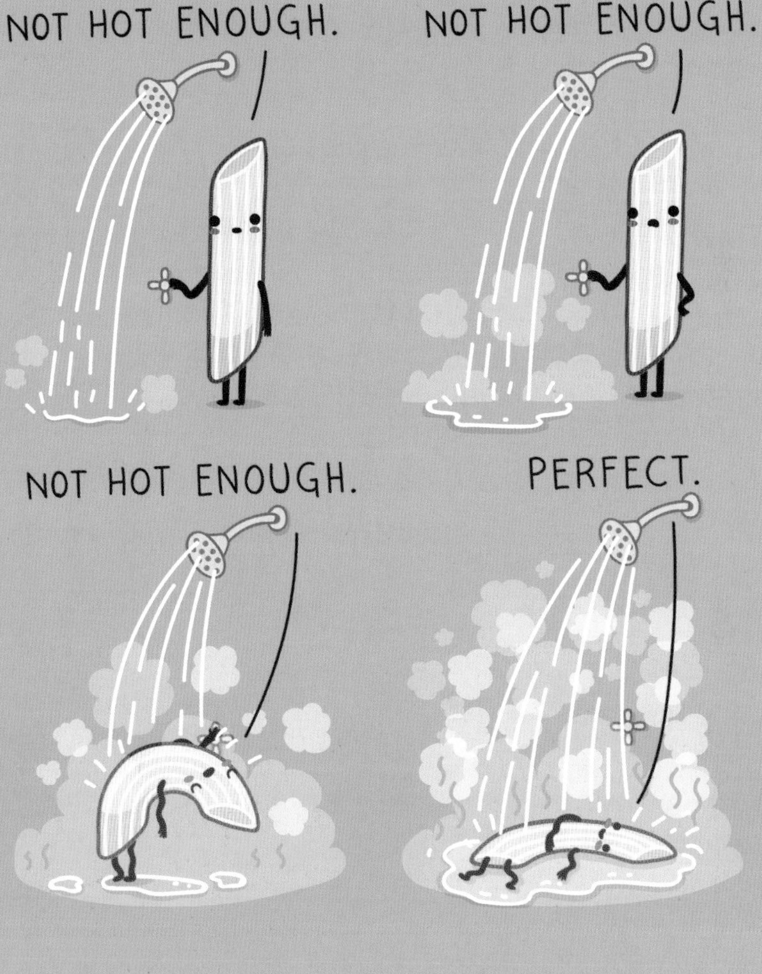
NOT HOT ENOUGH.
NOT HOT ENOUGH.
NOT HOT ENOUGH.
PERFECT.

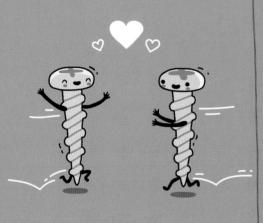

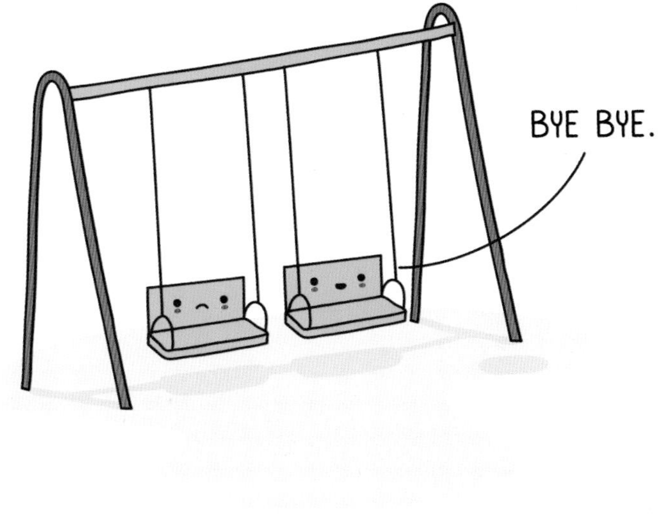
BYE BYE.

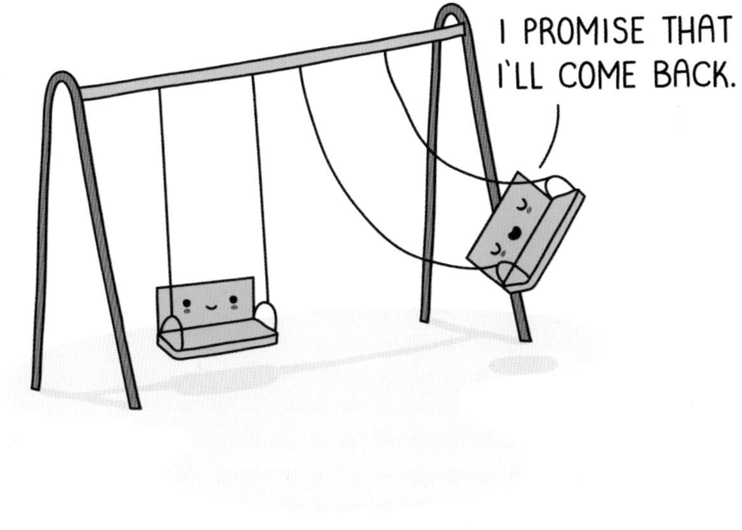
I PROMISE THAT I'LL COME BACK.

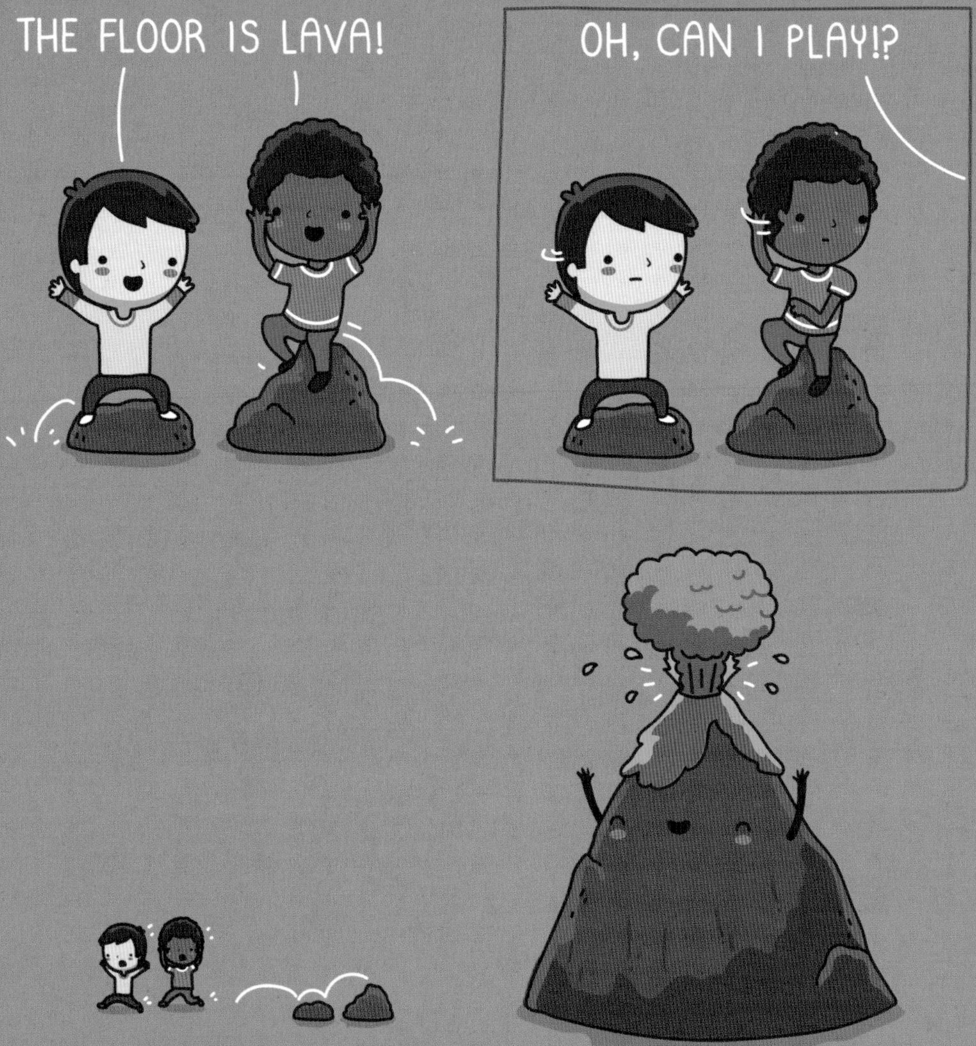
THE FLOOR IS LAVA!
OH, CAN I PLAY!?

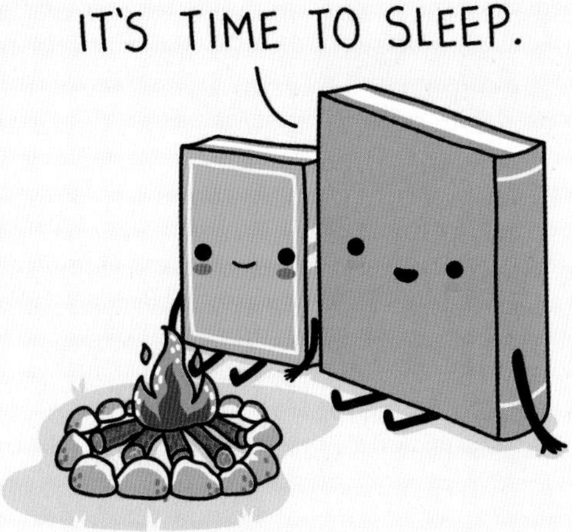
IT'S TIME TO SLEEP.

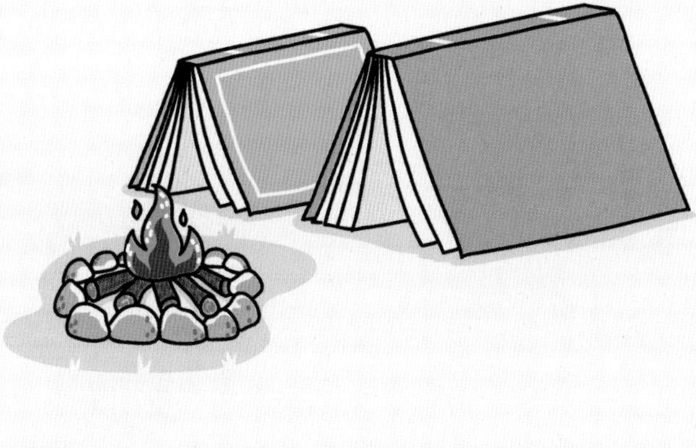

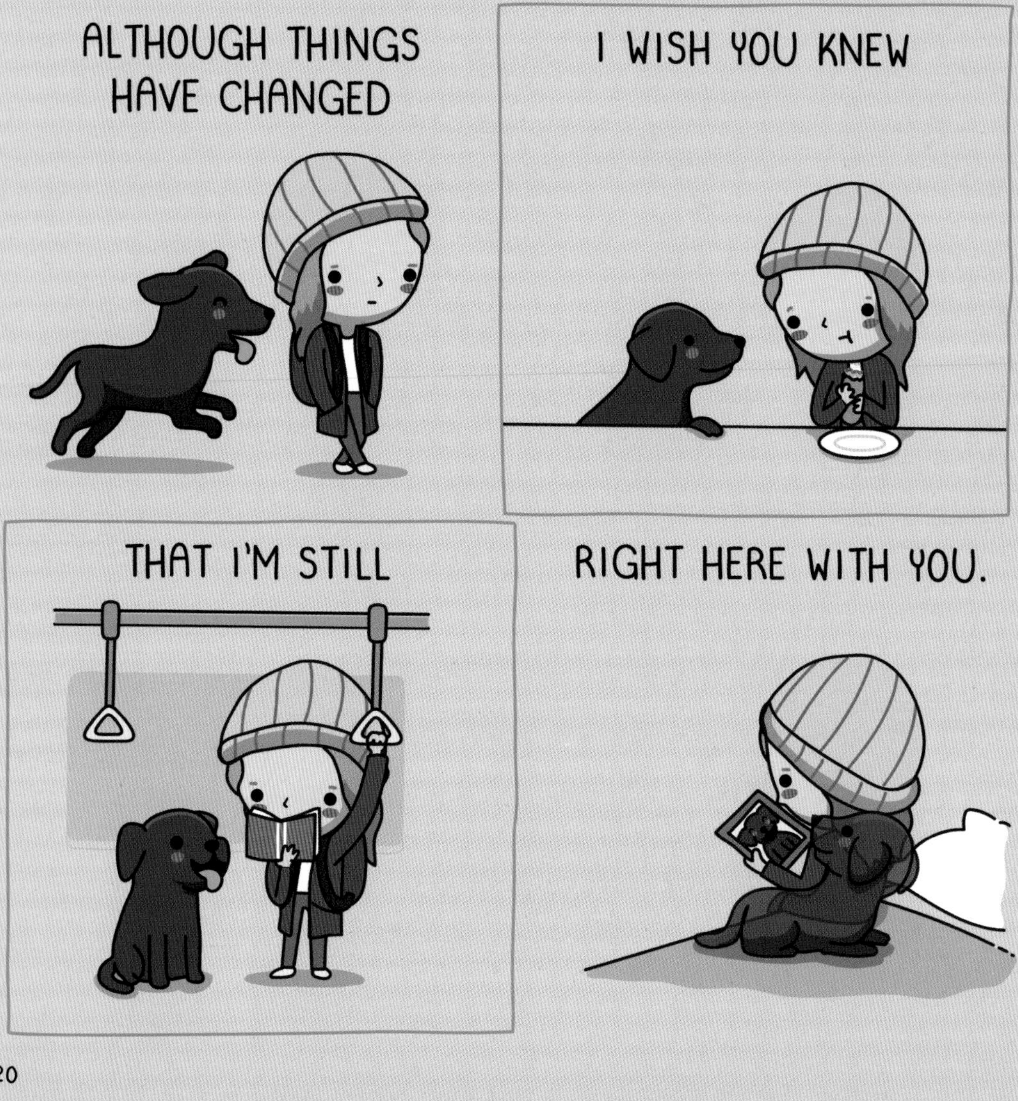
ALTHOUGH THINGS HAVE CHANGED
I WISH YOU KNEW
THAT I'M STILL
RIGHT HERE WITH YOU.

COLLECT POLLEN,
WORK, WORK, WORK.

I NEED A BREAK
FROM ROUTINE.

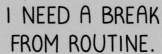

WELL, I'M STUCK IN BED.

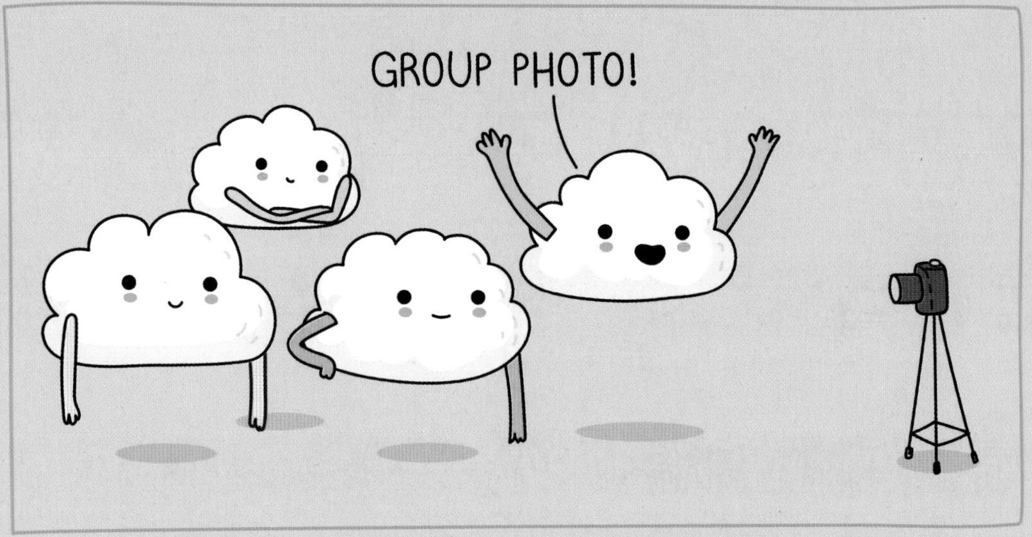
GROUP PHOTO!

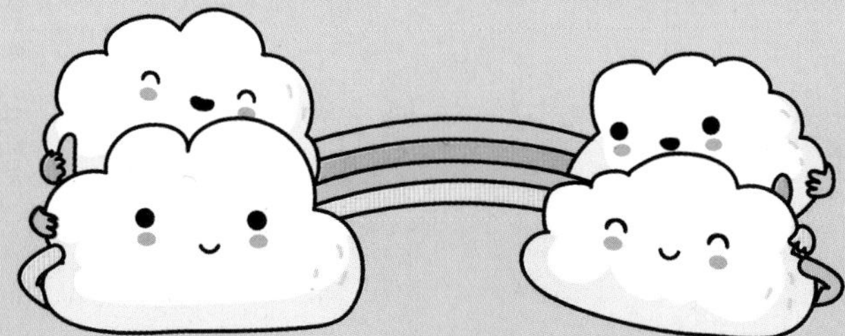

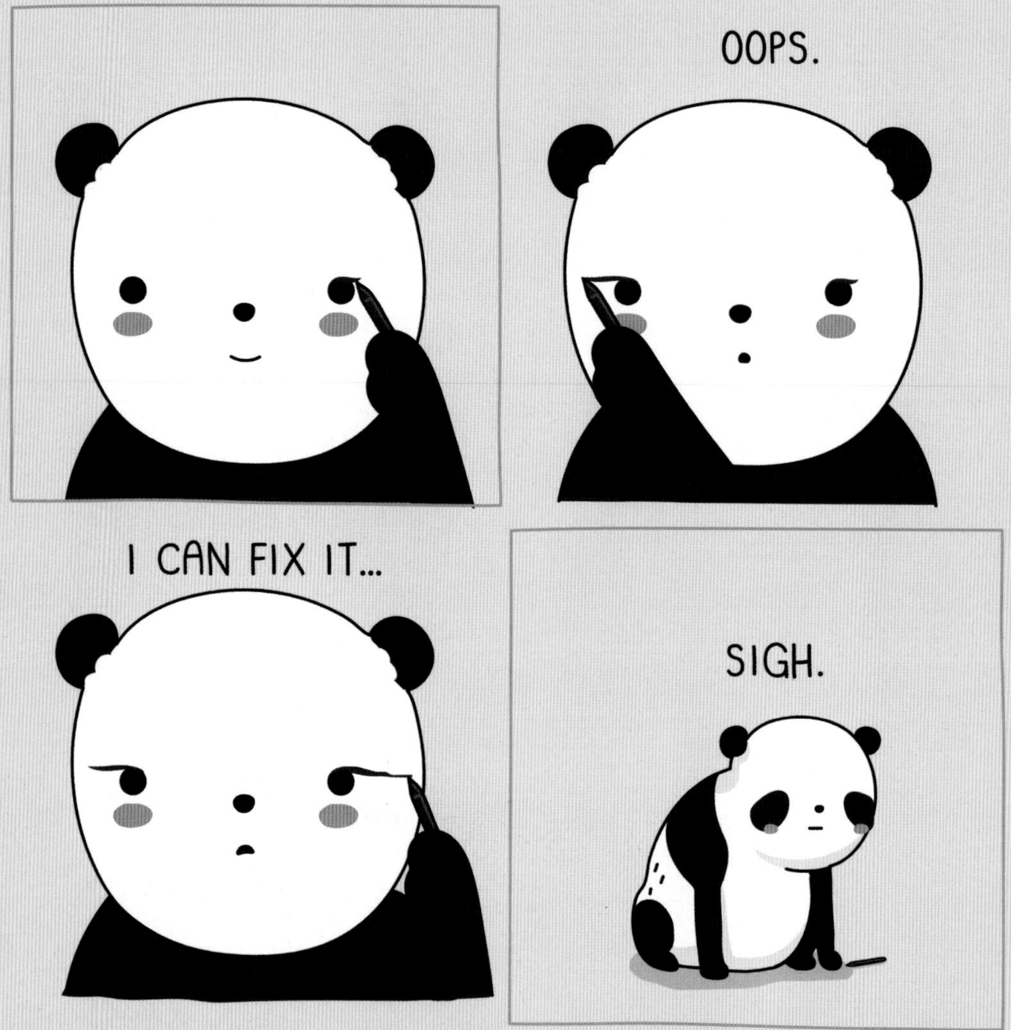
OOPS.
I CAN FIX IT...
SIGH.

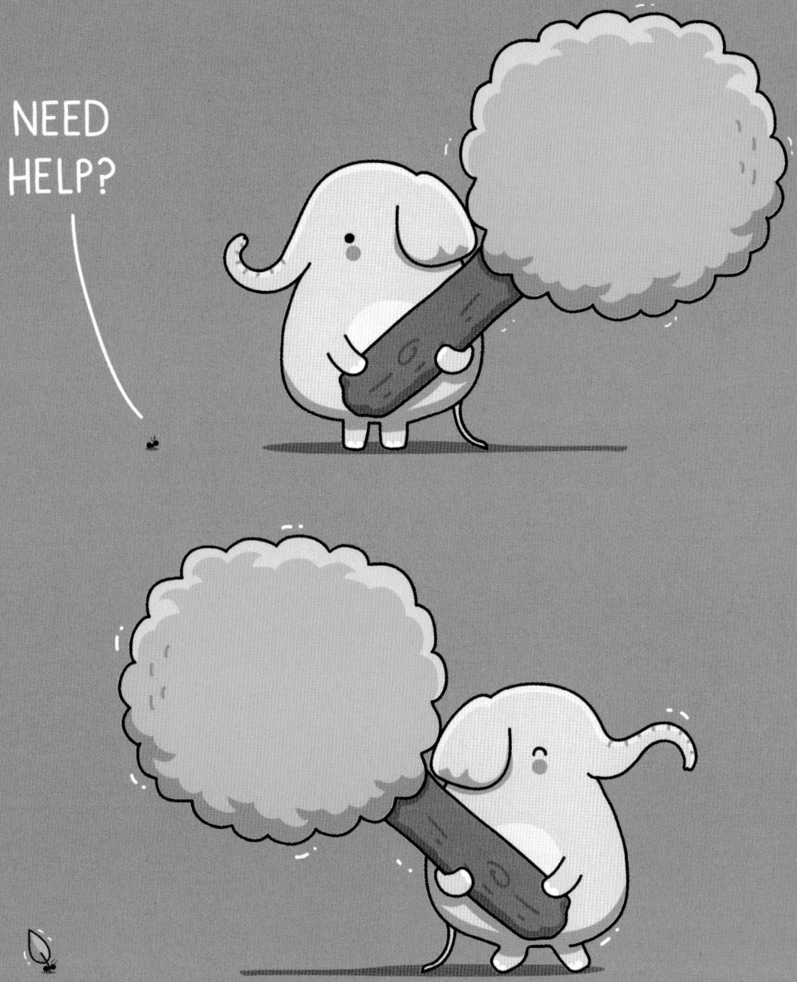
NEED
HELP?

GOD, WHY DID
YOU TAKE HIM?!

I'M DOING
YOGA.

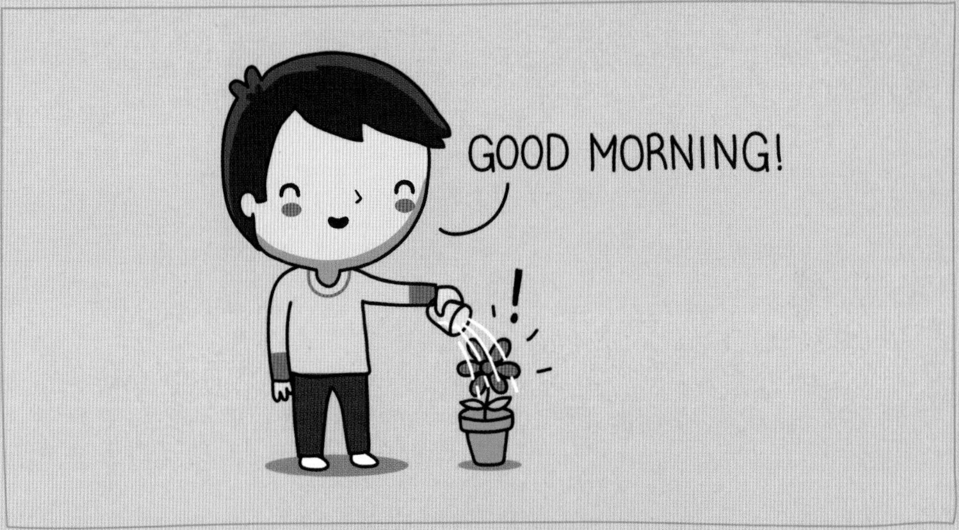
GOOD MORNING!

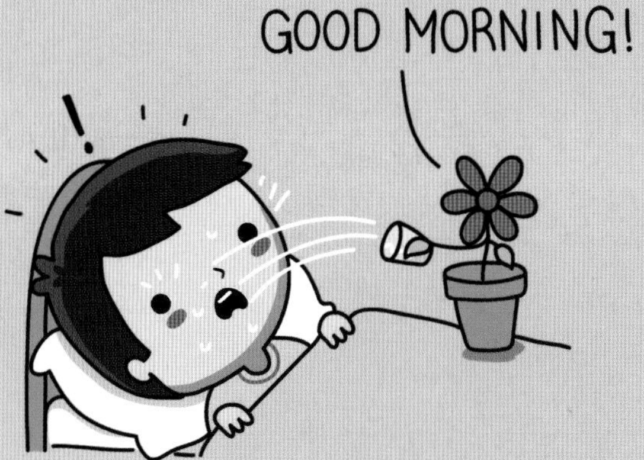
GOOD MORNING!

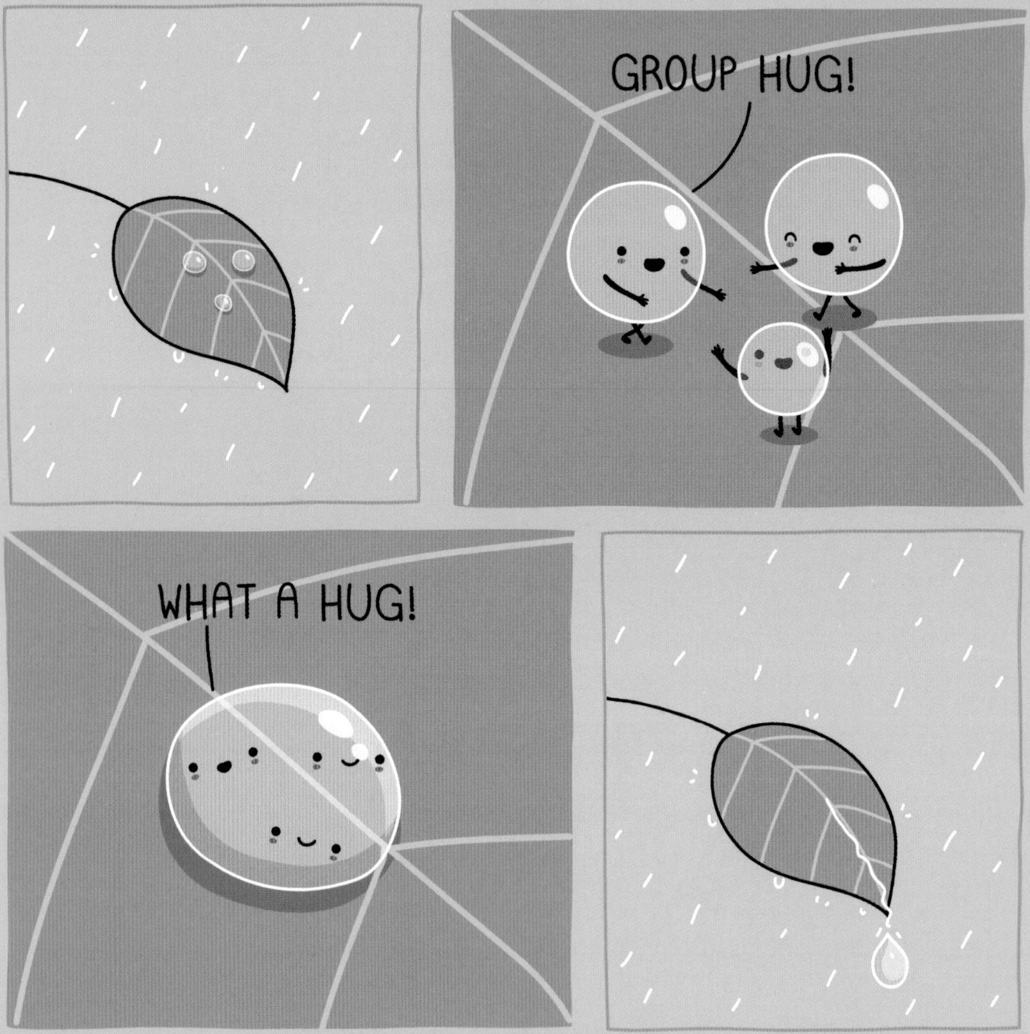
GROUP HUG!
WHAT A HUG!

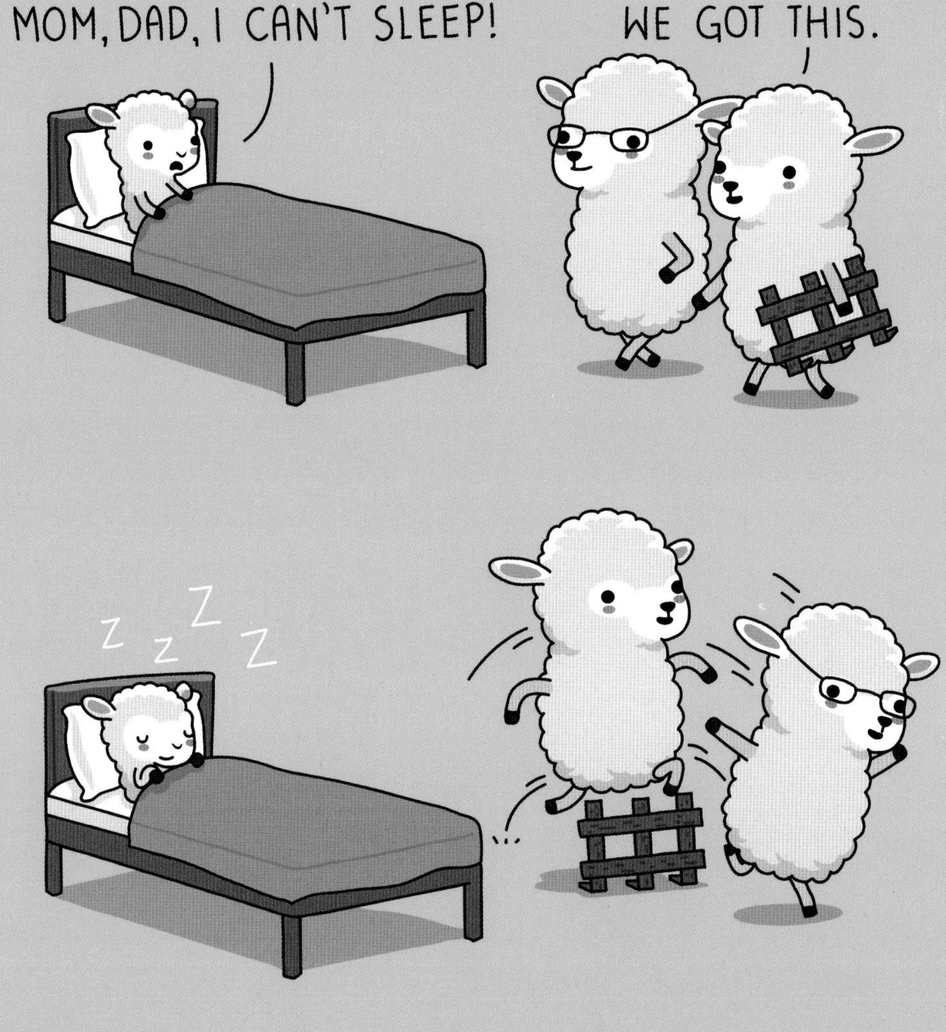
MOM, DAD, I CAN'T SLEEP!
WE GOT THIS.
Z Z Z Z

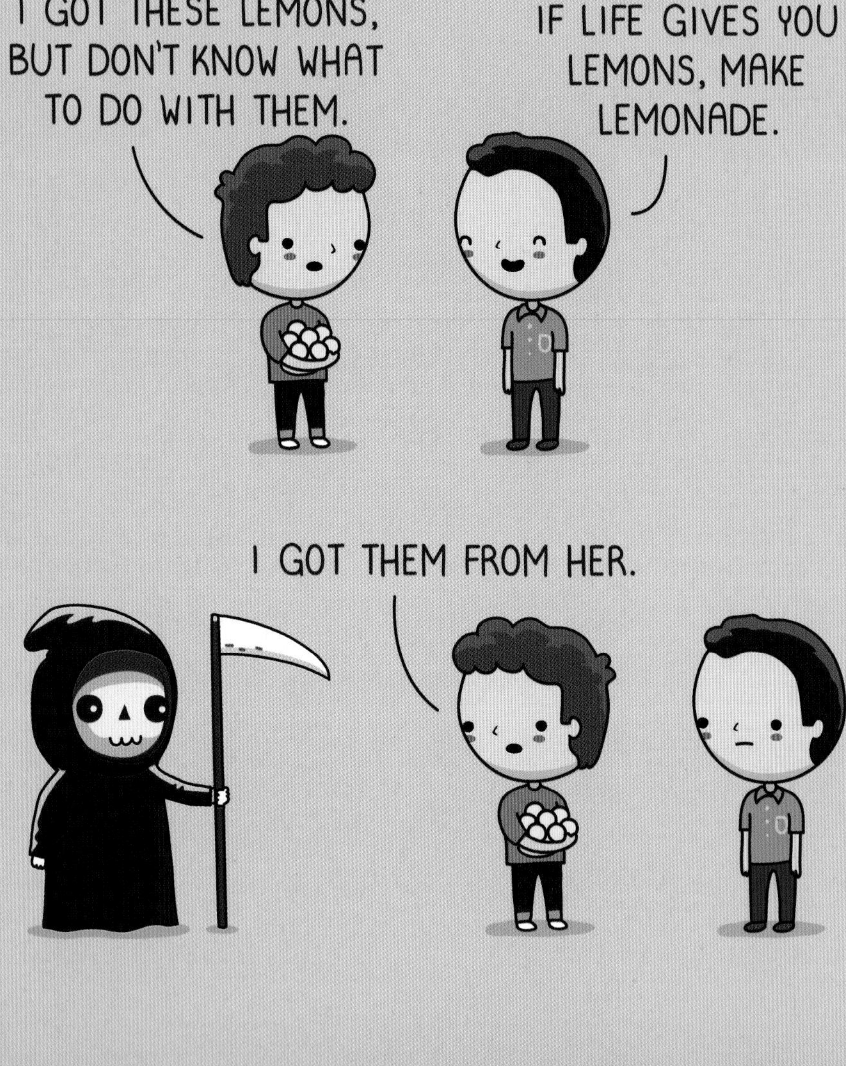
I GOT THESE LEMONS, BUT DON'T KNOW WHAT TO DO WITH THEM.
IF LIFE GIVES YOU LEMONS, MAKE LEMONADE.
I GOT THEM FROM HER.

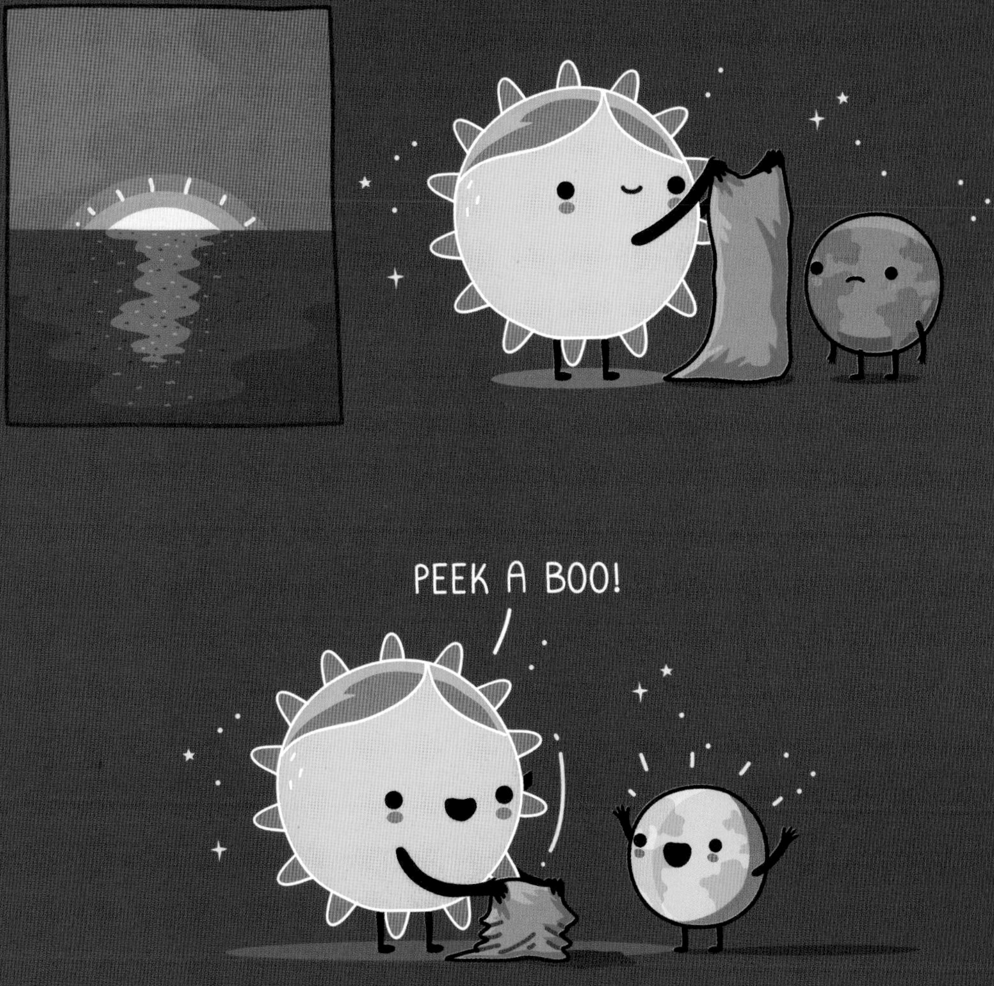
PEEK A BOO!

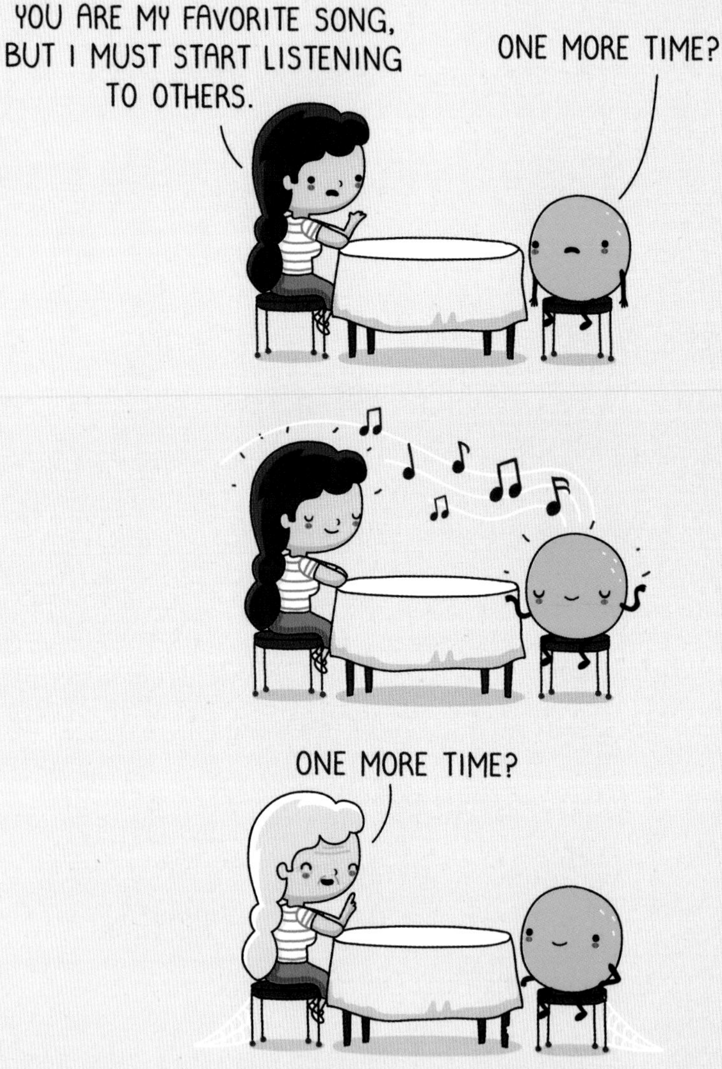
YOU ARE MY FAVORITE SONG, BUT I MUST START LISTENING TO OTHERS.
ONE MORE TIME?
ONE MORE TIME?

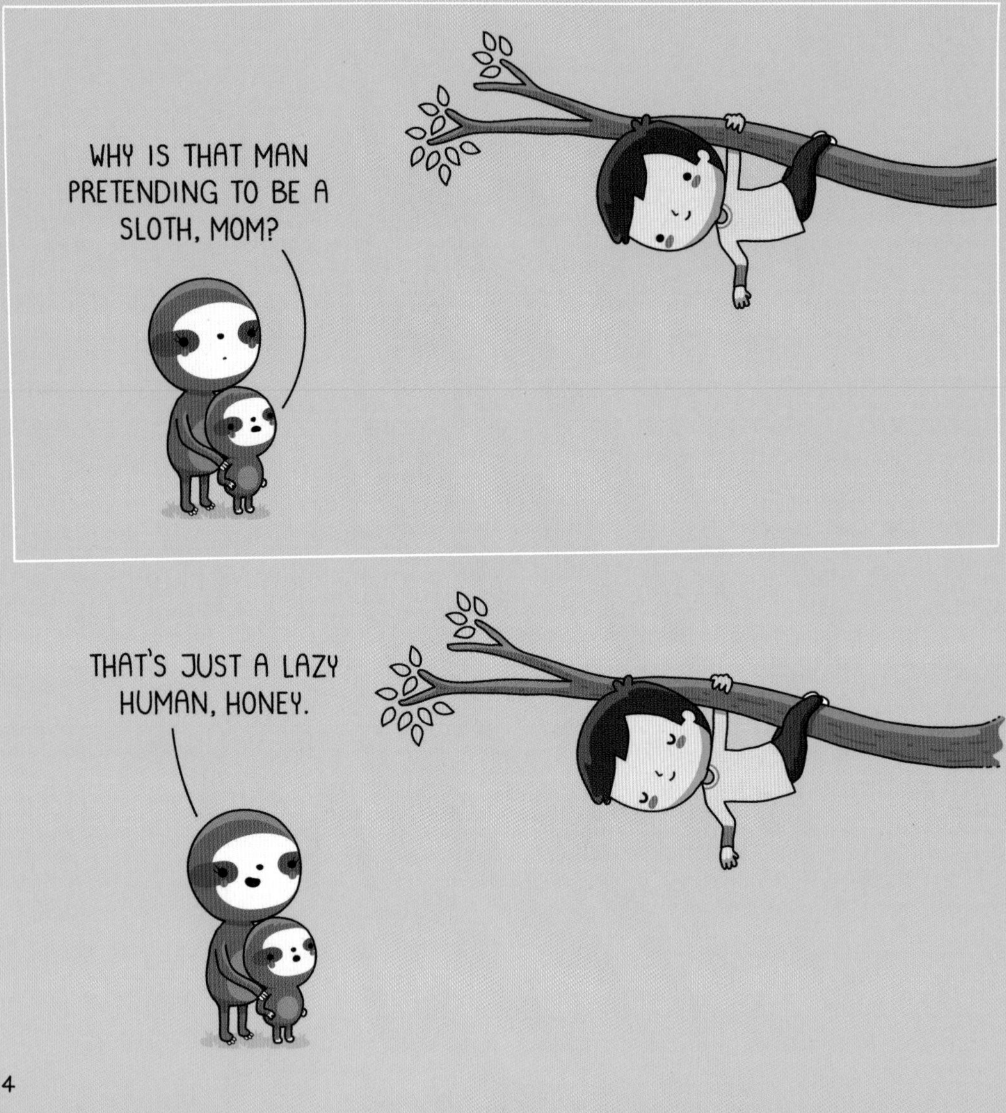
WHY IS THAT MAN PRETENDING TO BE A SLOTH, MOM?
THAT'S JUST A LAZY HUMAN, HONEY.

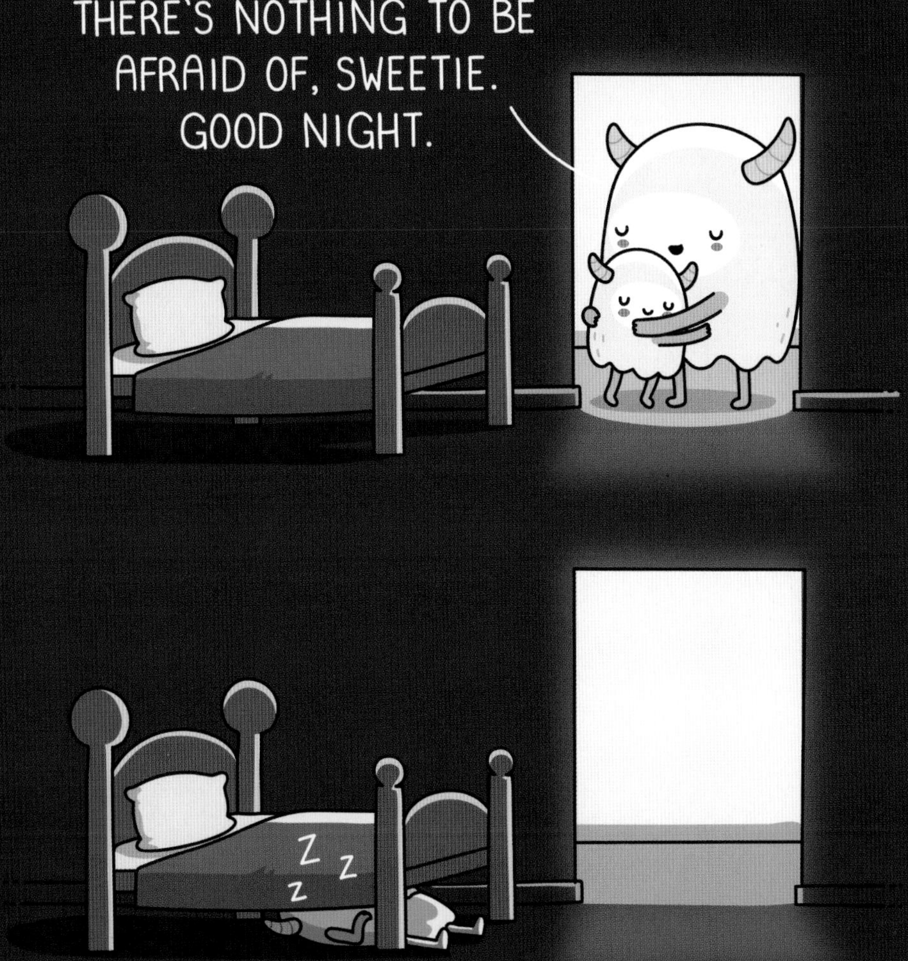
THERE'S NOTHING TO BE AFRAID OF, SWEETIE. GOOD NIGHT.
Z Z Z

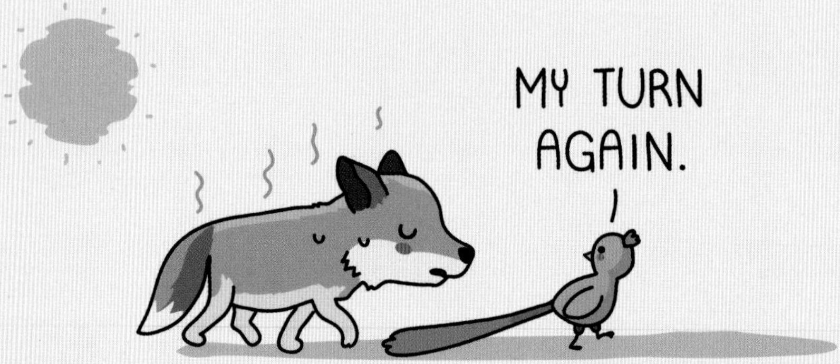
MY TURN
AGAIN.

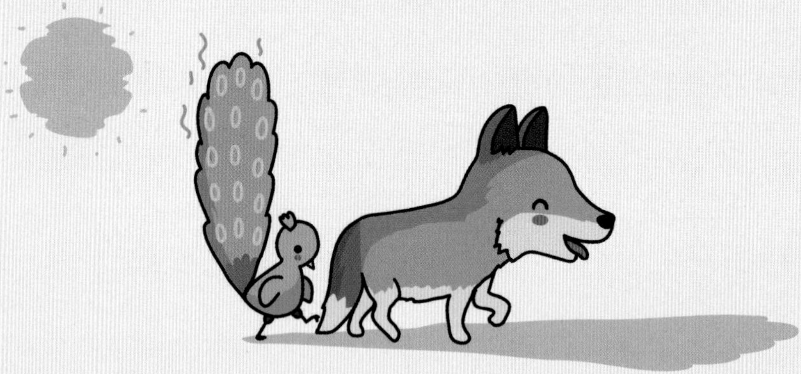

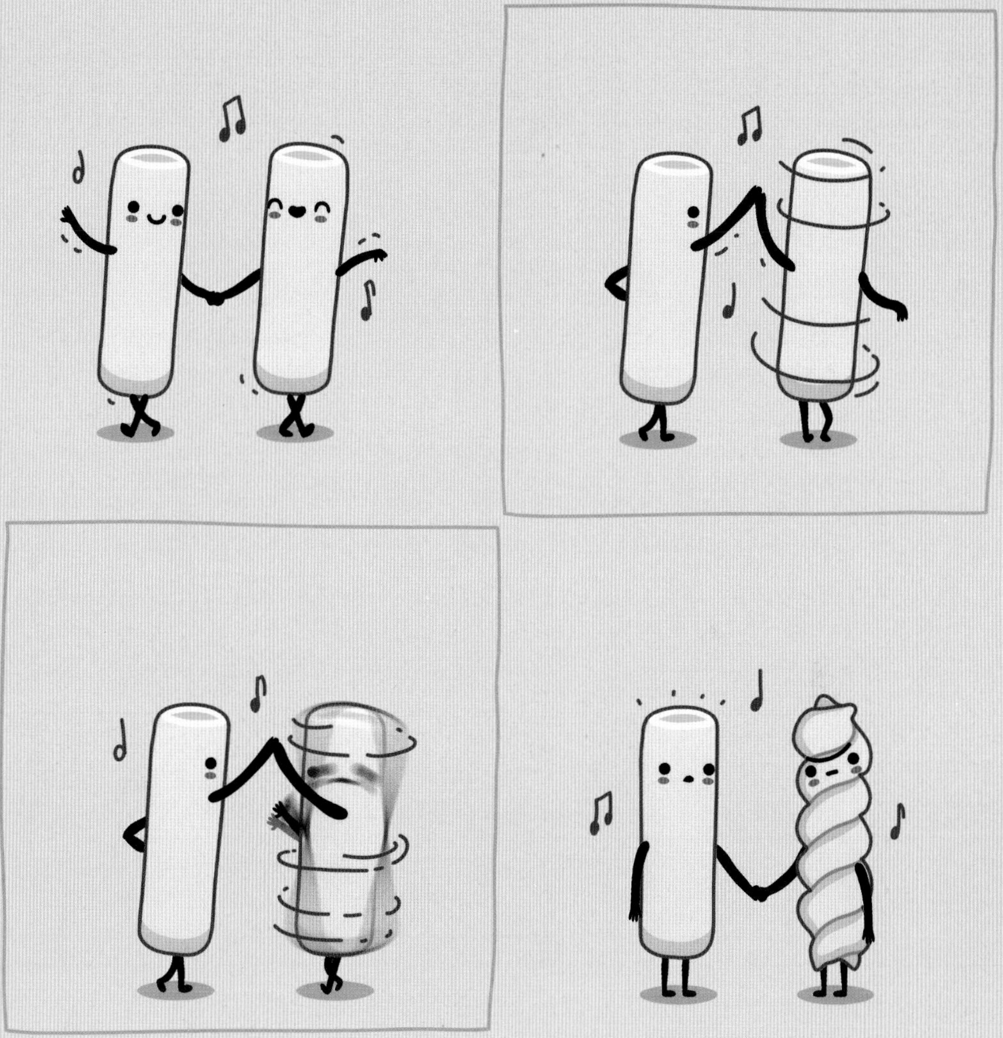

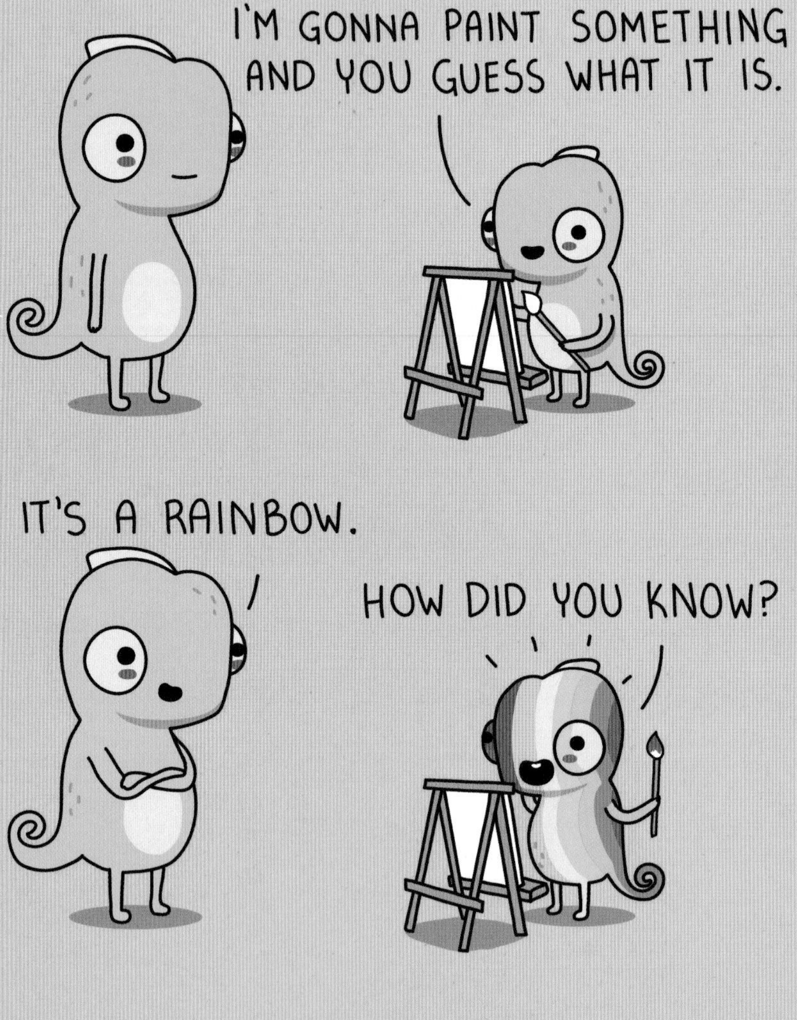
I'M GONNA PAINT SOMETHING AND YOU GUESS WHAT IT IS.
IT'S A RAINBOW.
HOW DID YOU KNOW?

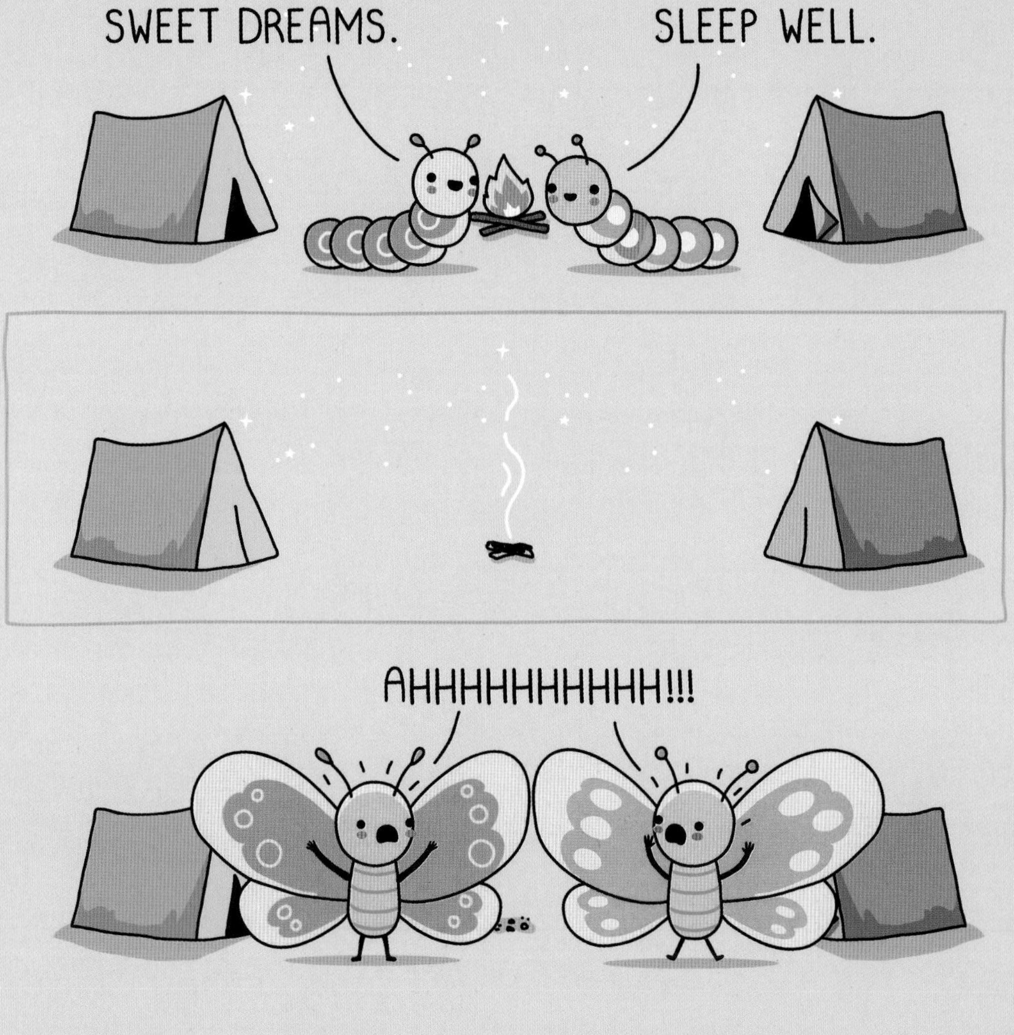
SWEET DREAMS.
SLEEP WELL.
AHHHHHHHHHHH!!!

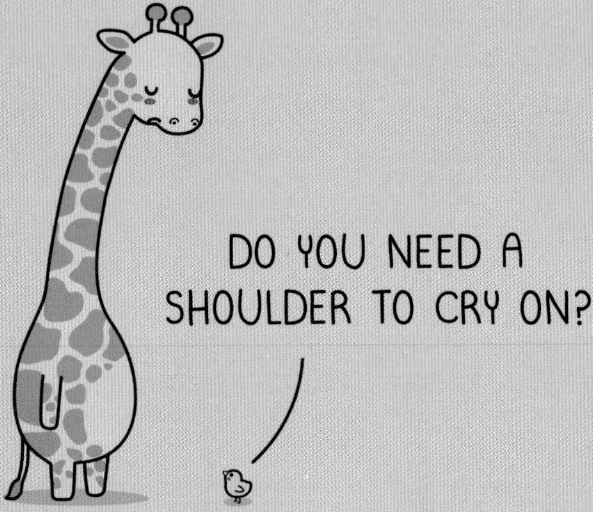
DO YOU NEED A
SHOULDER TO CRY ON?

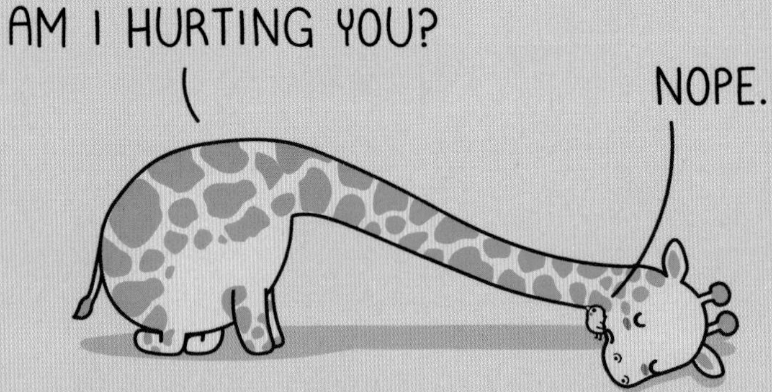
AM I HURTING YOU?
NOPE.

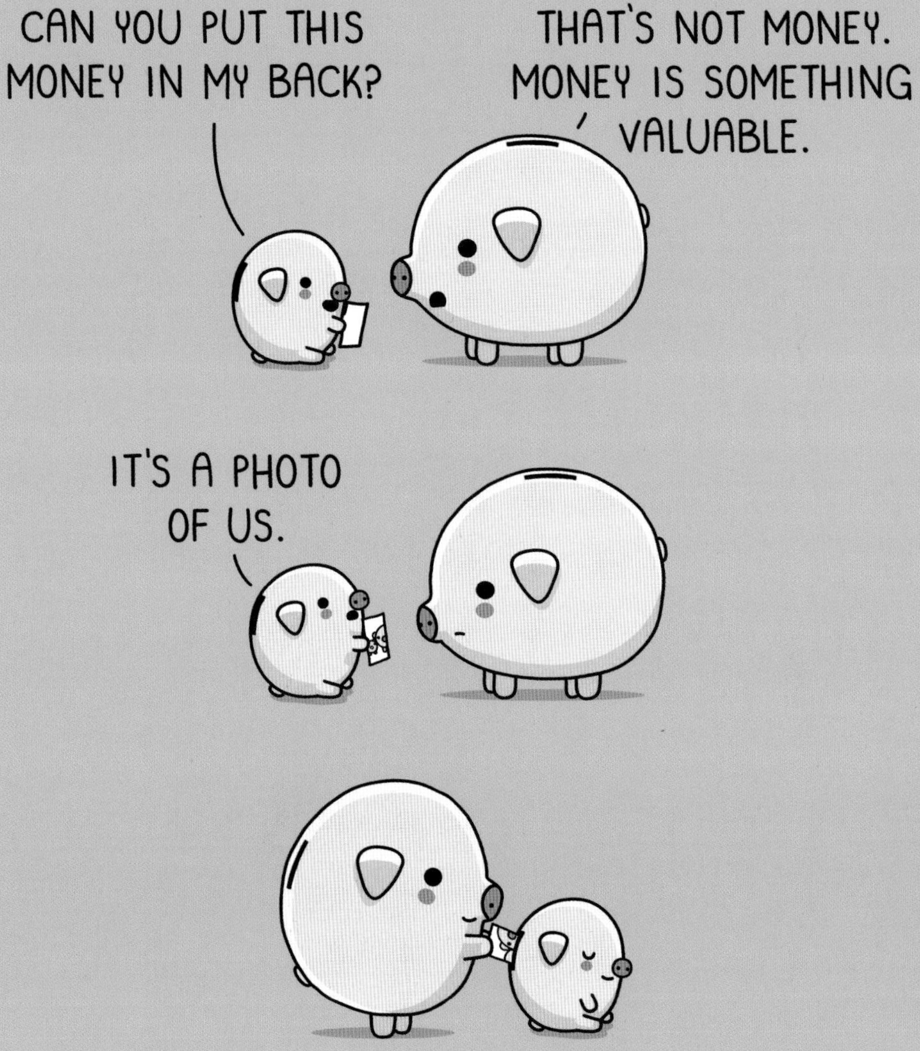
CAN YOU PUT THIS MONEY IN MY BACK?
THAT'S NOT MONEY. MONEY IS SOMETHING VALUABLE.
IT'S A PHOTO OF US.

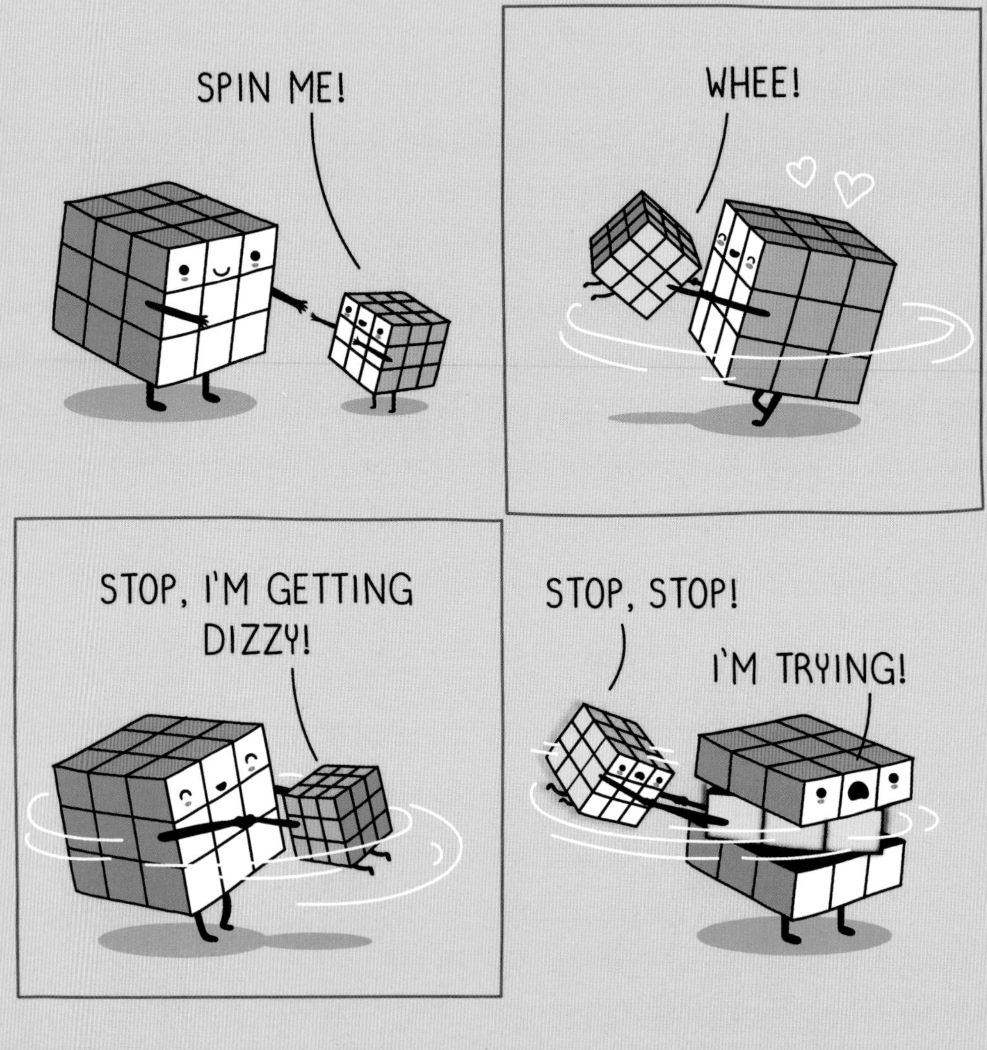
SPIN ME!
WHEE!
STOP, I'M GETTING DIZZY!
STOP, STOP!
I'M TRYING!

MAY I HOLD YOU?   ONLY IF YOU'RE PATIENT ENOUGH.

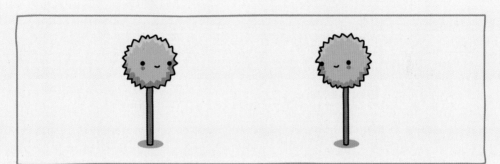

143

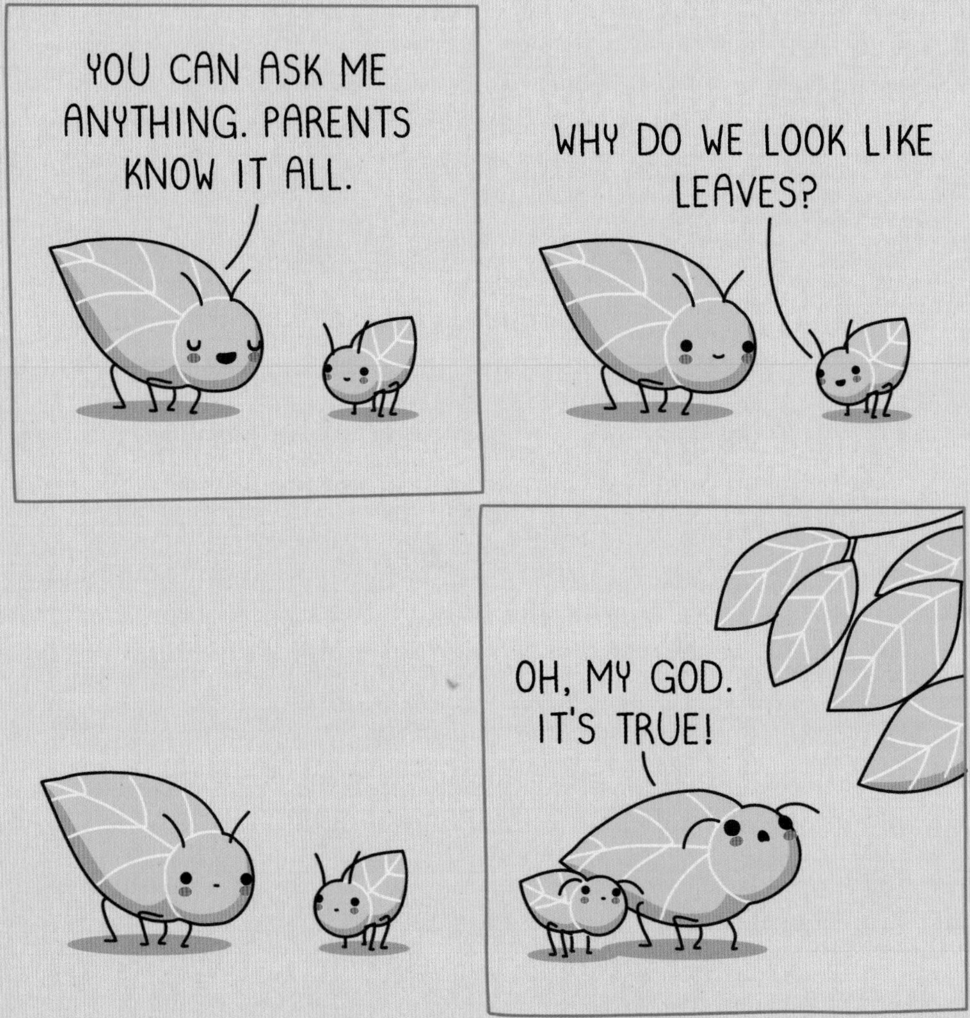
YOU CAN ASK ME ANYTHING. PARENTS KNOW IT ALL.
WHY DO WE LOOK LIKE LEAVES?
OH, MY GOD. IT'S TRUE!

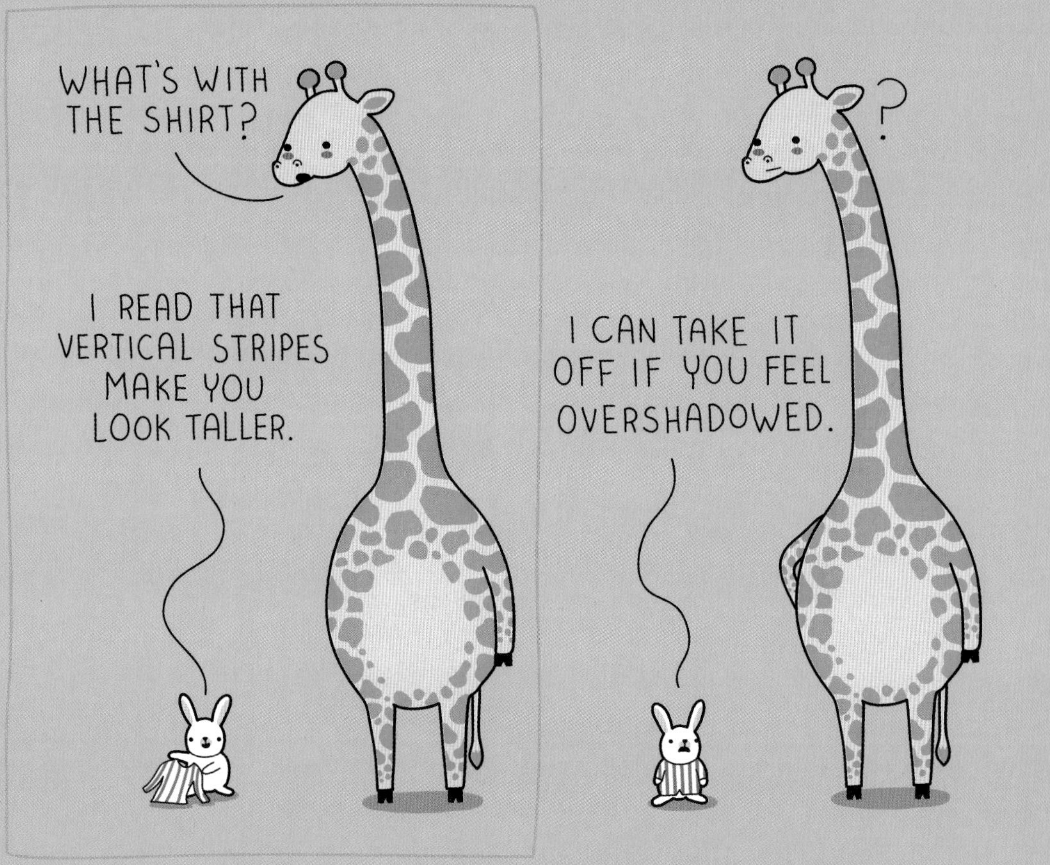
WHAT'S WITH THE SHIRT?
I READ THAT VERTICAL STRIPES MAKE YOU LOOK TALLER.
?
I CAN TAKE IT OFF IF YOU FEEL OVERSHADOWED.

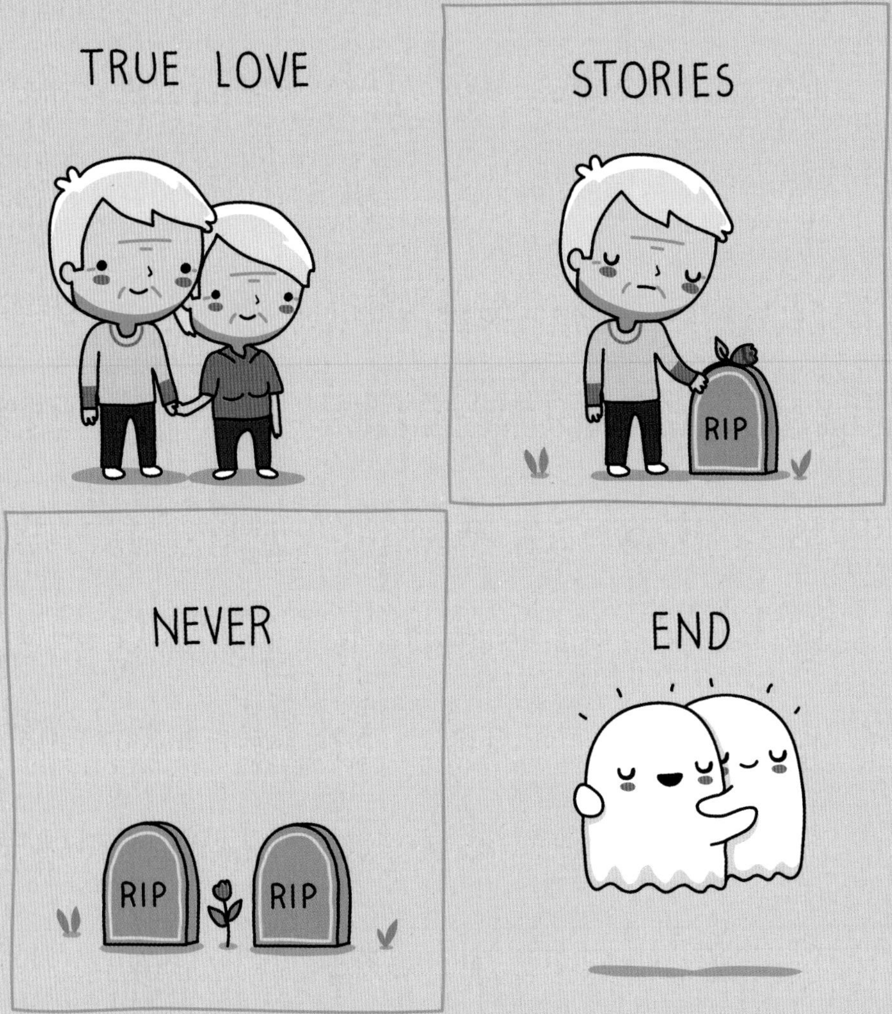
TRUE LOVE
STORIES
RIP
NEVER
RIP
RIP
END

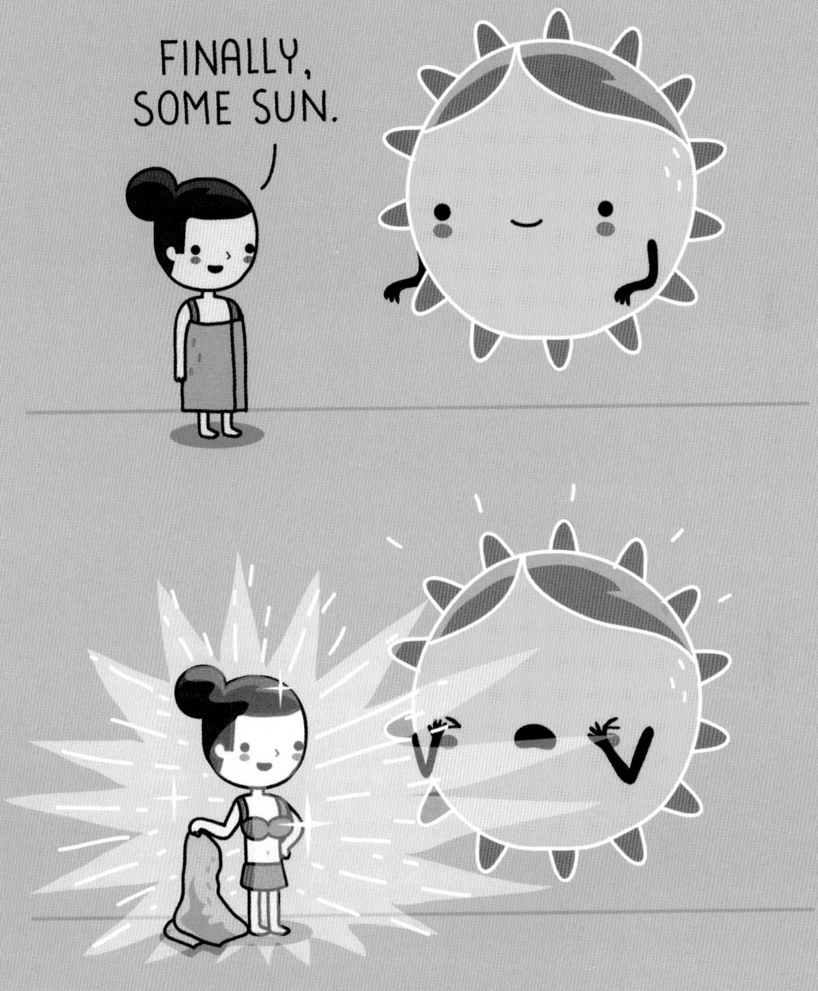
FINALLY,
SOME SUN.

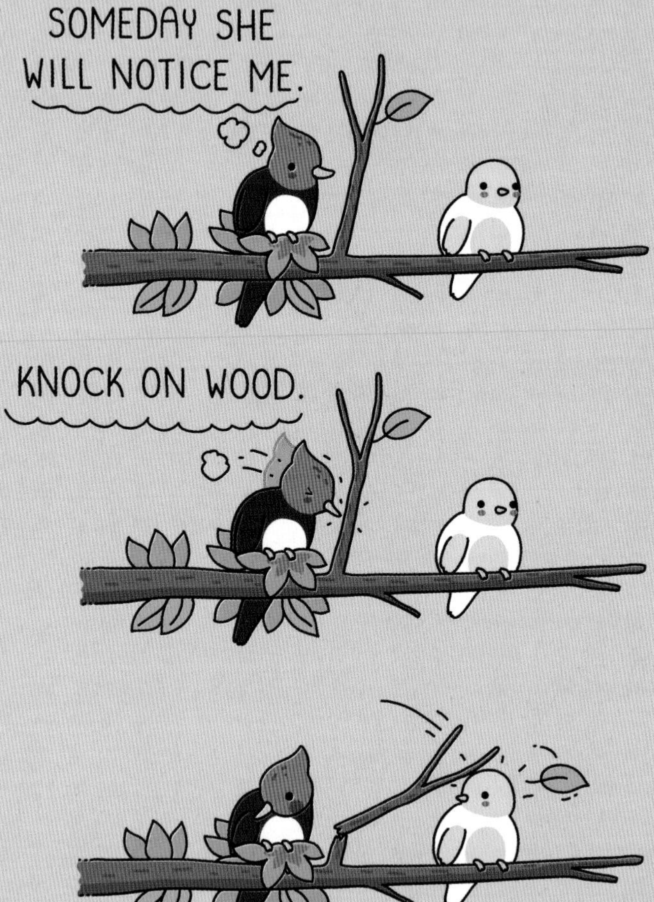
SOMEDAY SHE WILL NOTICE ME.
KNOCK ON WOOD.

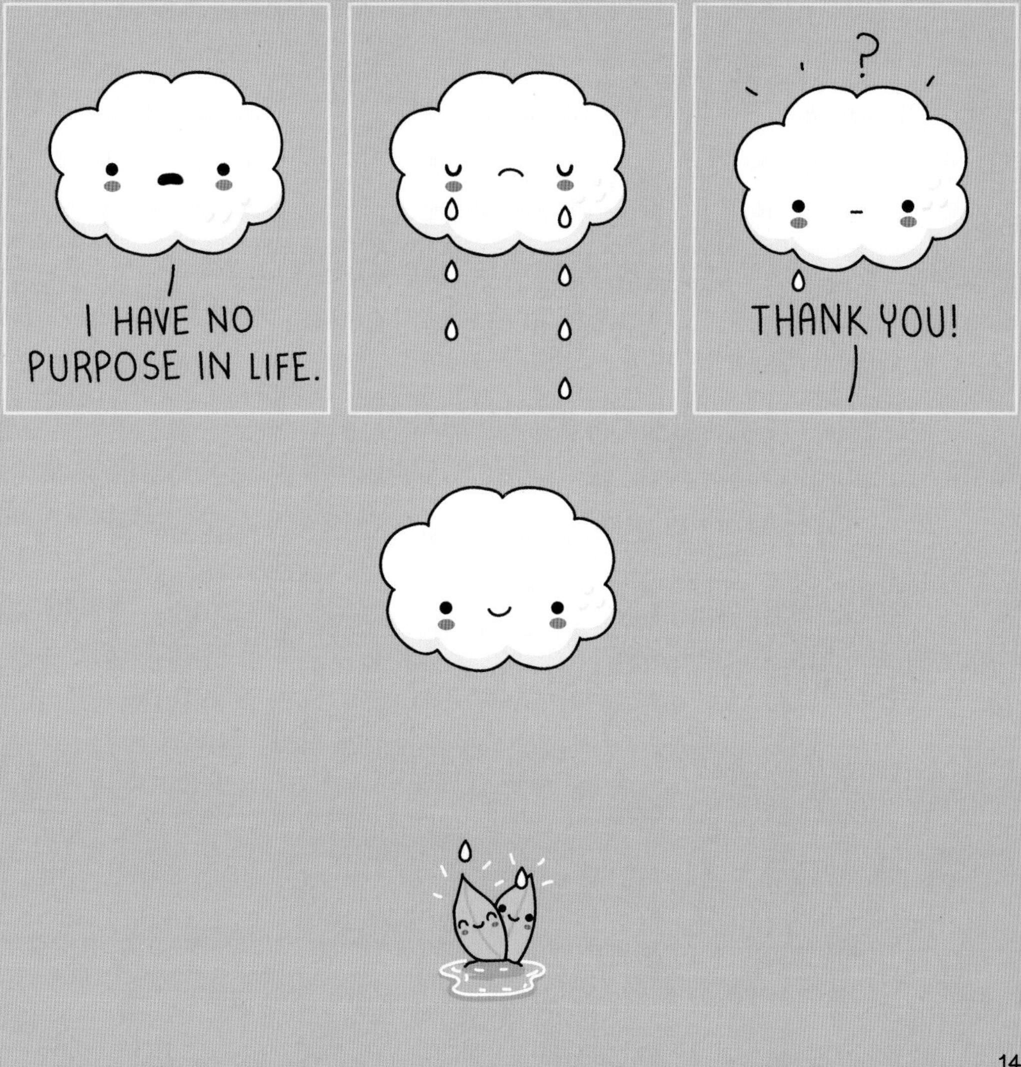
I HAVE NO PURPOSE IN LIFE.
?
THANK YOU!

MAY I BORROW YOUR BOOK?

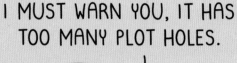

I MUST WARN YOU, IT HAS TOO MANY PLOT HOLES.

DID YOU STICK YOUR TUSKS THROUGH THE PAGES AGAIN?

MAYBE...

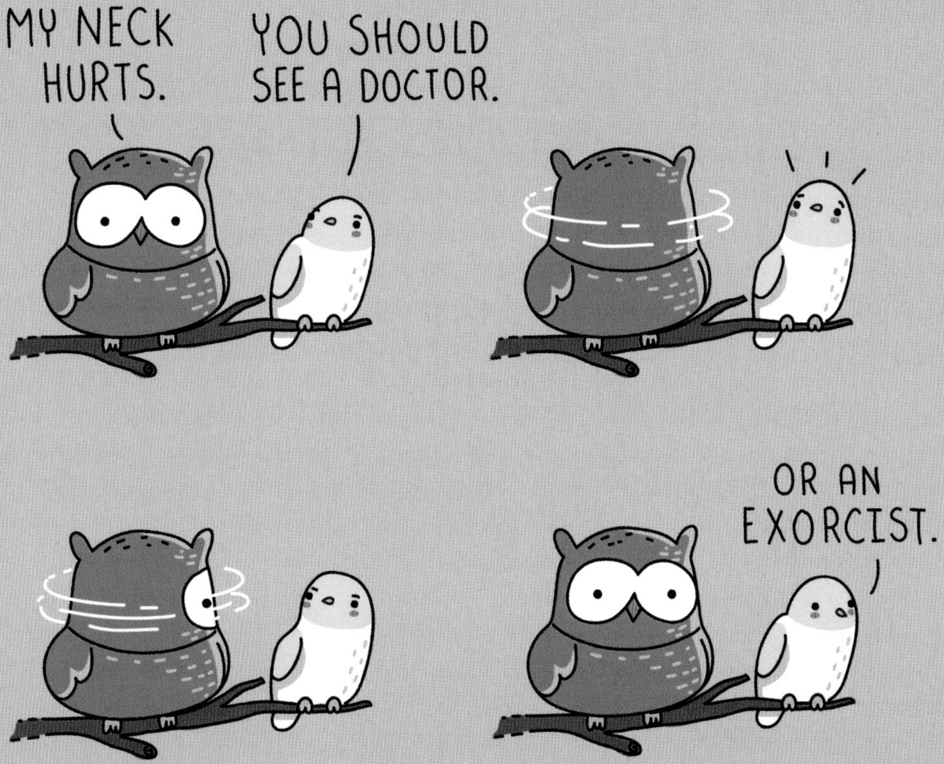
MY NECK HURTS.
YOU SHOULD SEE A DOCTOR.
OR AN EXORCIST.

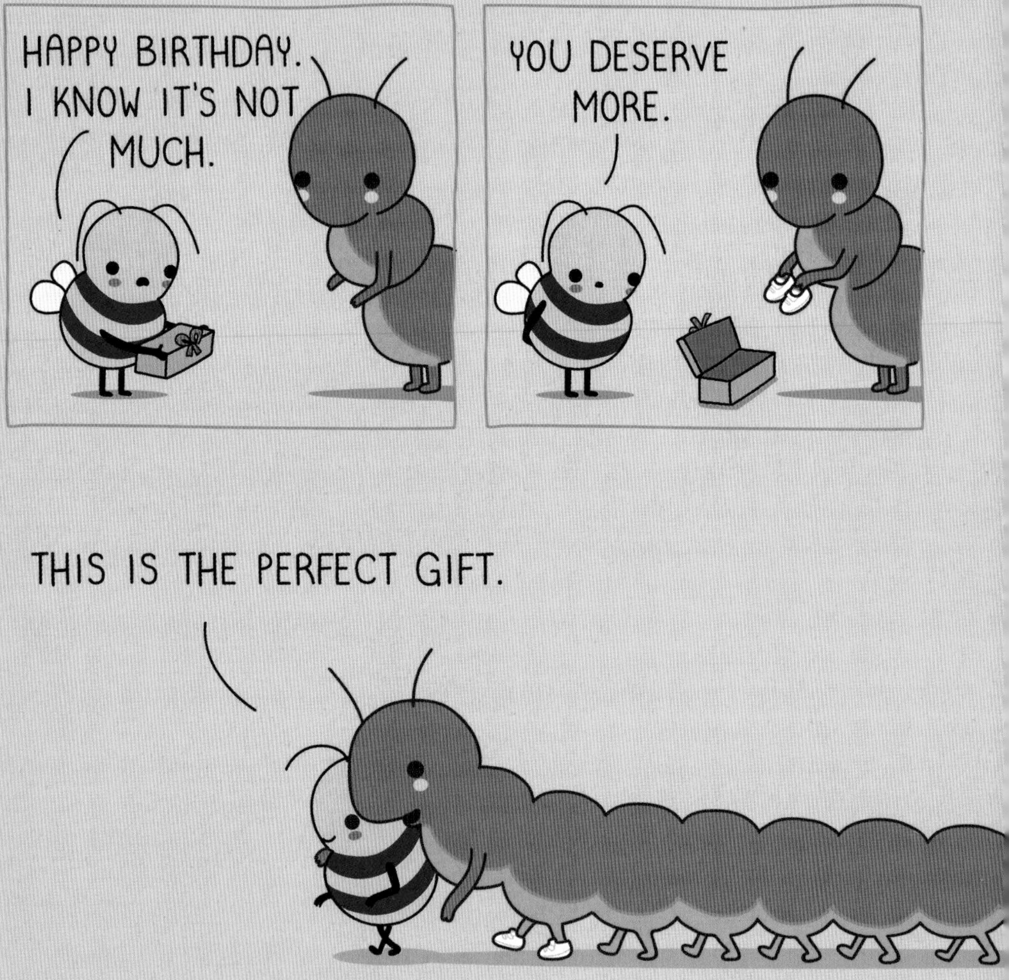
HAPPY BIRTHDAY. I KNOW IT'S NOT MUCH.
YOU DESERVE MORE.
THIS IS THE PERFECT GIFT.

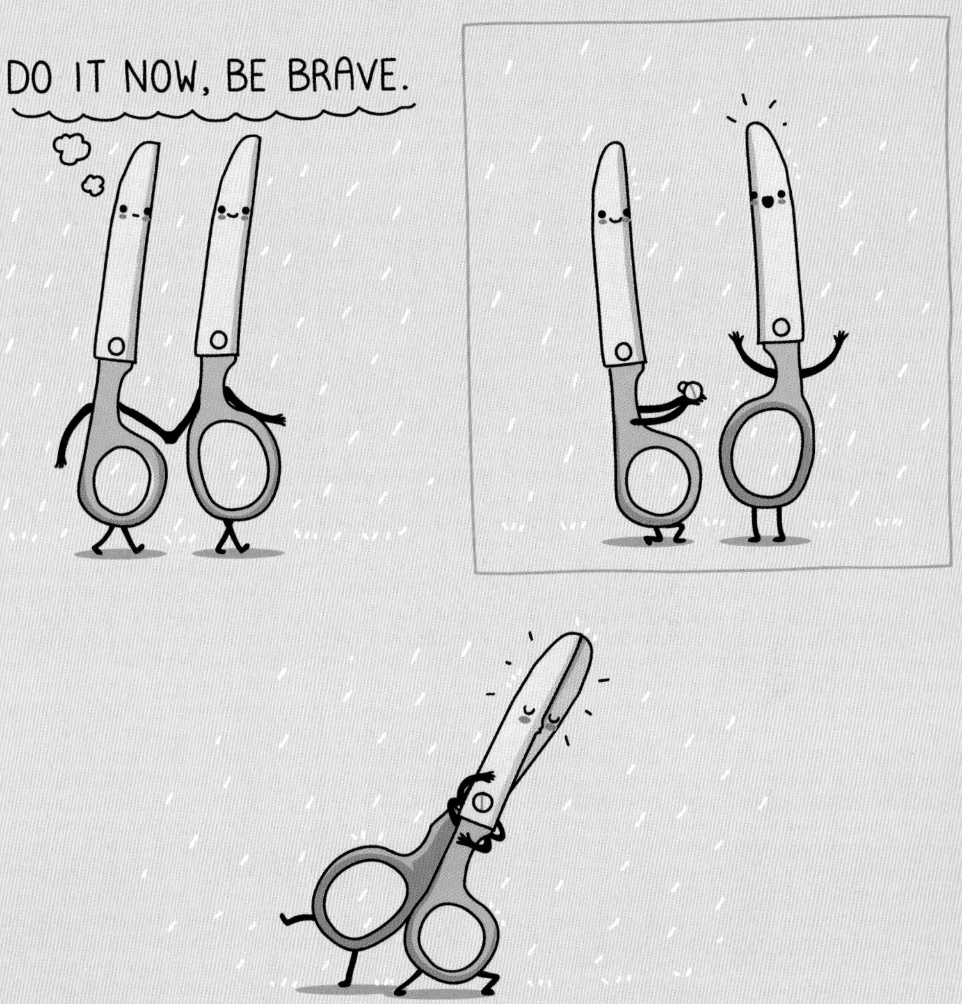
DO IT NOW, BE BRAVE.

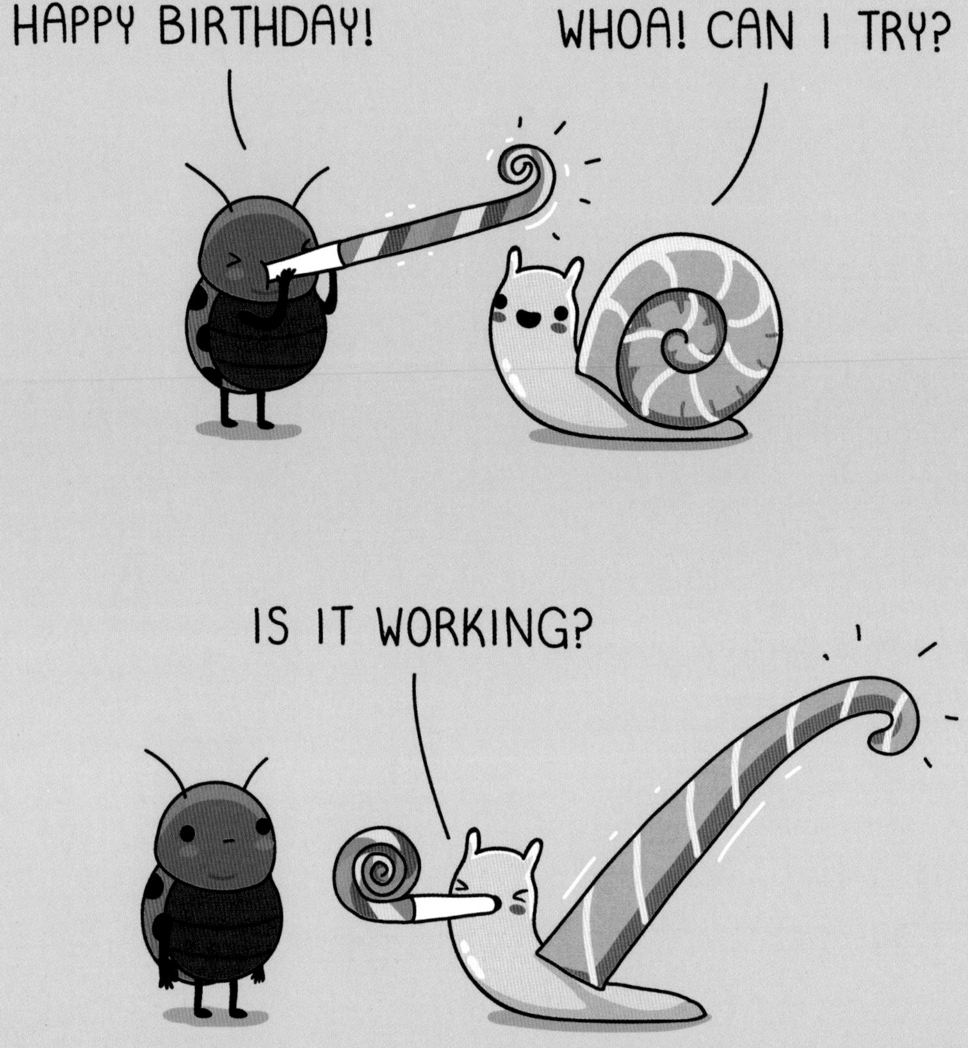
HAPPY BIRTHDAY!
WHOA! CAN I TRY?
IS IT WORKING?

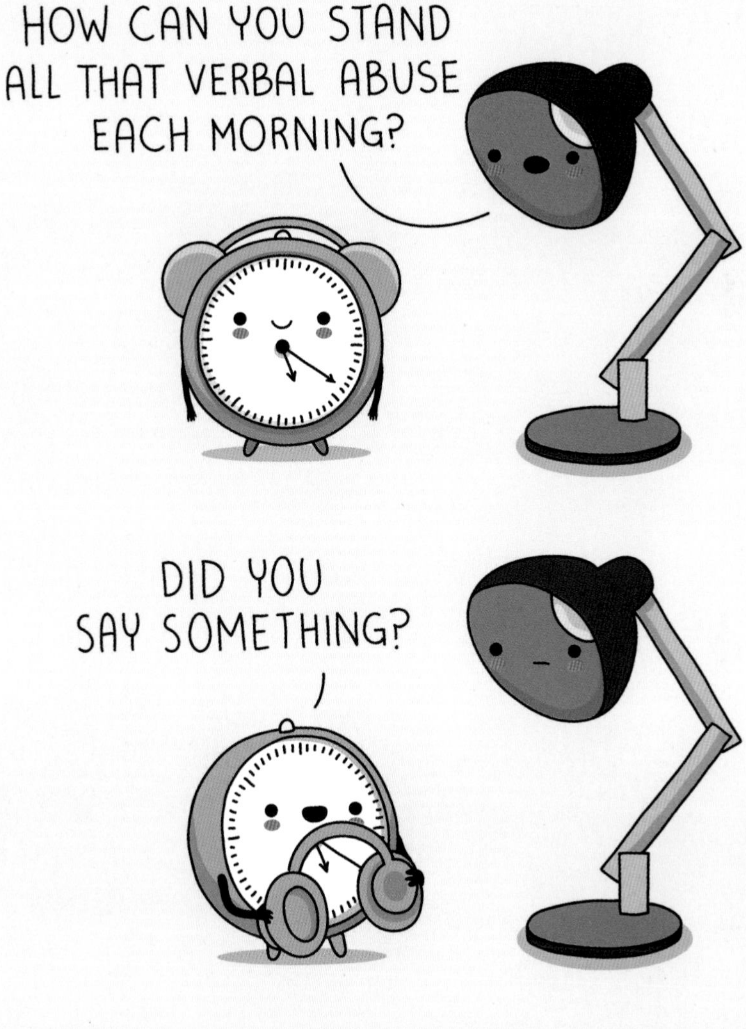
HOW CAN YOU STAND ALL THAT VERBAL ABUSE EACH MORNING?
DID YOU SAY SOMETHING?

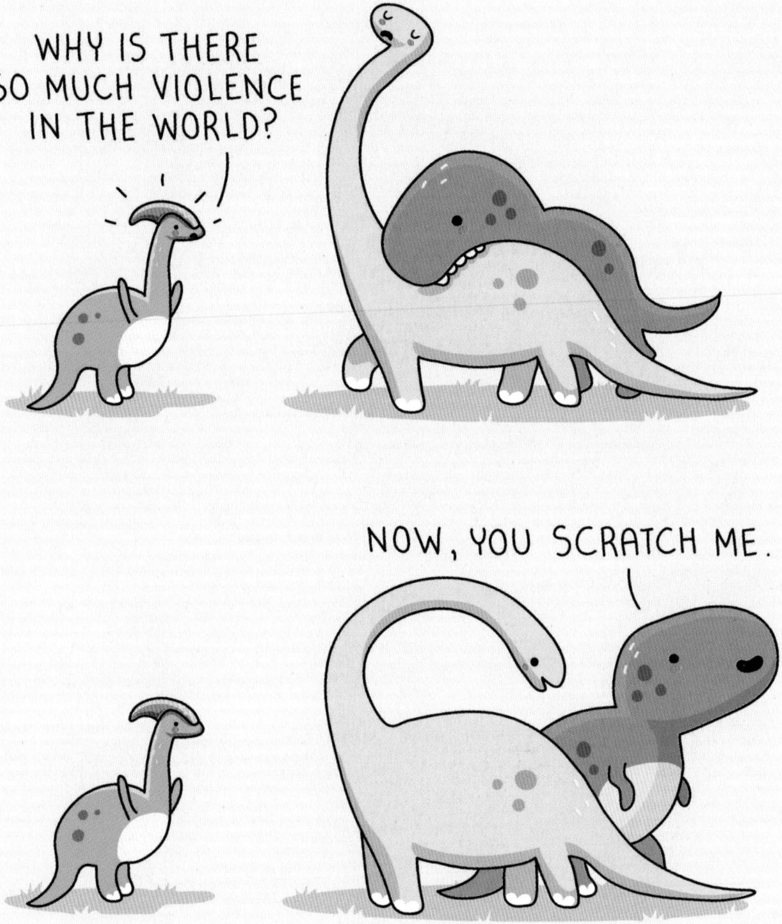
WHY IS THERE SO MUCH VIOLENCE IN THE WORLD?
NOW, YOU SCRATCH ME.

THAT'S ENOUGH!

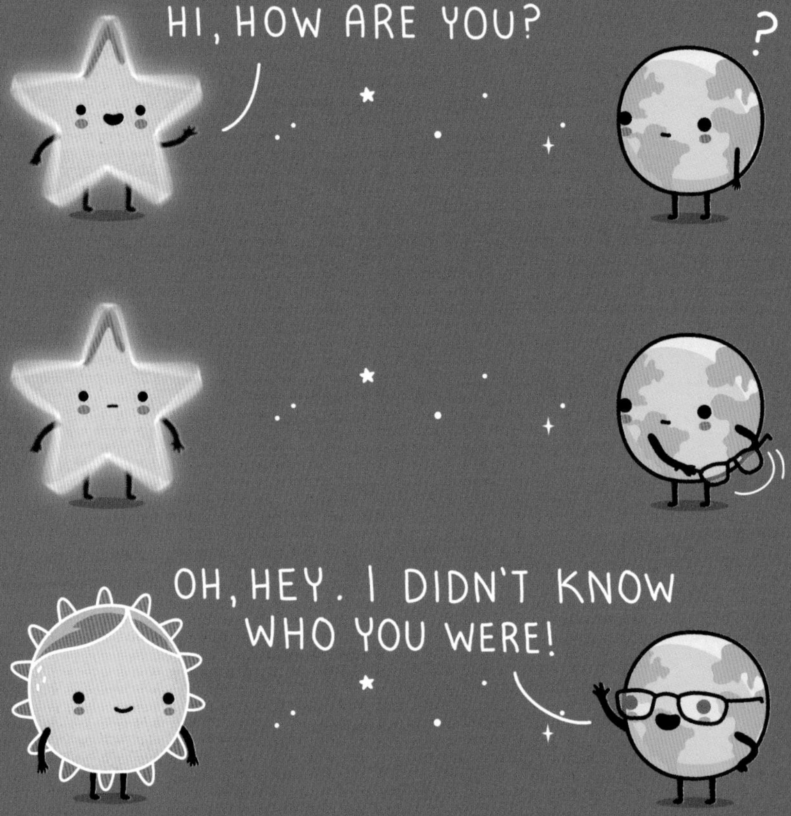
HI, HOW ARE YOU?
?
OH, HEY. I DIDN'T KNOW WHO YOU WERE!

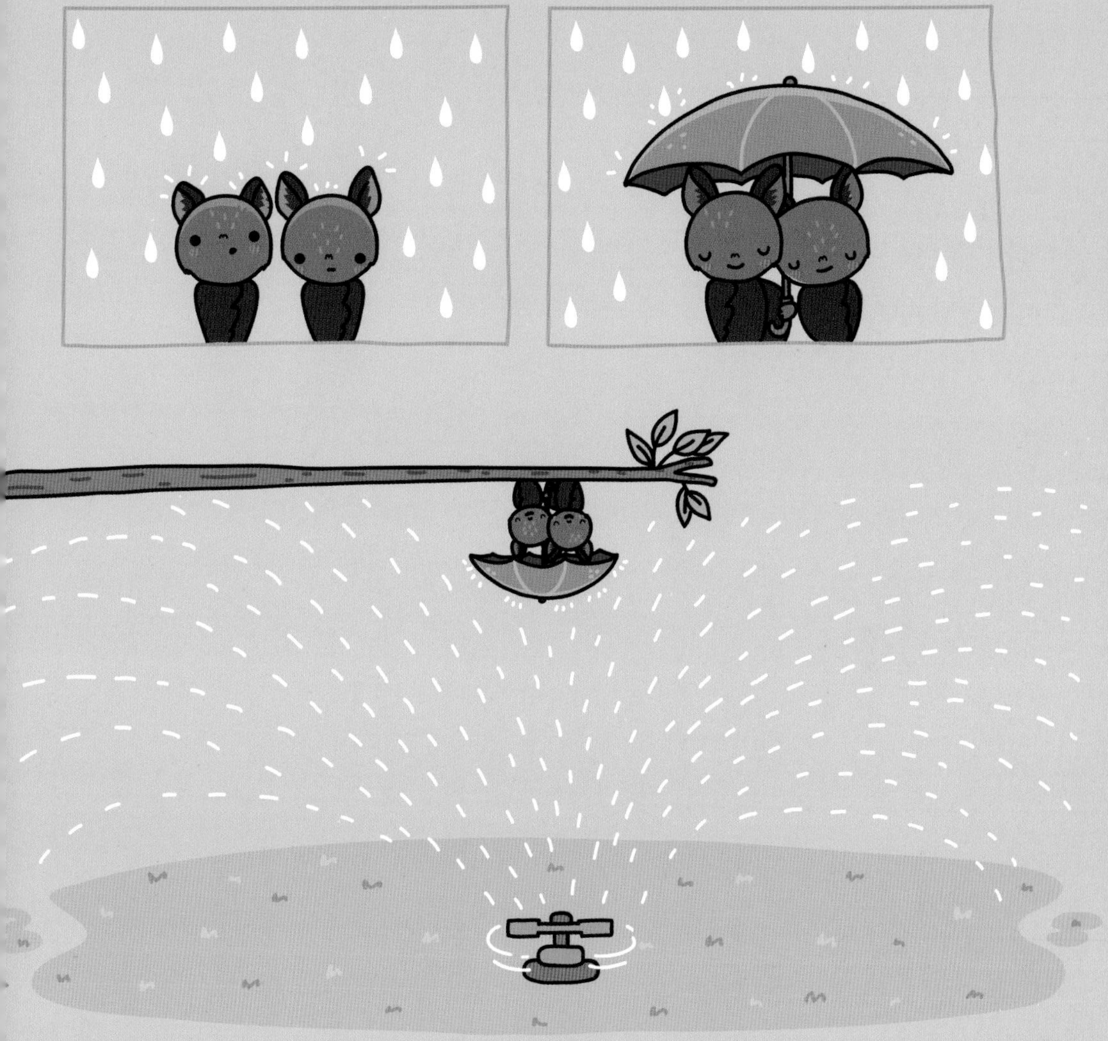

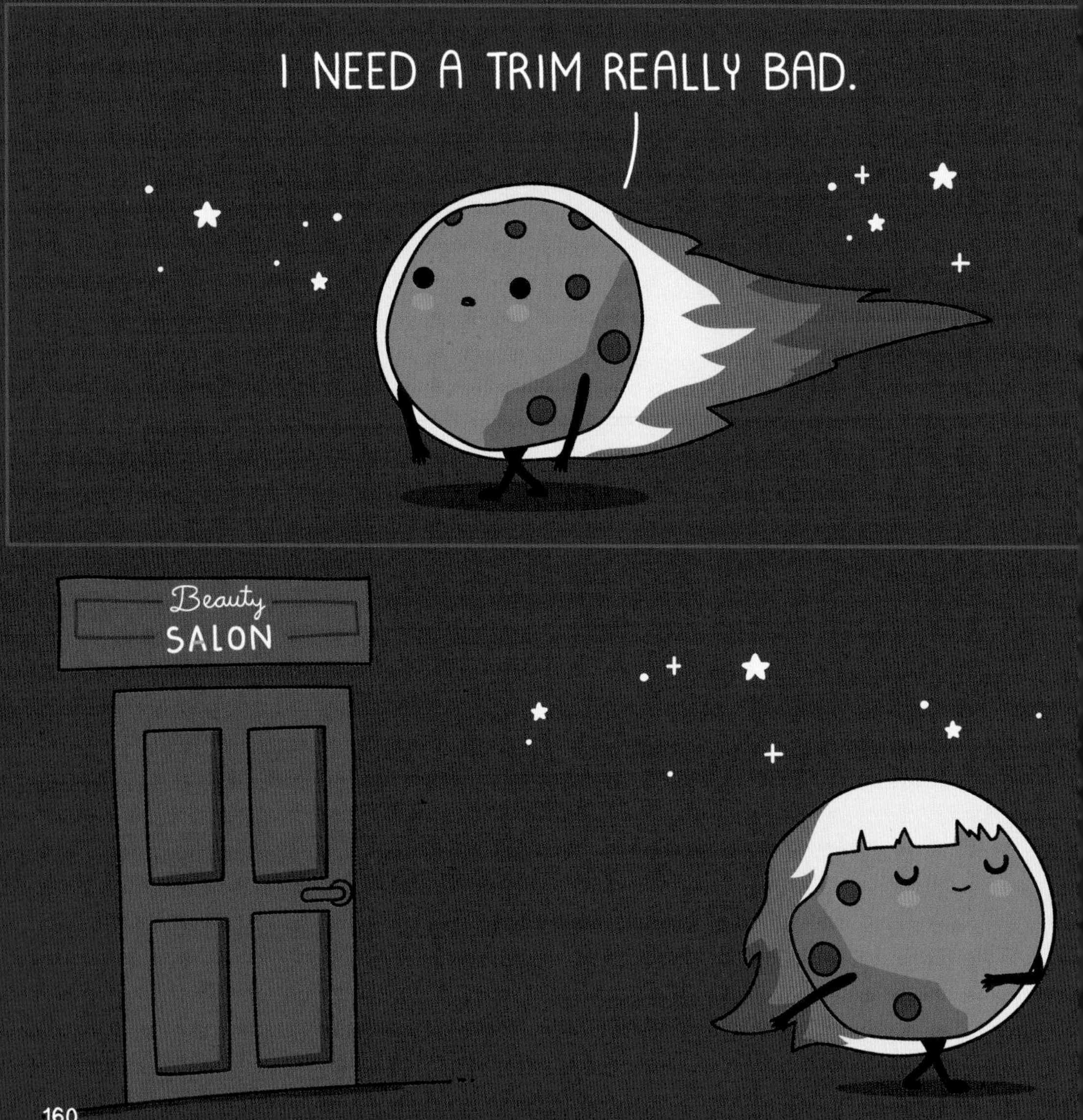
I NEED A TRIM REALLY BAD.
Beauty
SALON

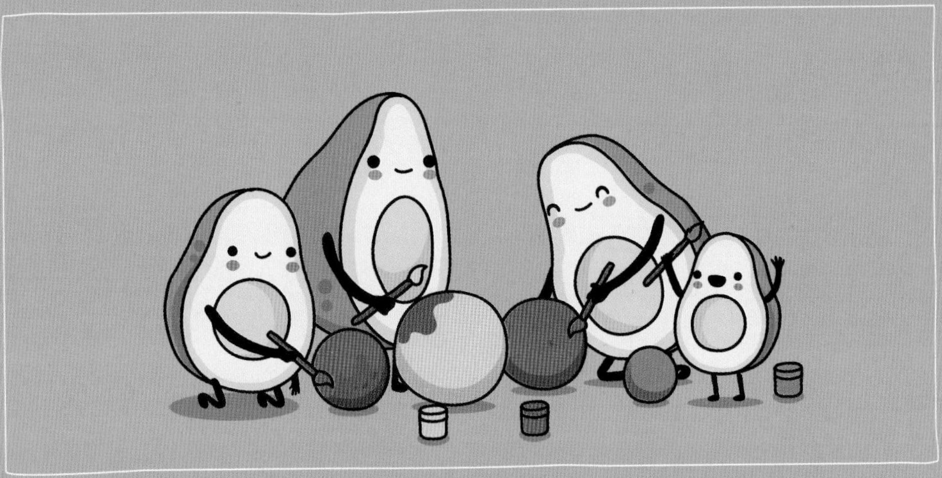

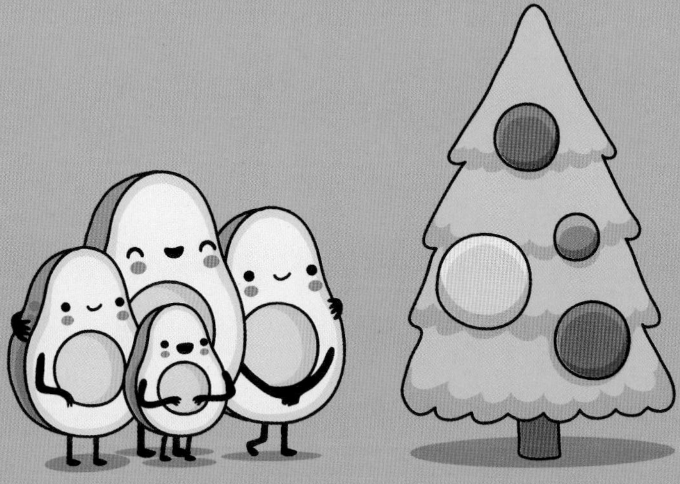

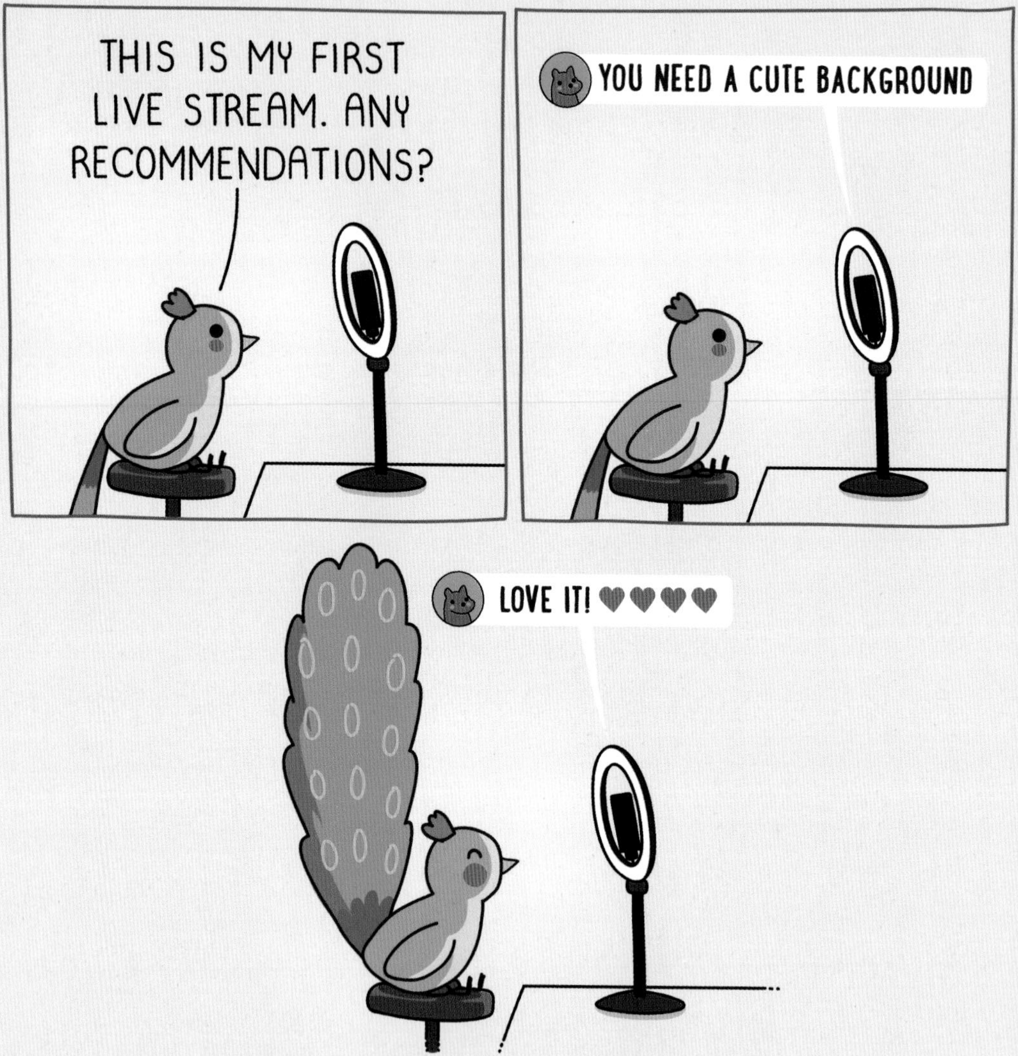
THIS IS MY FIRST LIVE STREAM. ANY RECOMMENDATIONS?
YOU NEED A CUTE BACKGROUND
LOVE IT!

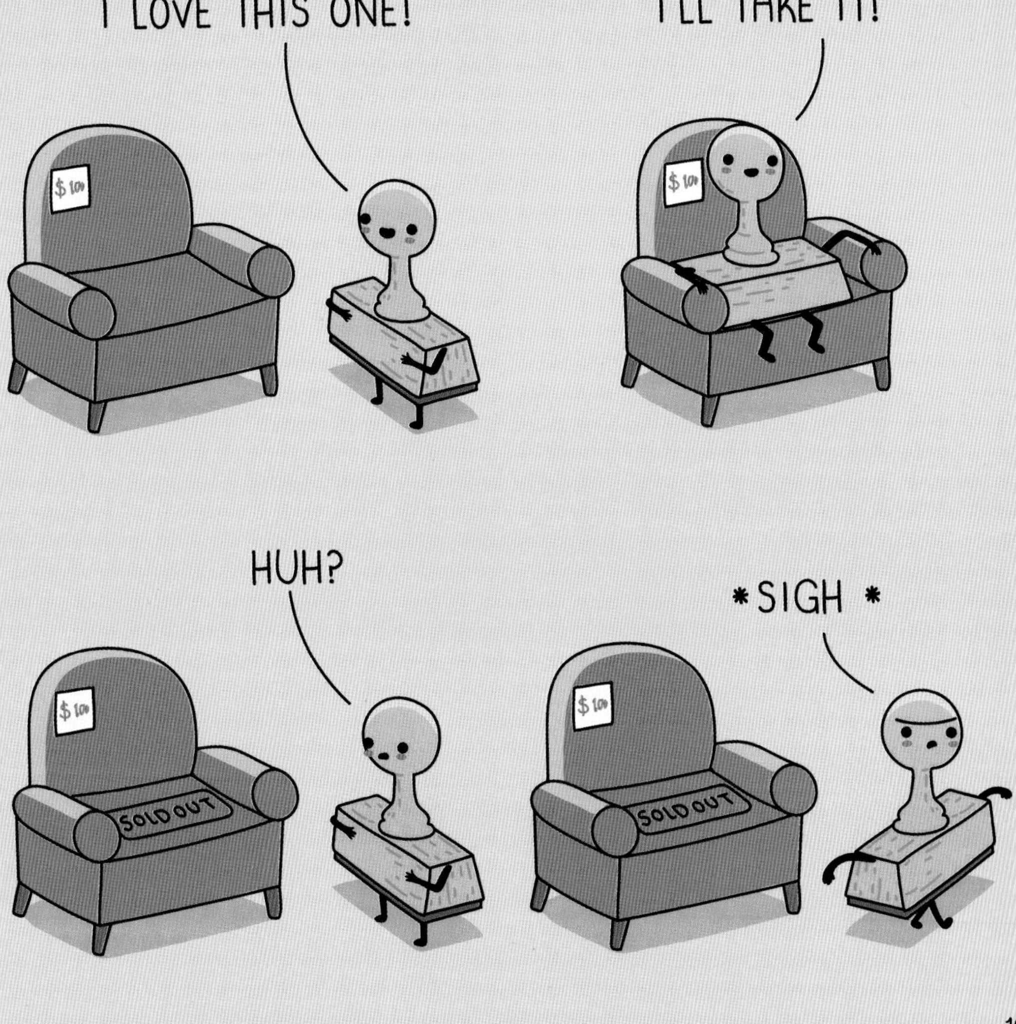
I LOVE THIS ONE!
$ 100
I'LL TAKE IT!
$ 100
HUH?
$ 100
SOLD OUT
*SIGH *
$ 100
SOLD OUT

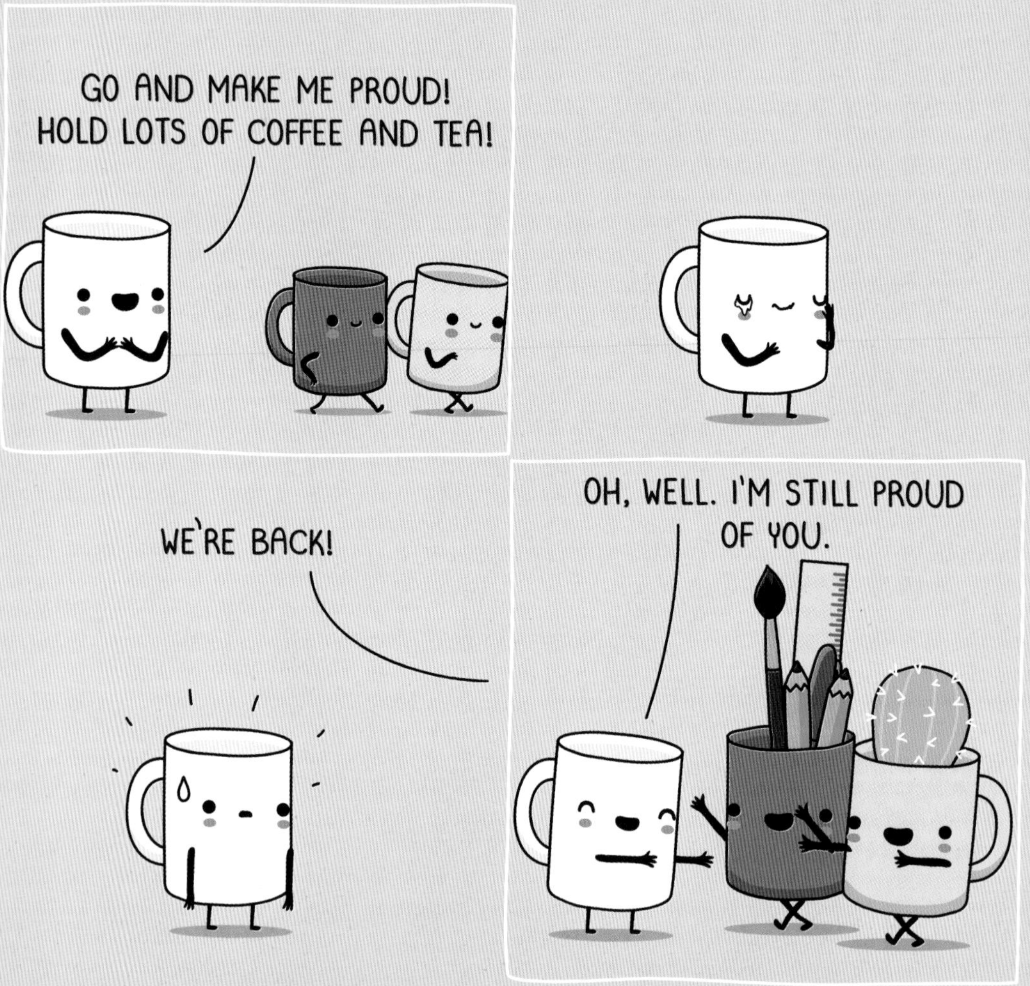
GO AND MAKE ME PROUD! HOLD LOTS OF COFFEE AND TEA!
WE'RE BACK!
OH, WELL. I'M STILL PROUD OF YOU.

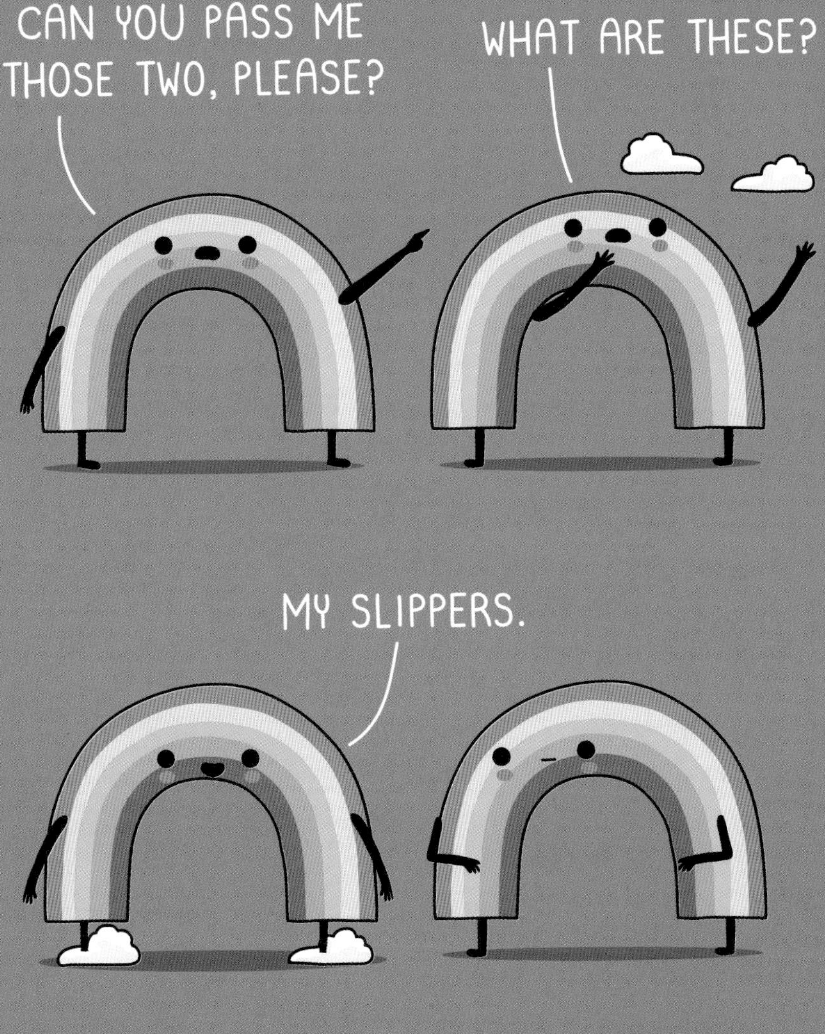
CAN YOU PASS ME THOSE TWO, PLEASE?
WHAT ARE THESE?
MY SLIPPERS.

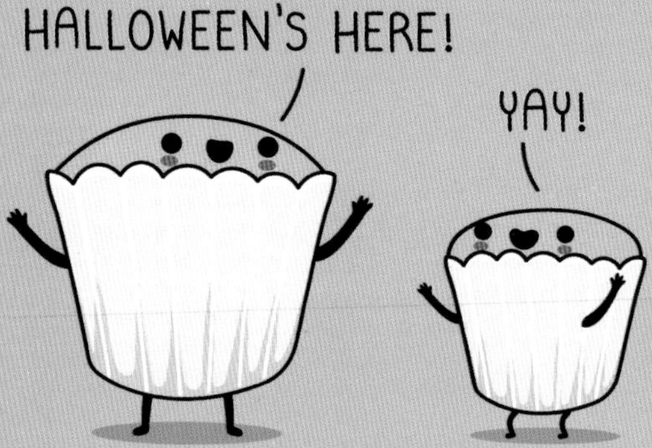
HALLOWEEN'S HERE!
YAY!

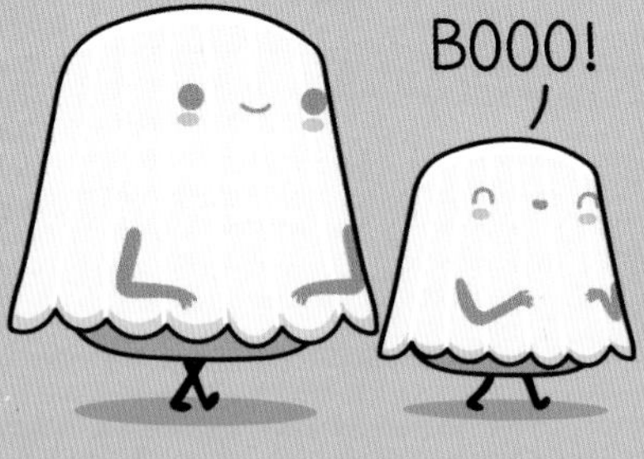
BOOO!

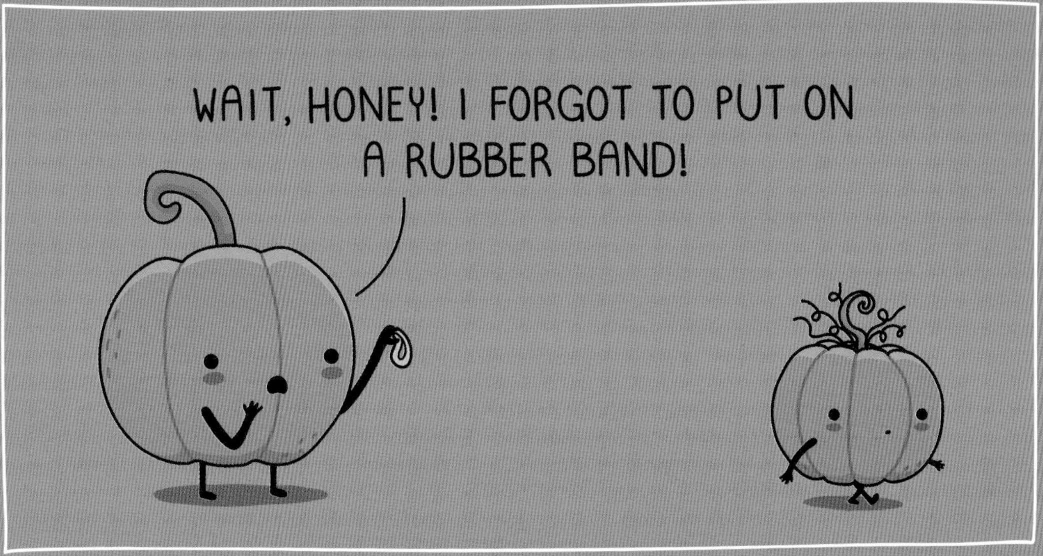
WAIT, HONEY! I FORGOT TO PUT ON A RUBBER BAND!

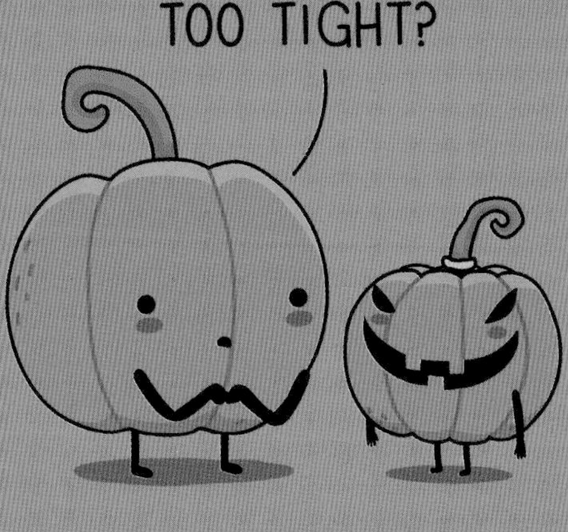
TOO TIGHT?

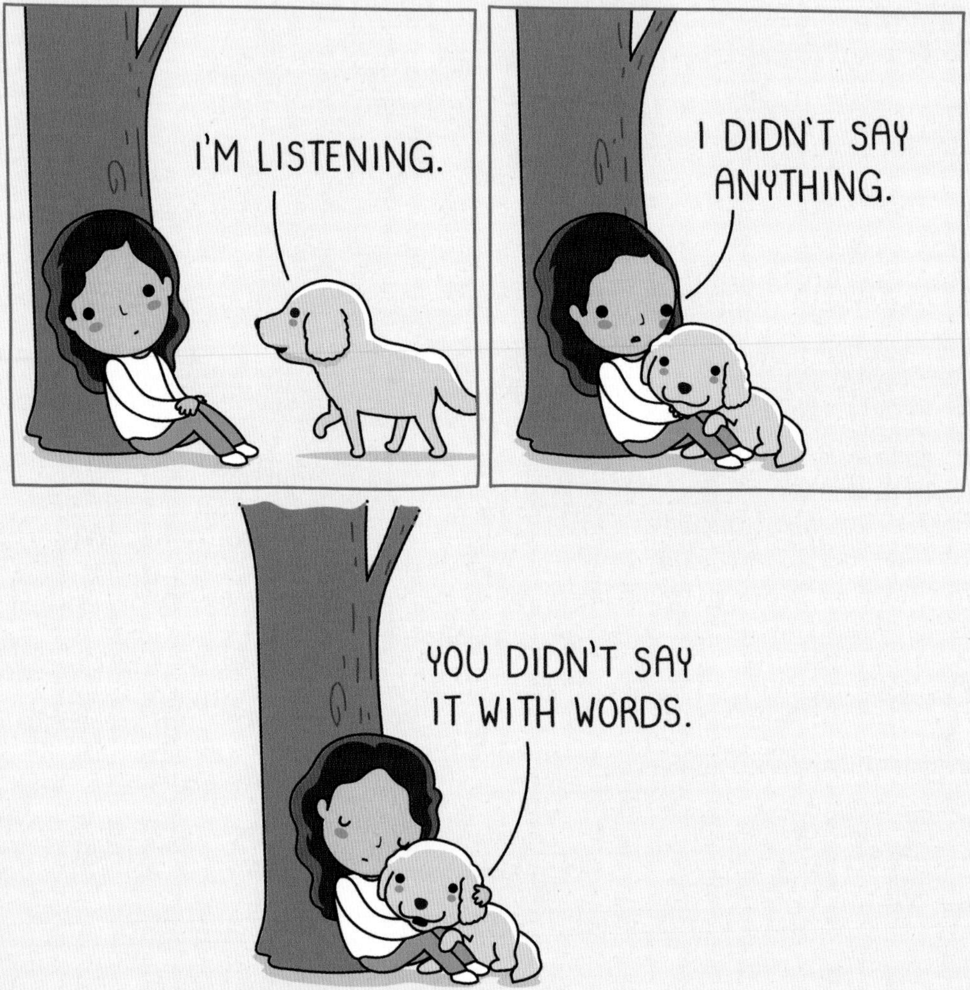
I'M LISTENING.
I DIDN'T SAY ANYTHING.
YOU DIDN'T SAY IT WITH WORDS.

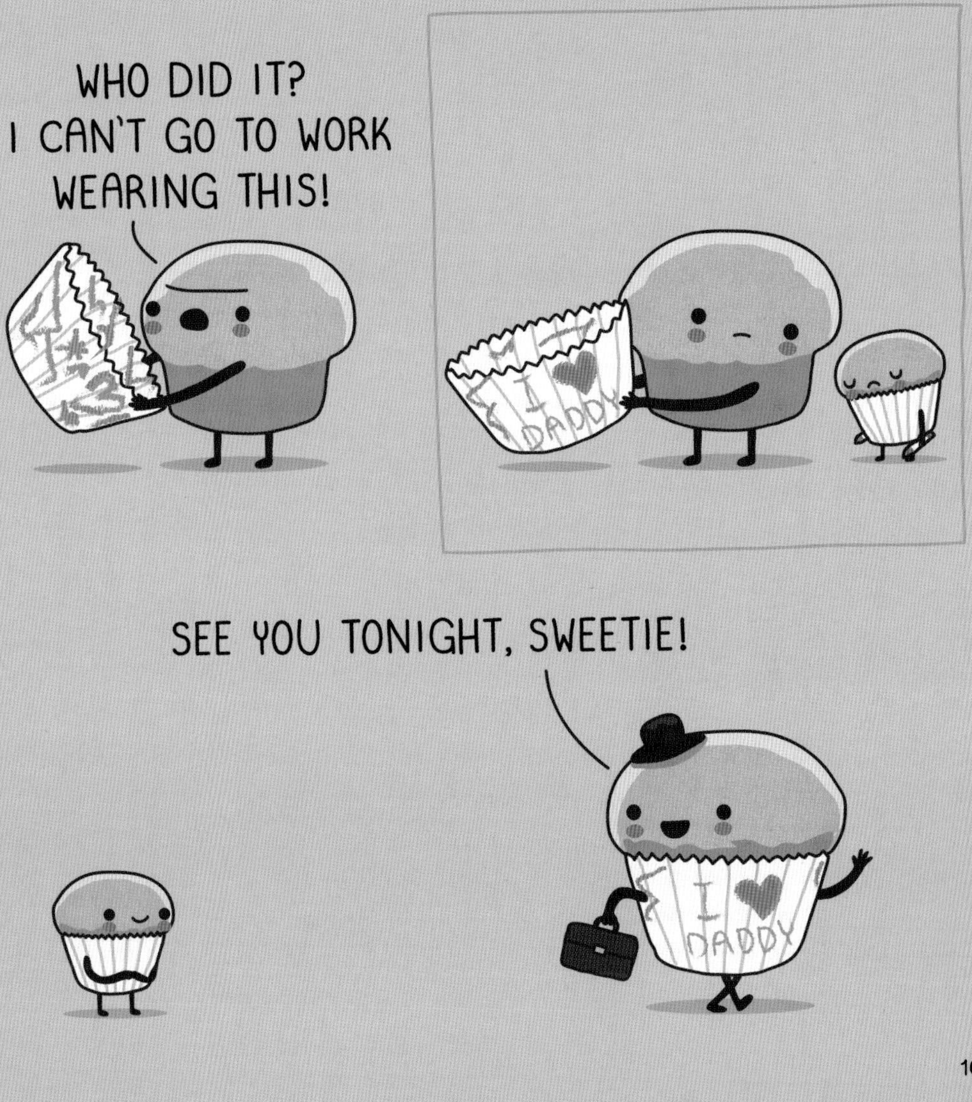
WHO DID IT?
I CAN'T GO TO WORK
WEARING THIS!
I ♥ DADDY
SEE YOU TONIGHT, SWEETIE!
I ♥ DADDY

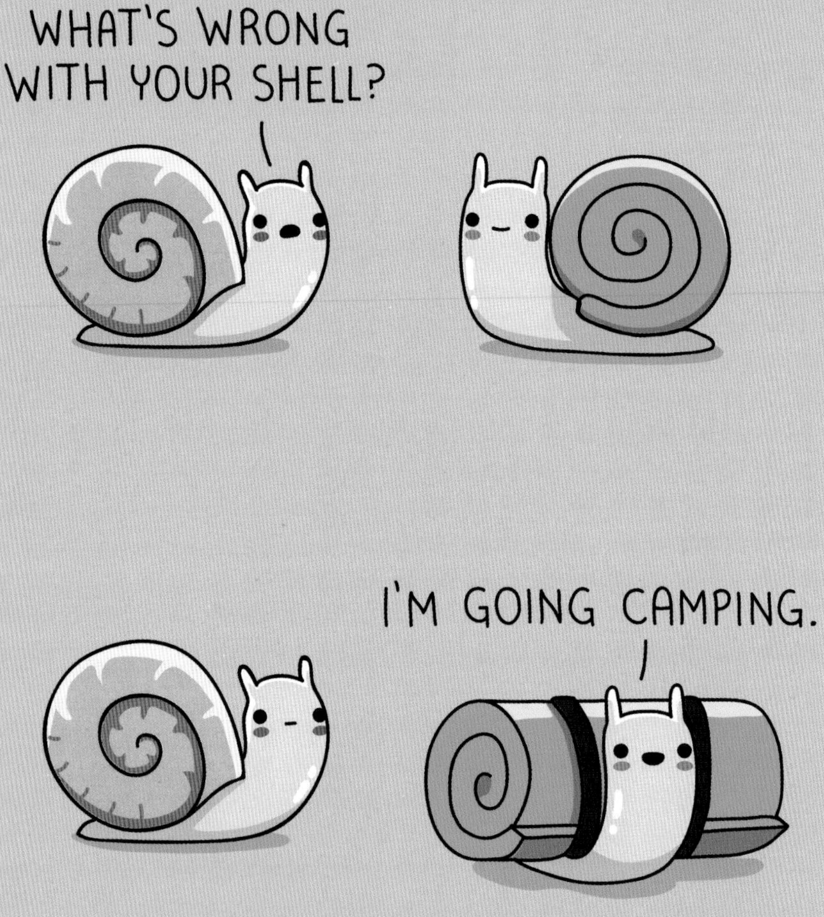
WHAT'S WRONG WITH YOUR SHELL?
I'M GOING CAMPING.

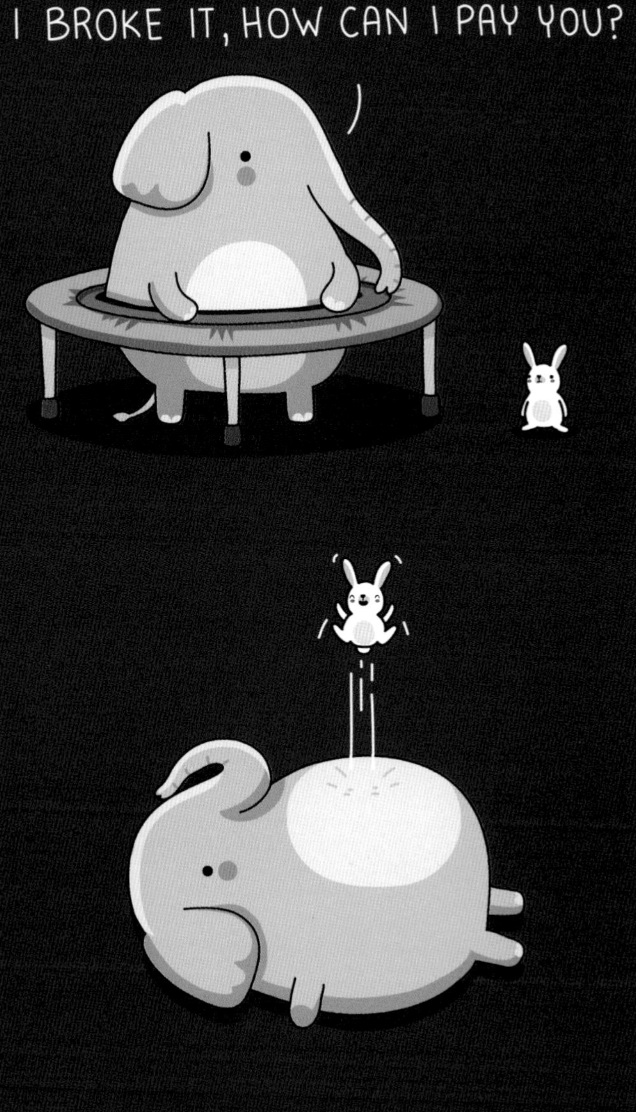
I BROKE IT, HOW CAN I PAY YOU?

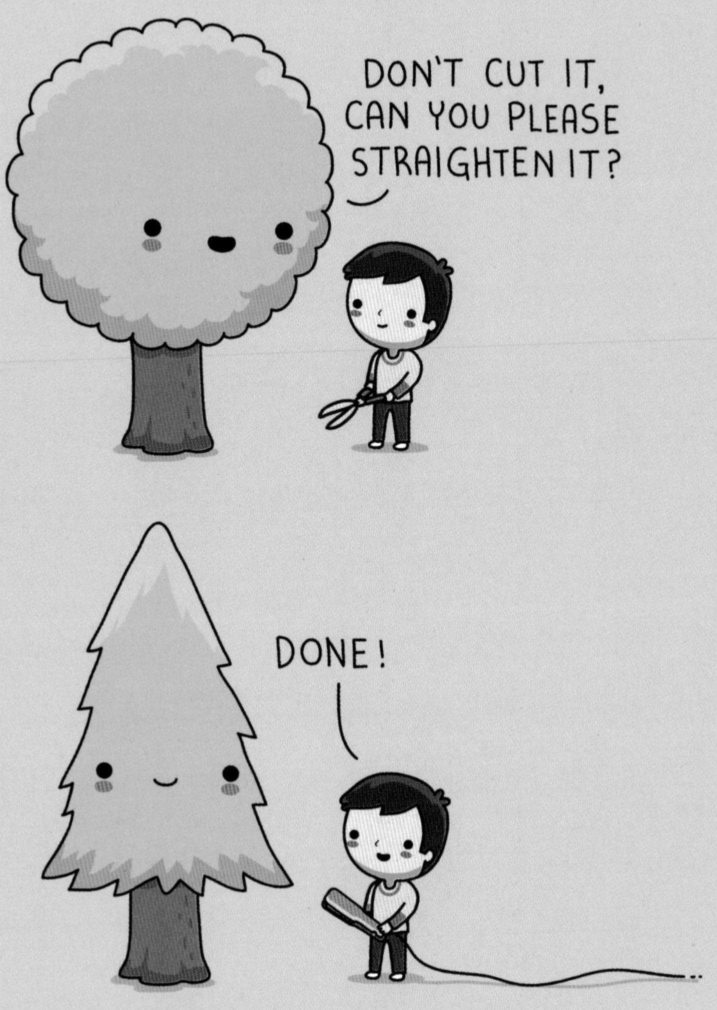
DON'T CUT IT,
CAN YOU PLEASE
STRAIGHTEN IT?
DONE!

IT'S TIME TO SHOW YOU HOW
I USE THESE TUSKS.

GULP

LET'S READ!

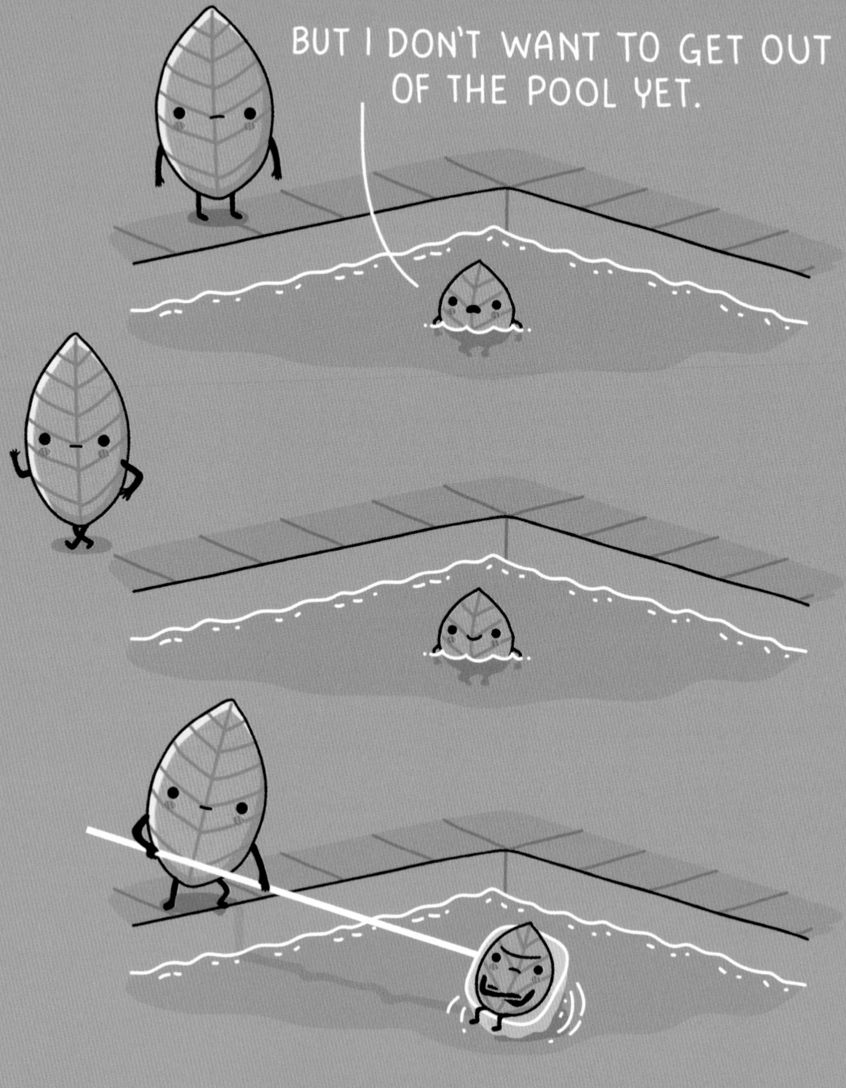
BUT I DON'T WANT TO GET OUT OF THE POOL YET.

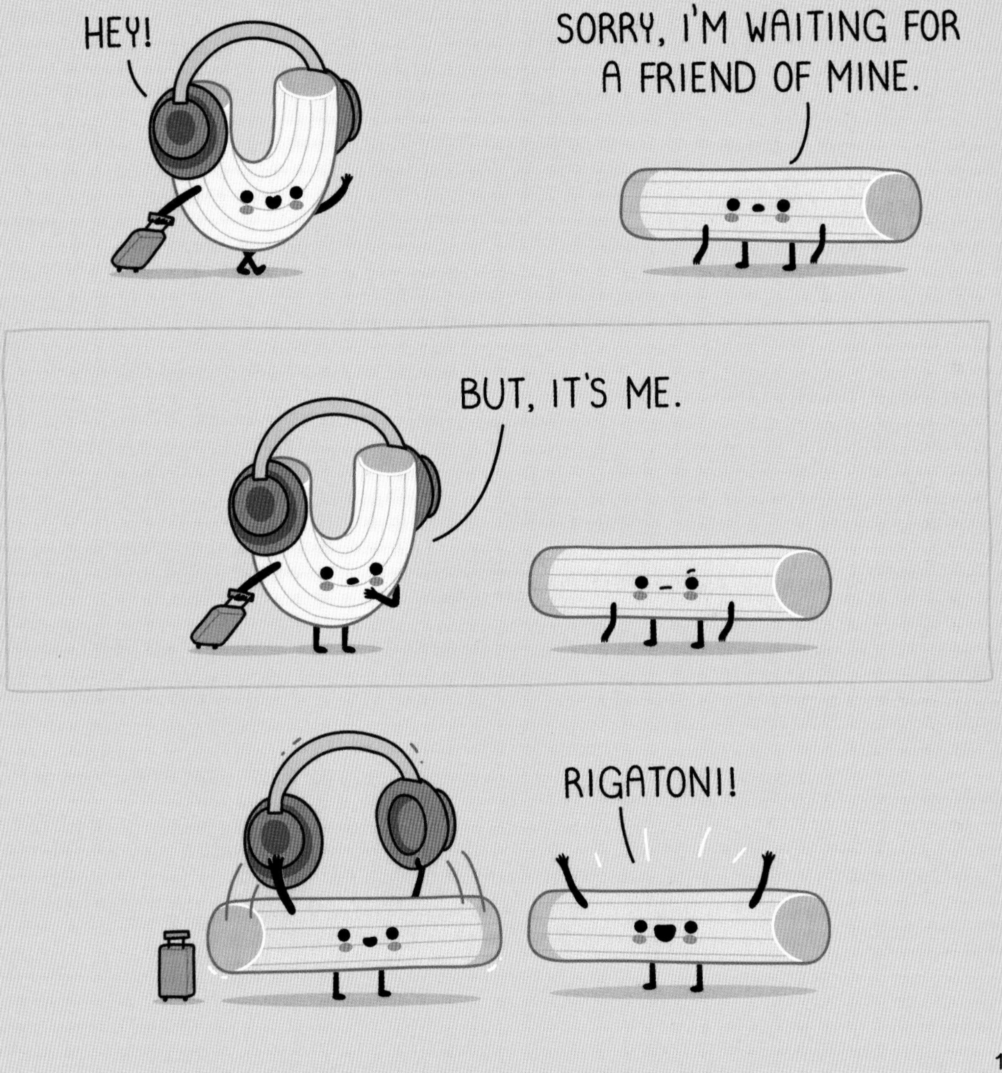
HEY!
SORRY, I'M WAITING FOR A FRIEND OF MINE.
BUT, IT'S ME.
RIGATONI!

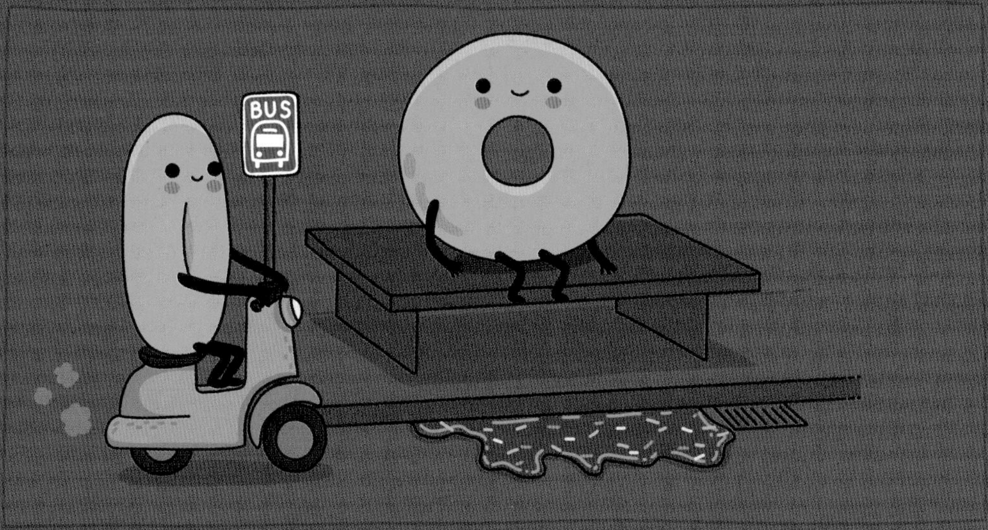
BUS

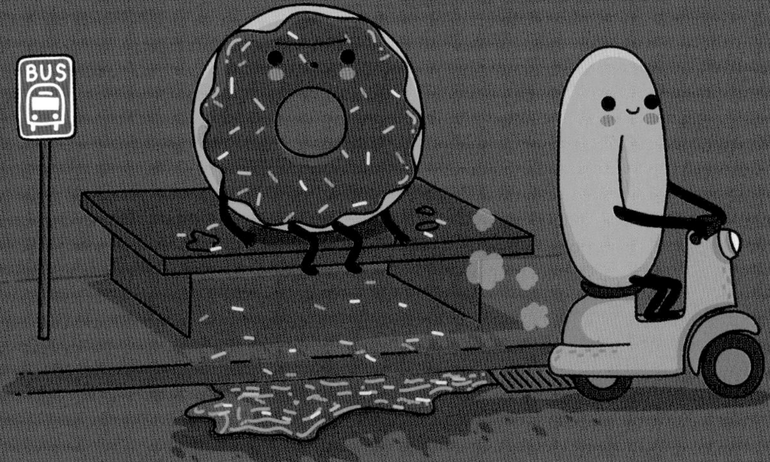
BUS

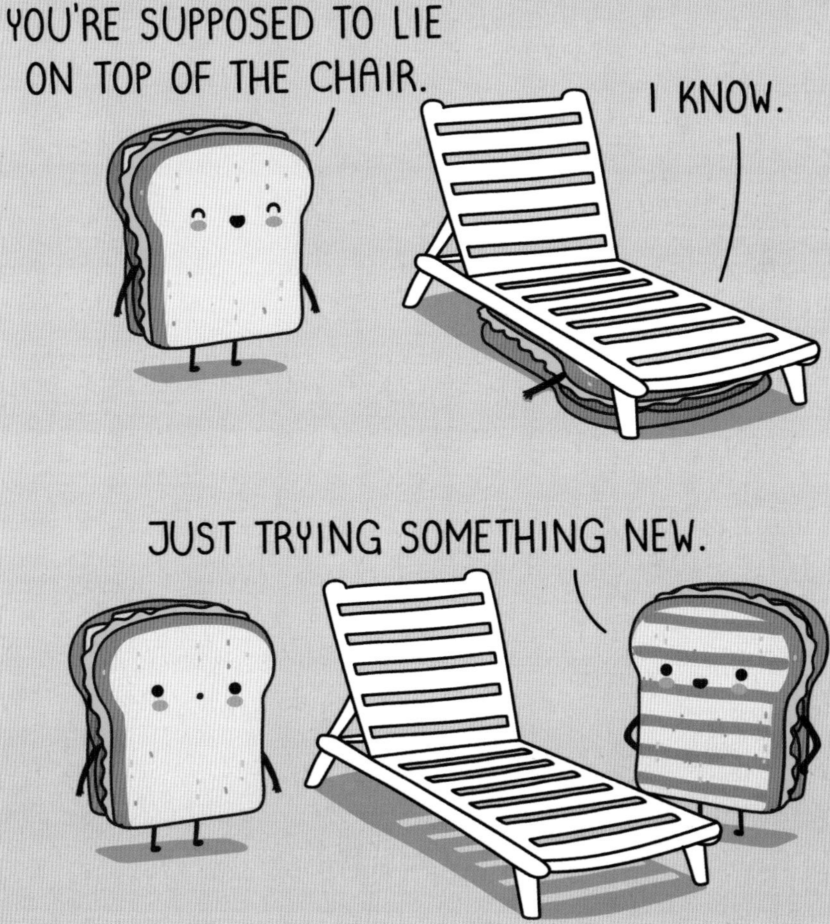
YOU'RE SUPPOSED TO LIE ON TOP OF THE CHAIR.
I KNOW.
JUST TRYING SOMETHING NEW.

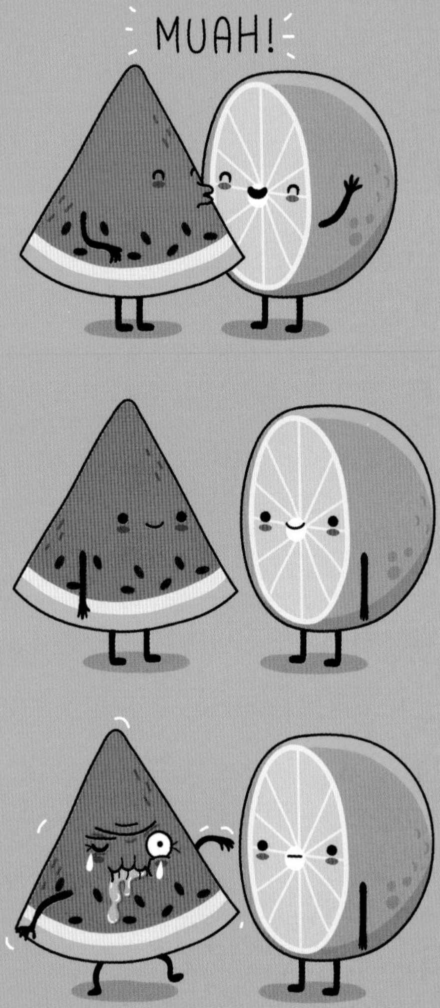
MUAH!

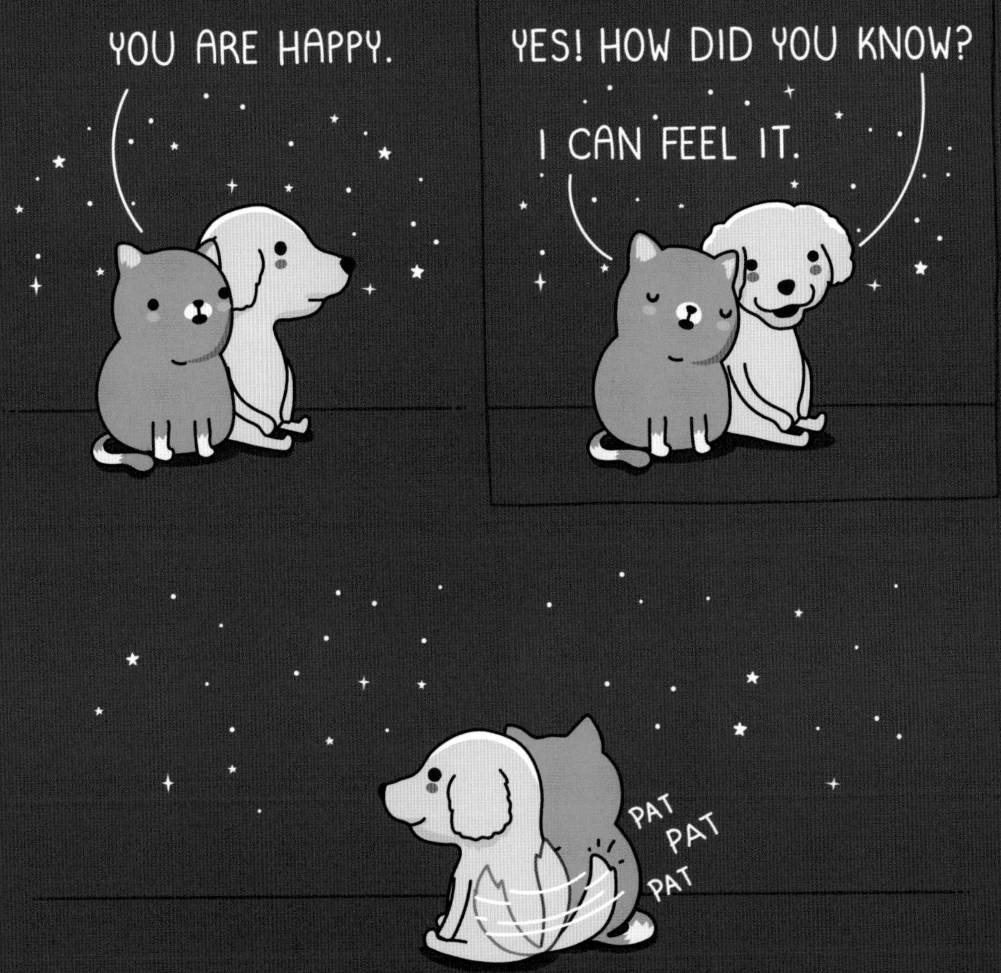
YOU ARE HAPPY.
YES! HOW DID YOU KNOW?
I CAN FEEL IT.
PAT
PAT
PAT

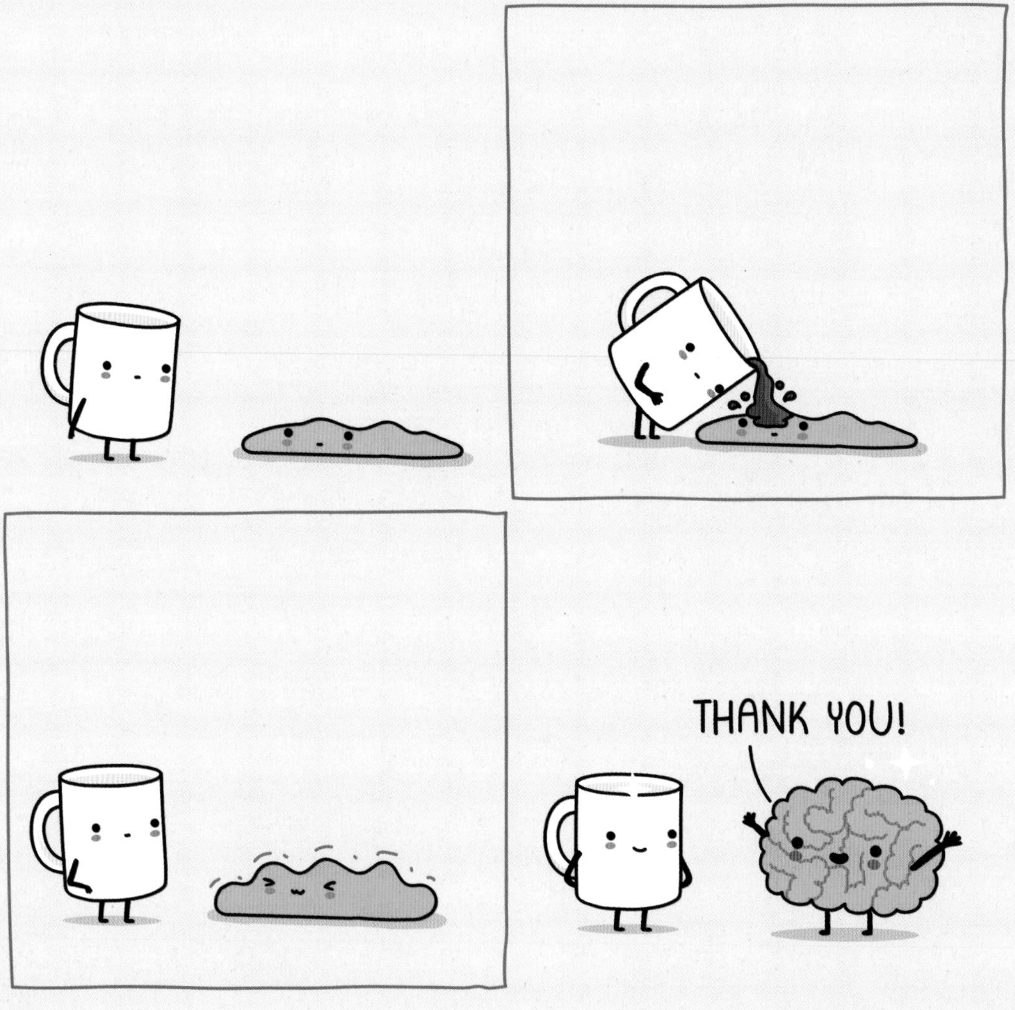
THANK YOU!

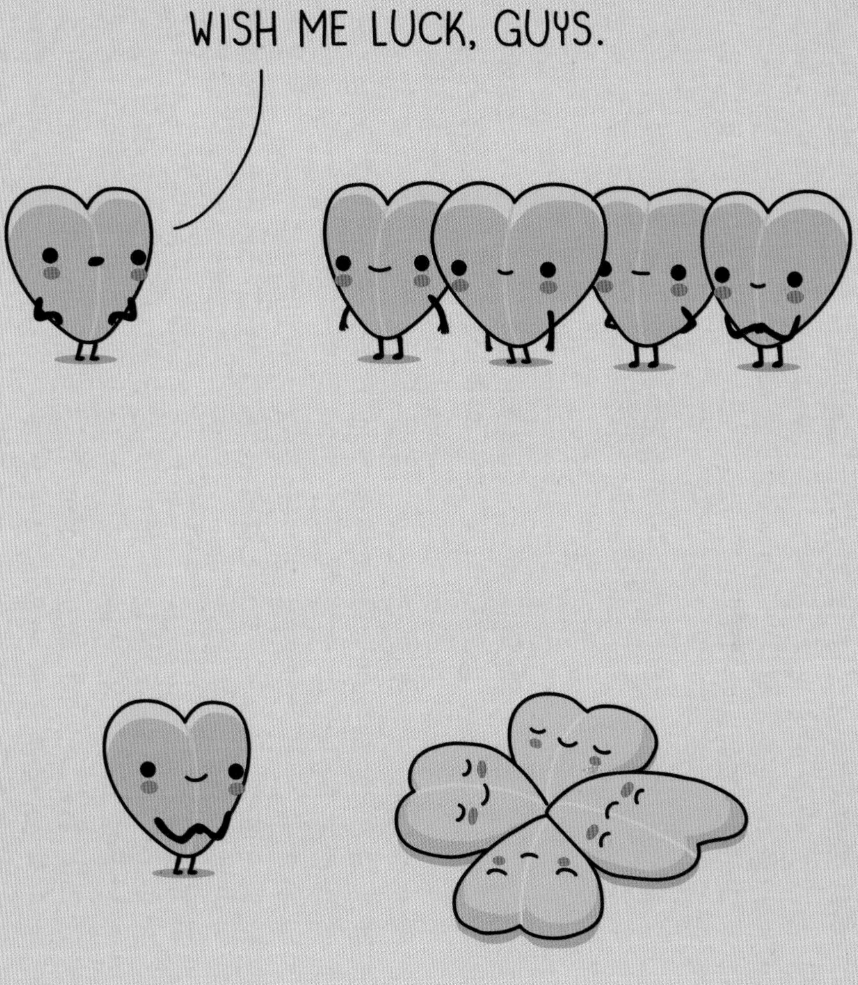
WISH ME LUCK, GUYS.

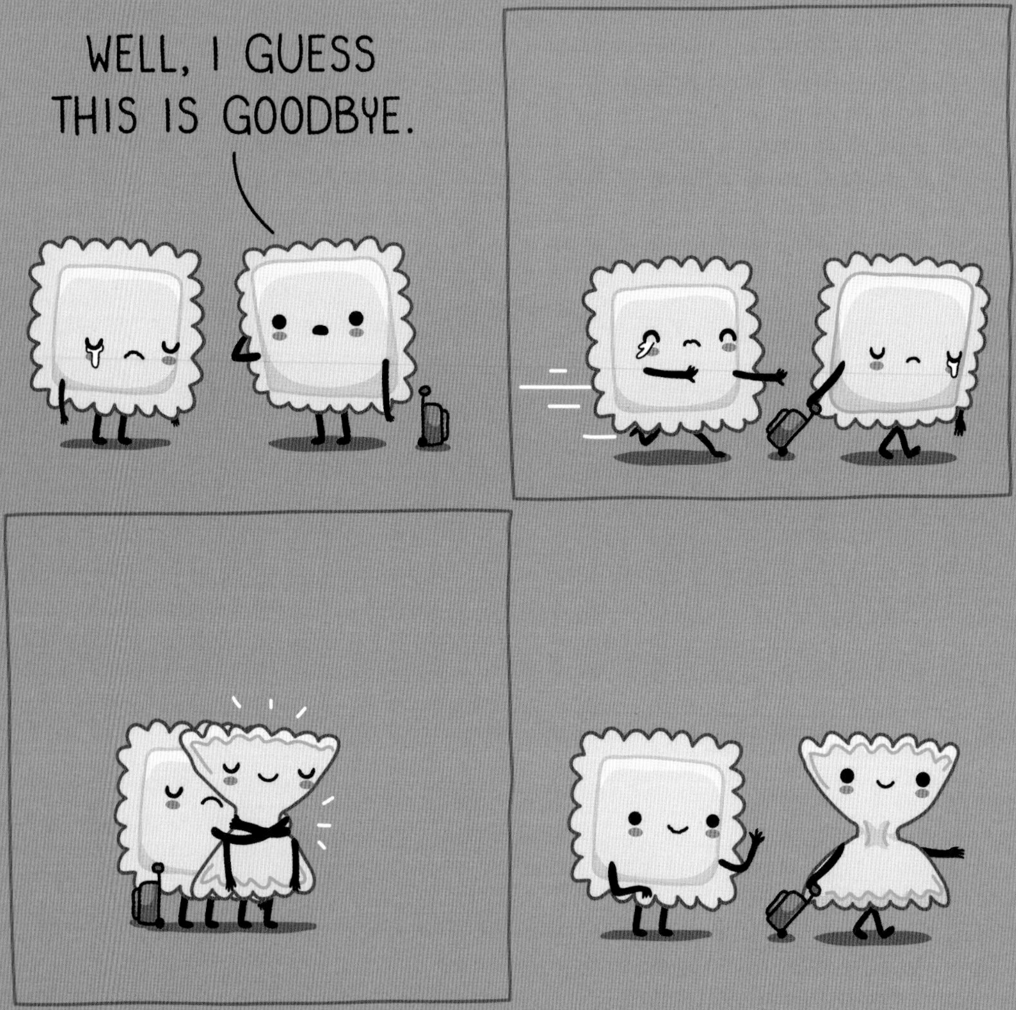
WELL, I GUESS THIS IS GOODBYE.

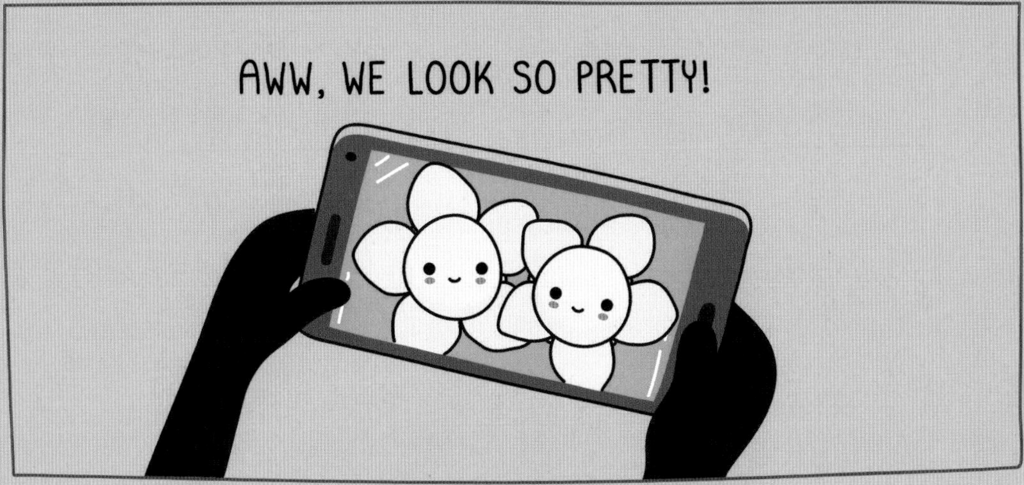
AWW, WE LOOK SO PRETTY!

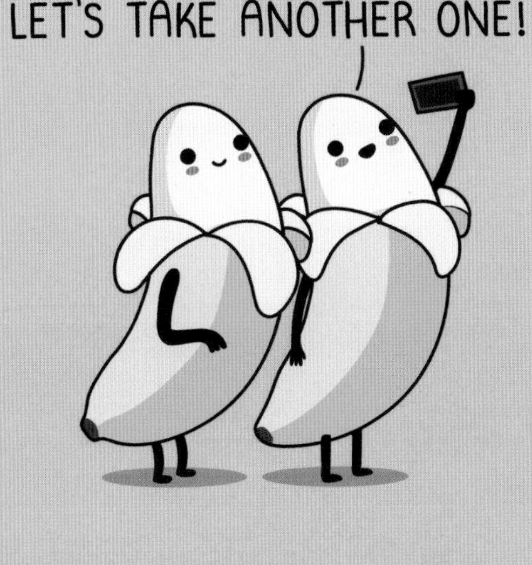
LET'S TAKE ANOTHER ONE!

I LOVE HUGGING YOU!
CALM DOWN... IT'LL ONLY BE FOR A YEAR OR TWO.
FINALLY!
HERE I COME!

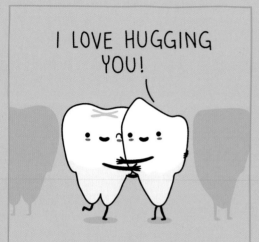

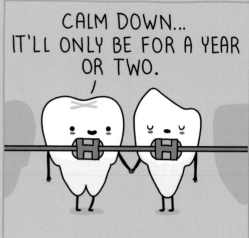

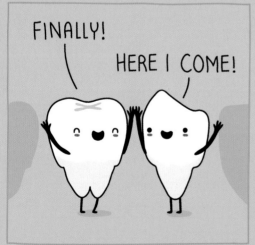

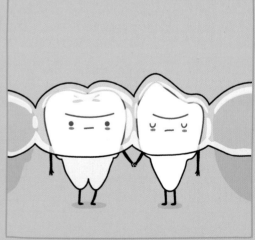

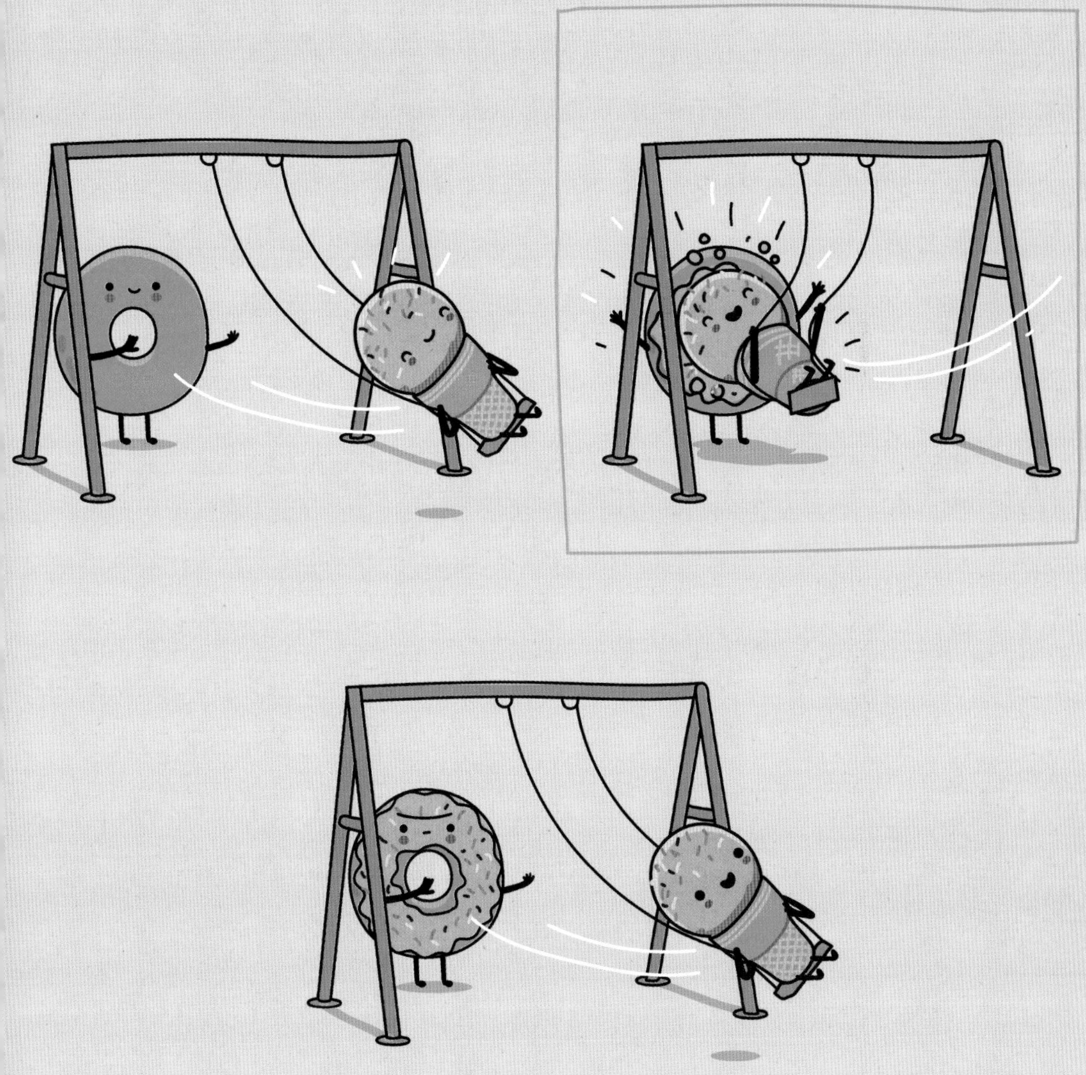

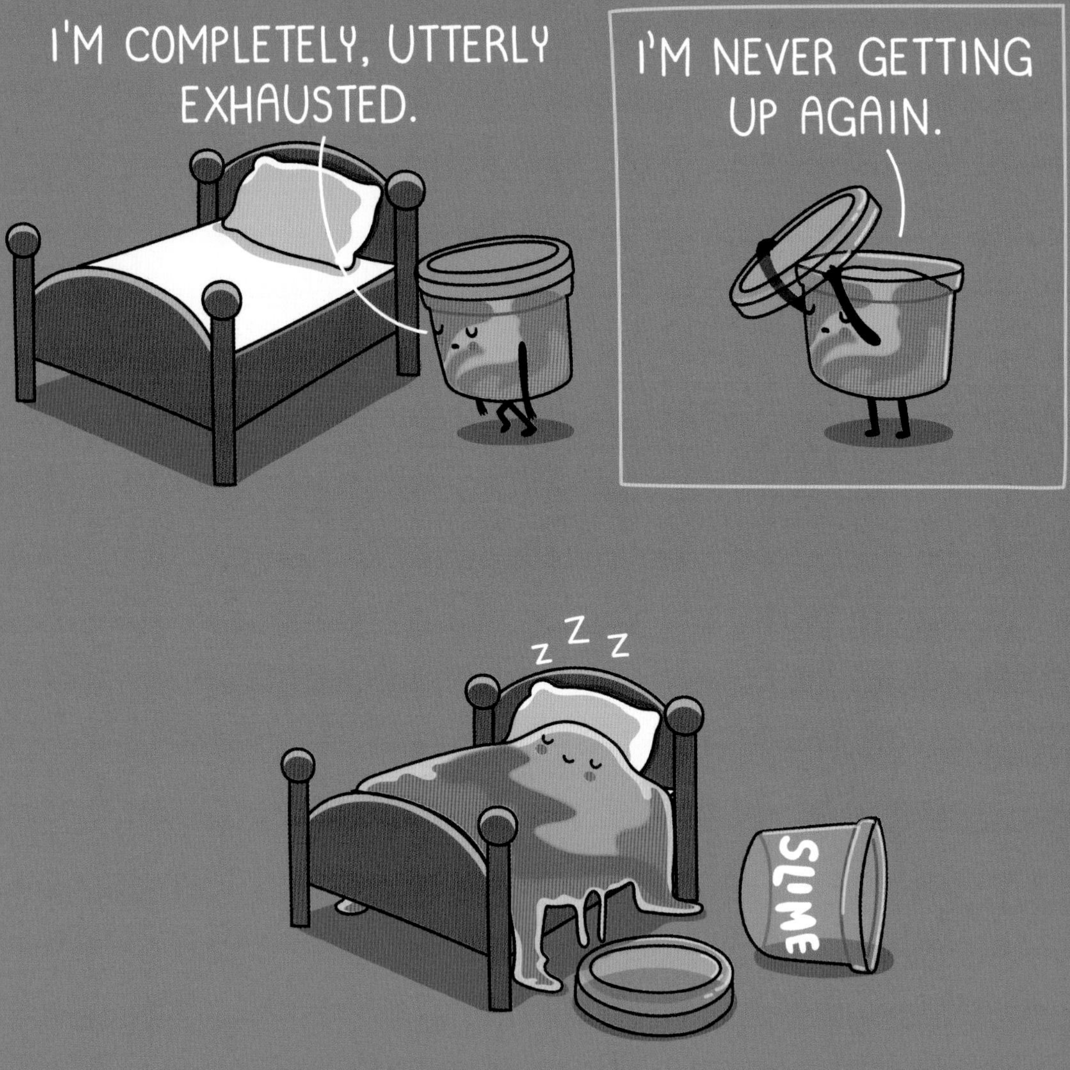
I'M COMPLETELY, UTTERLY EXHAUSTED.
I'M NEVER GETTING UP AGAIN.
Z Z Z
SLIME

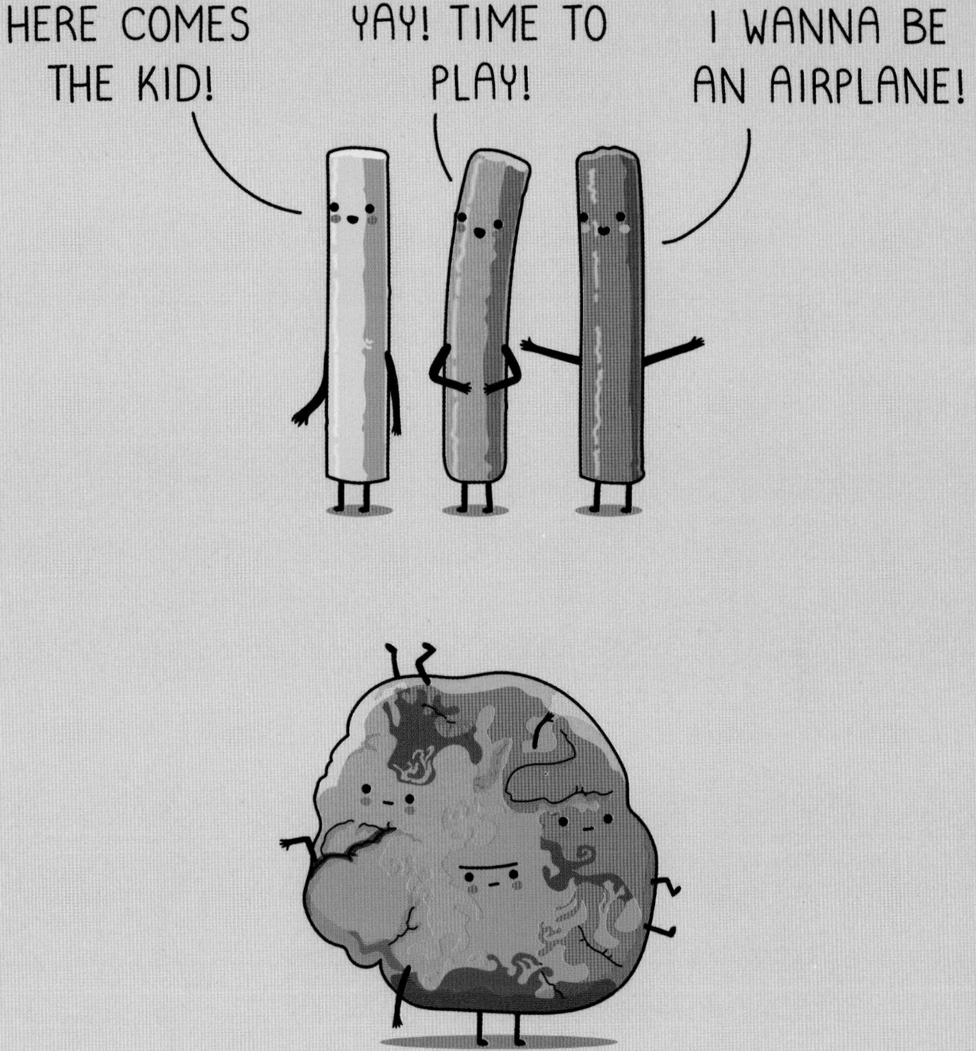
HERE COMES THE KID!
YAY! TIME TO PLAY!
I WANNA BE AN AIRPLANE!

HELP, I'VE FALLEN AND CAN'T GET OUT!

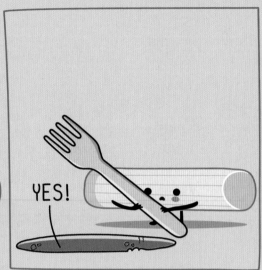

YES!

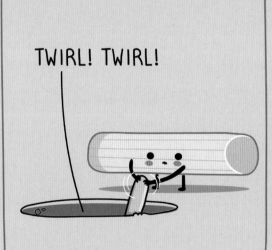

TWIRL! TWIRL!

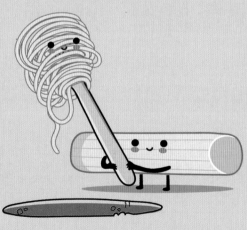

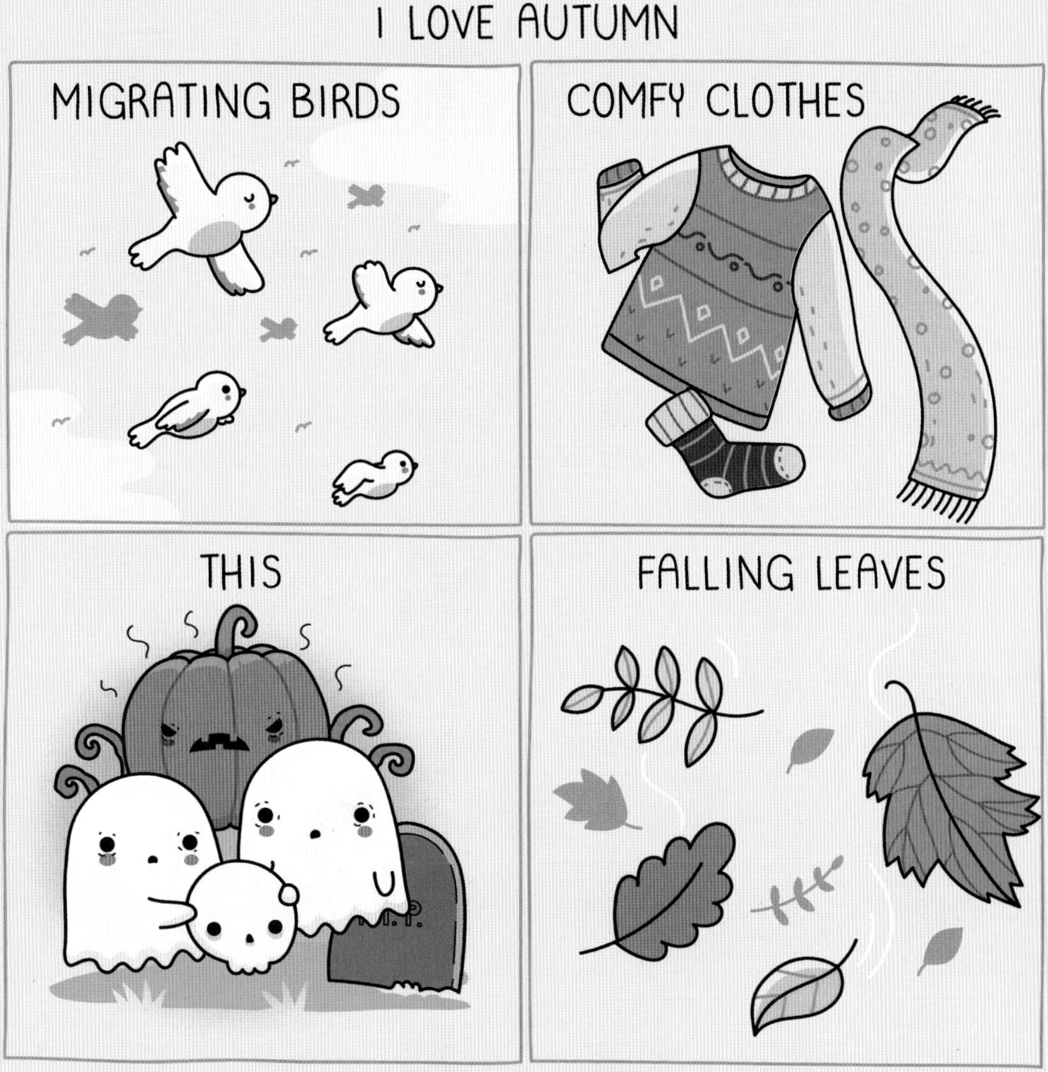
I LOVE AUTUMN
MIGRATING BIRDS
COMFY CLOTHES
THIS
FALLING LEAVES

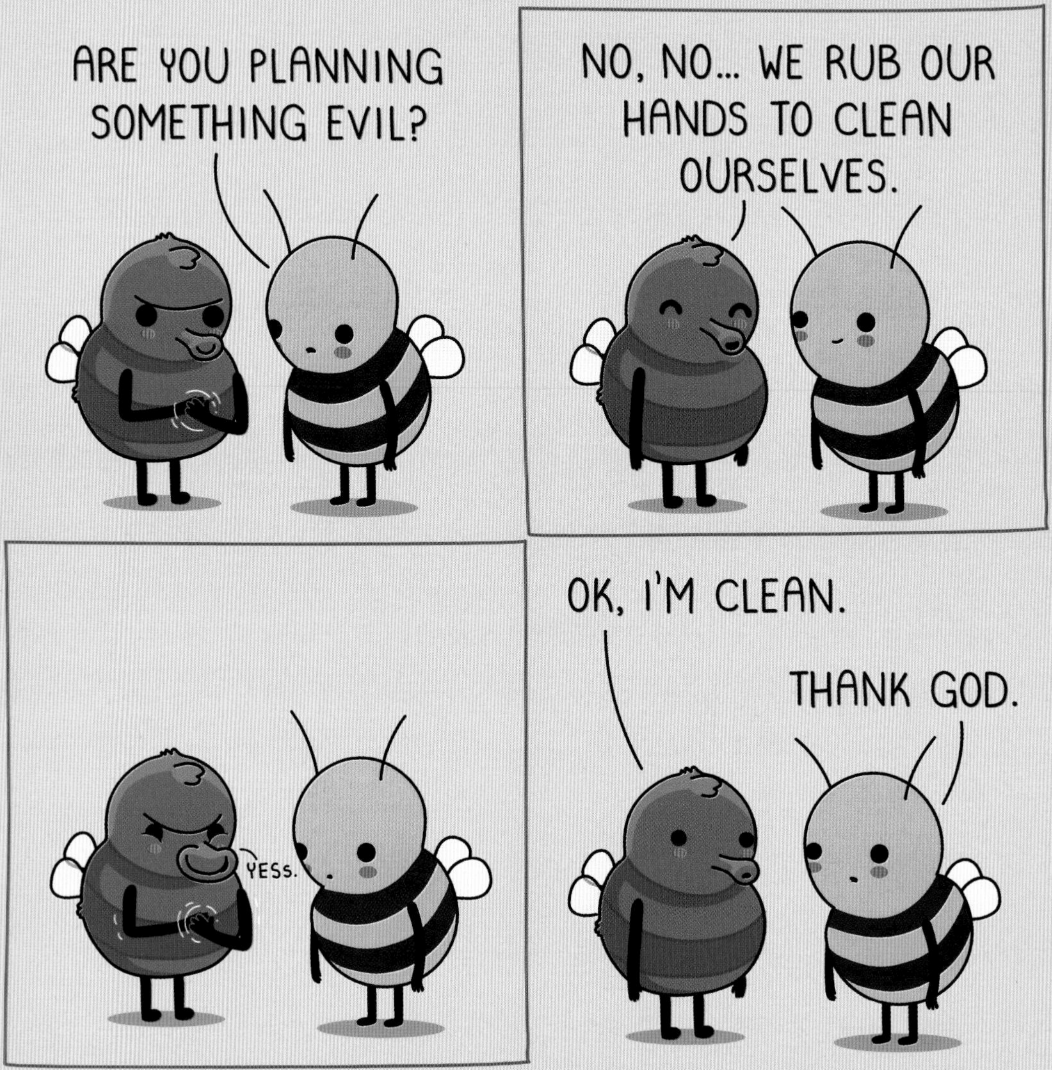
ARE YOU PLANNING SOMETHING EVIL?
NO, NO... WE RUB OUR HANDS TO CLEAN OURSELVES.
YESS.
OK, I'M CLEAN.
THANK GOD.

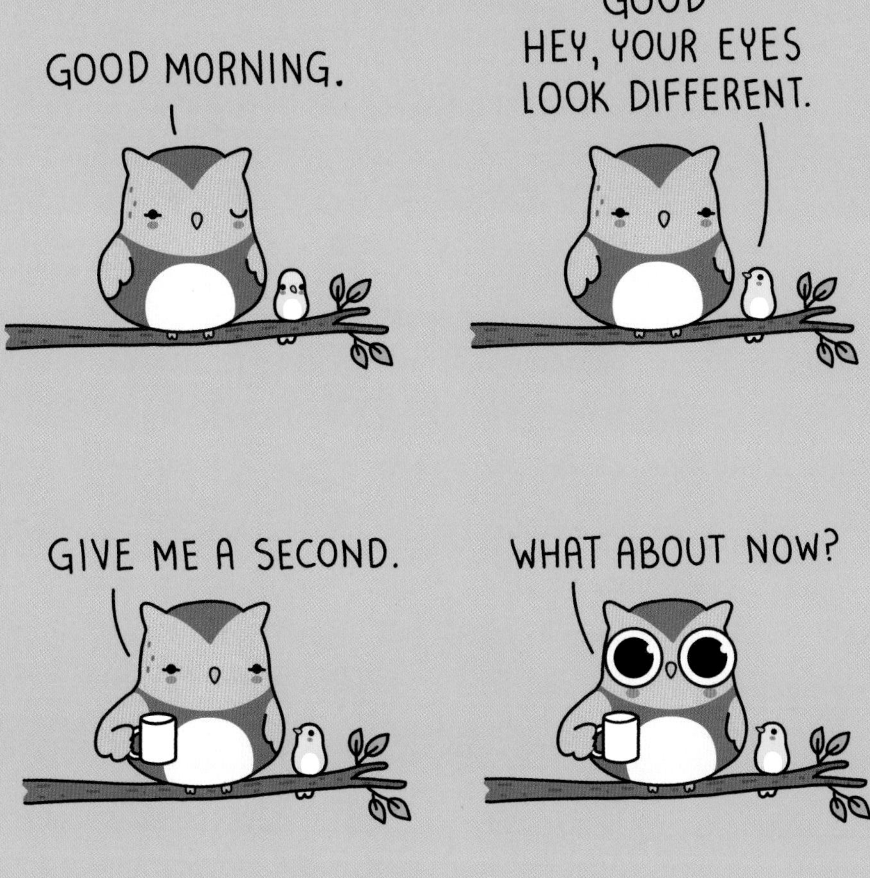
GOOD MORNING.
GOOD-
HEY, YOUR EYES
LOOK DIFFERENT.
GIVE ME A SECOND.
WHAT ABOUT NOW?

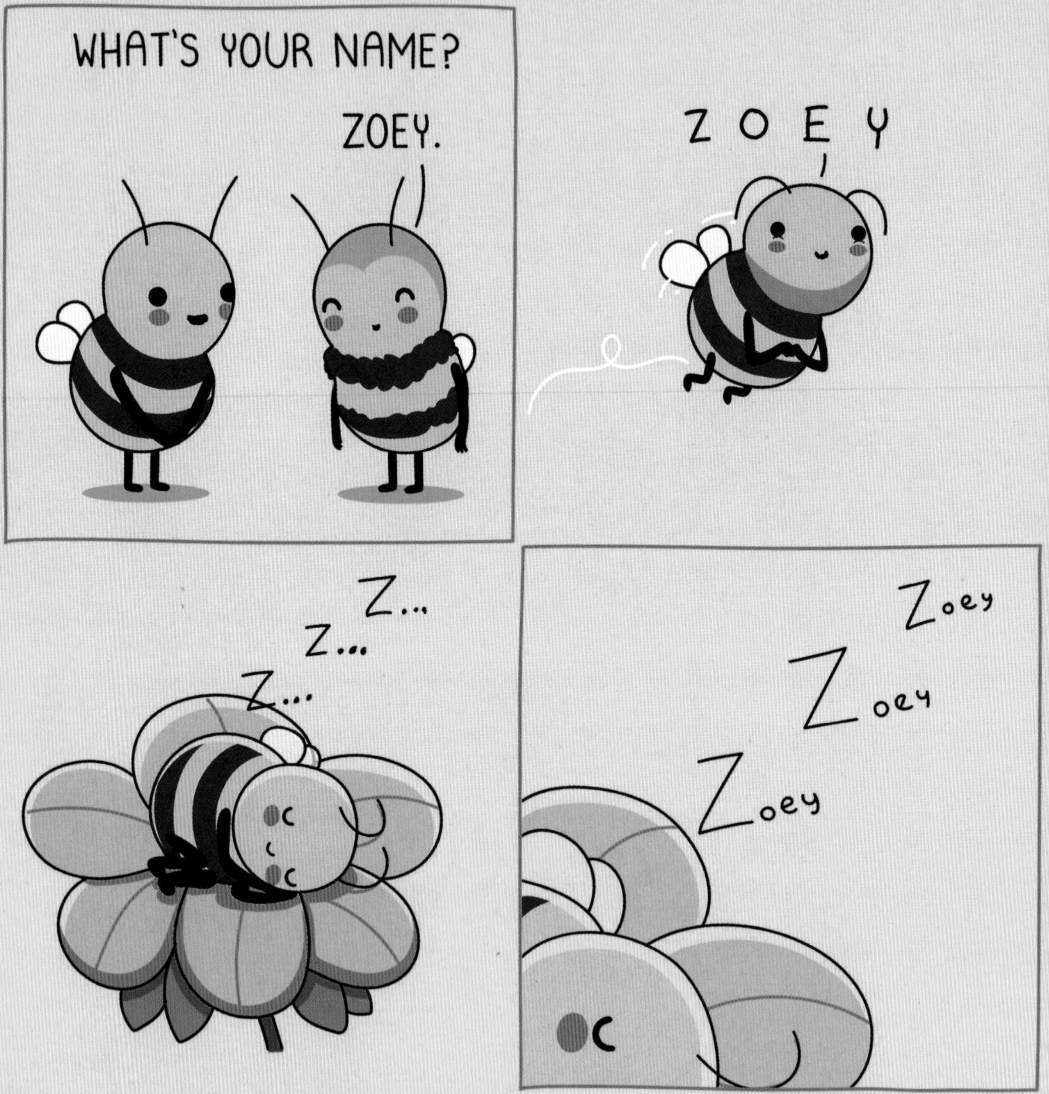
WHAT'S YOUR NAME?
ZOEY.
Z O E Y
Z...
Z...
Z...
Zoey
Zoey
Zoey

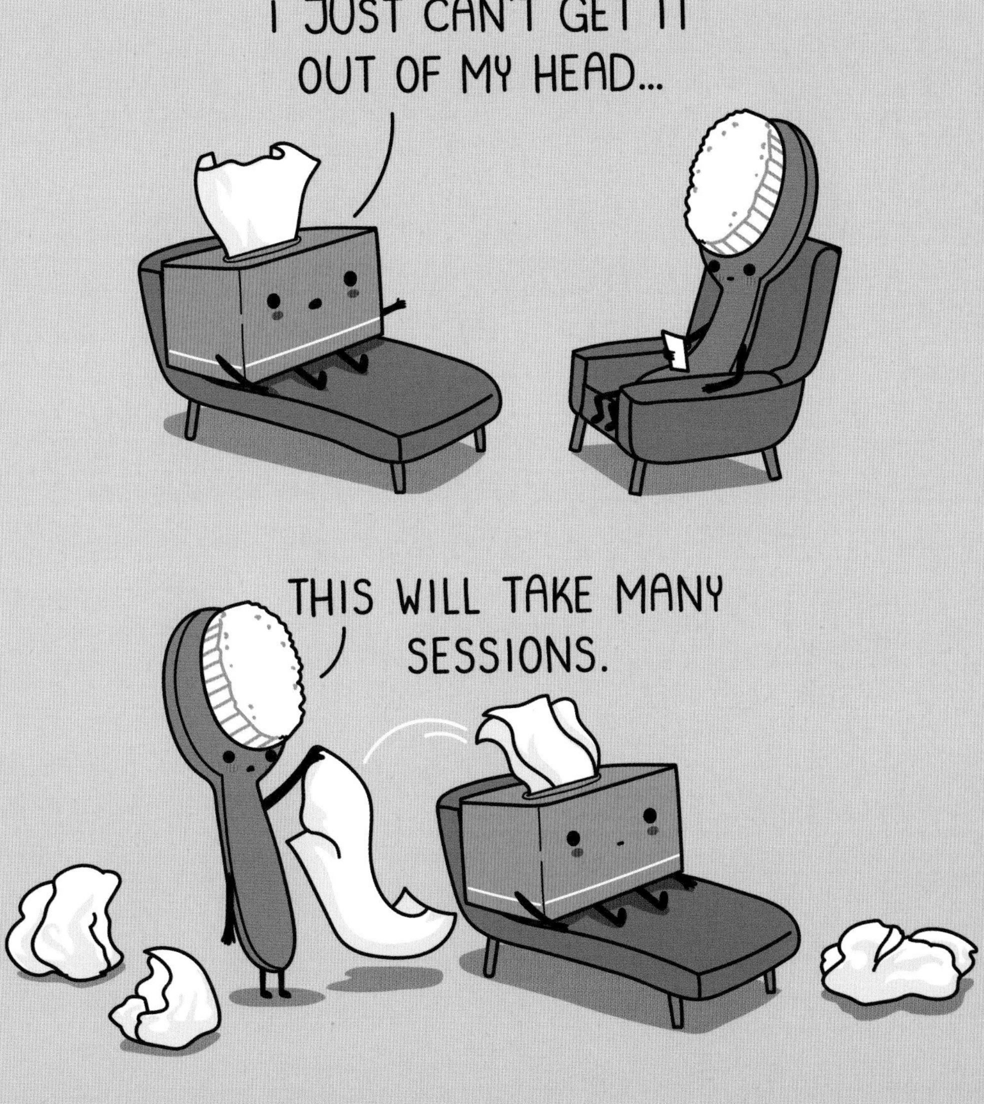
I JUST CAN'T GET IT OUT OF MY HEAD...
THIS WILL TAKE MANY SESSIONS.

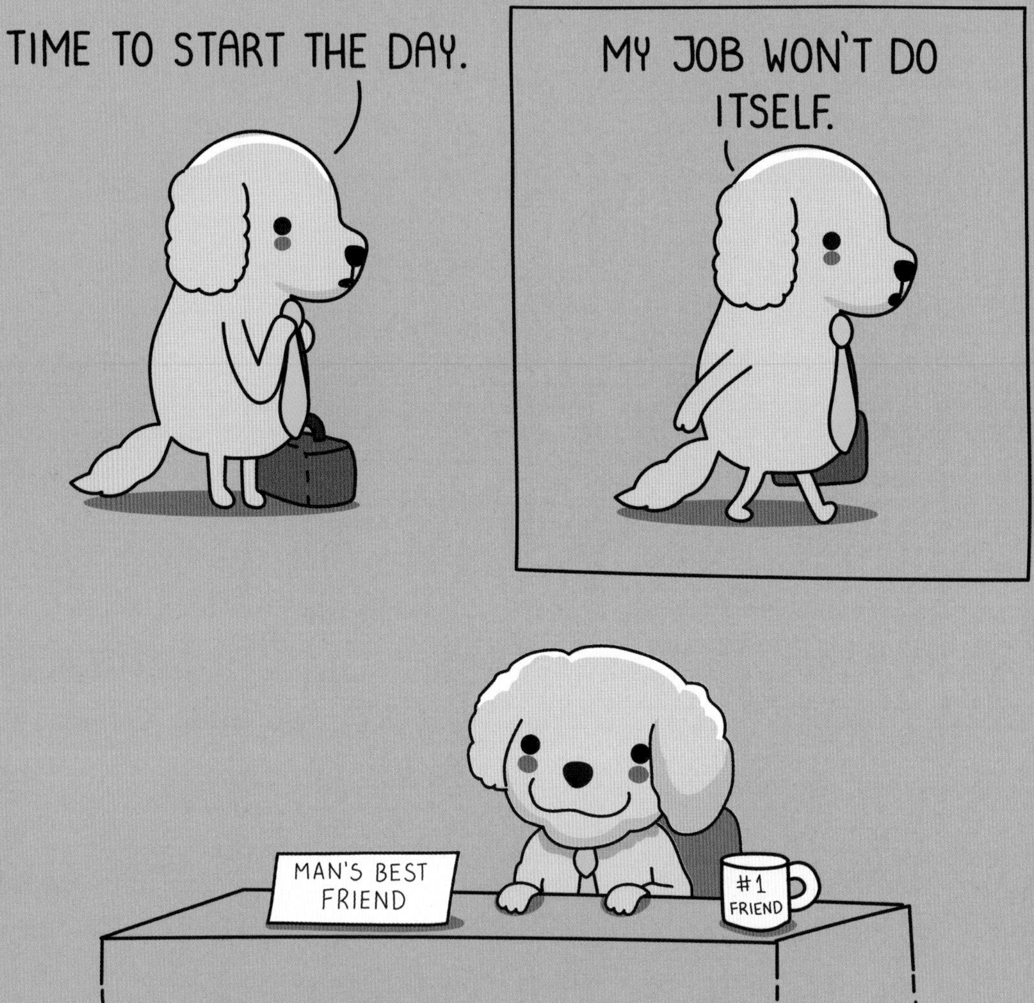
TIME TO START THE DAY.
MY JOB WON'T DO ITSELF.
MAN'S BEST FRIEND
#1 FRIEND

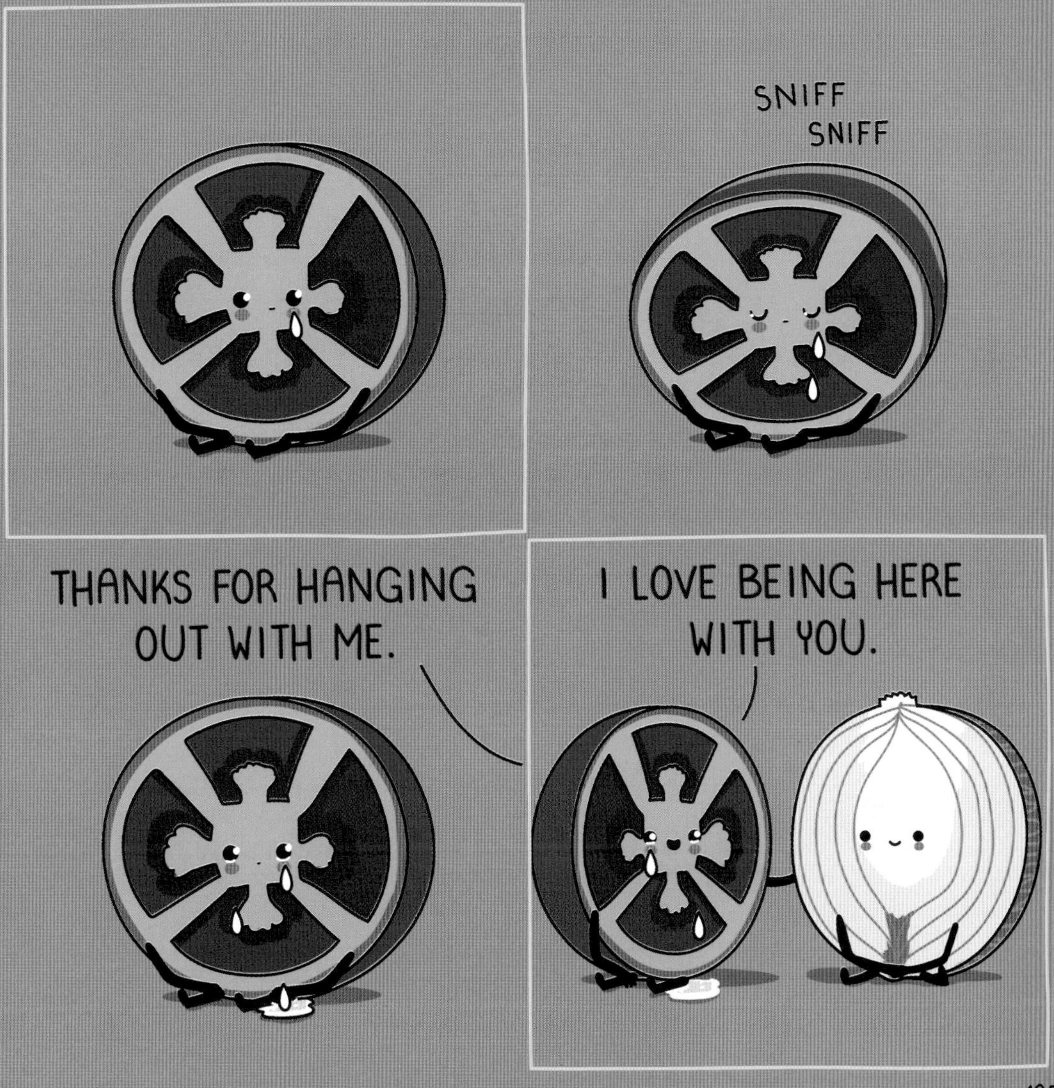
SNIFF
SNIFF
THANKS FOR HANGING OUT WITH ME.
I LOVE BEING HERE WITH YOU.

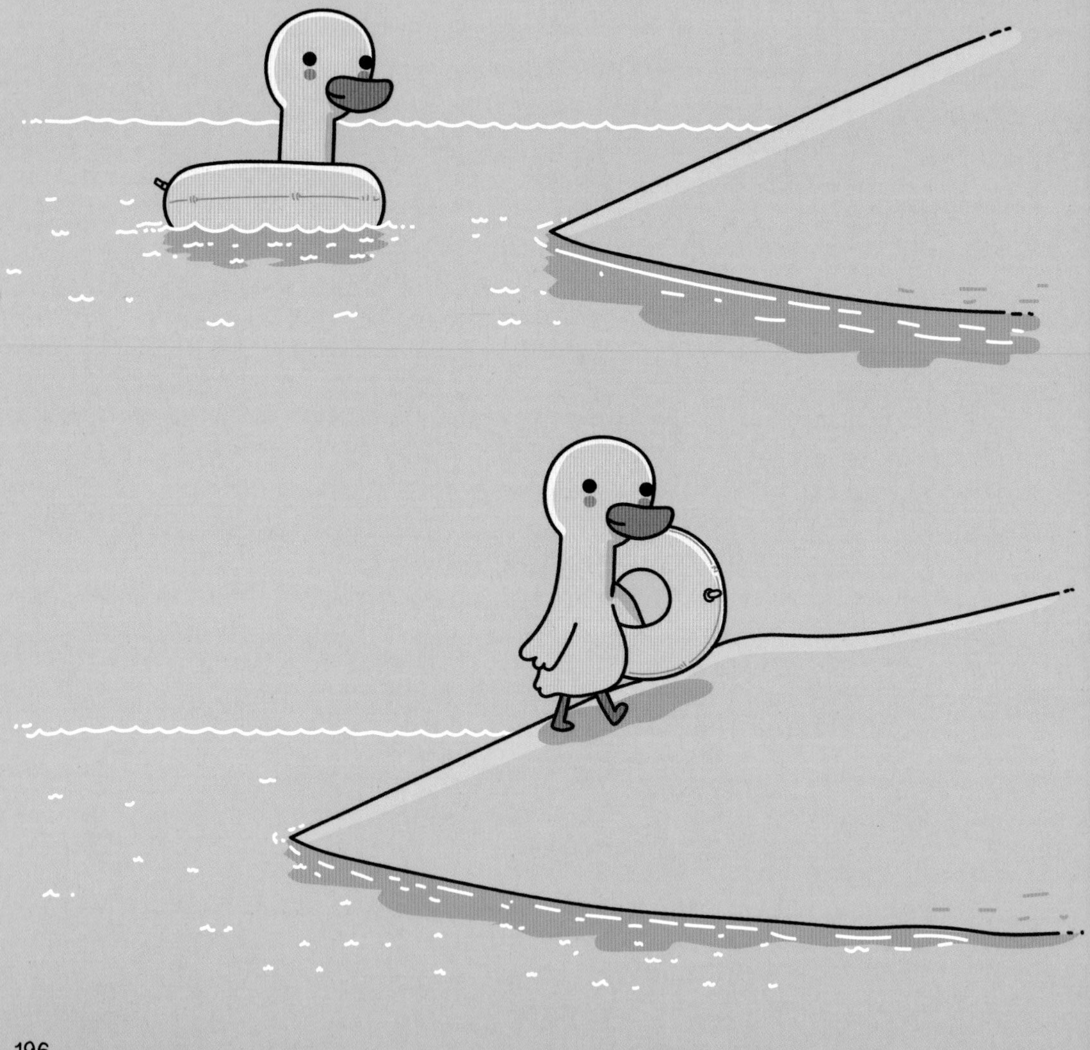

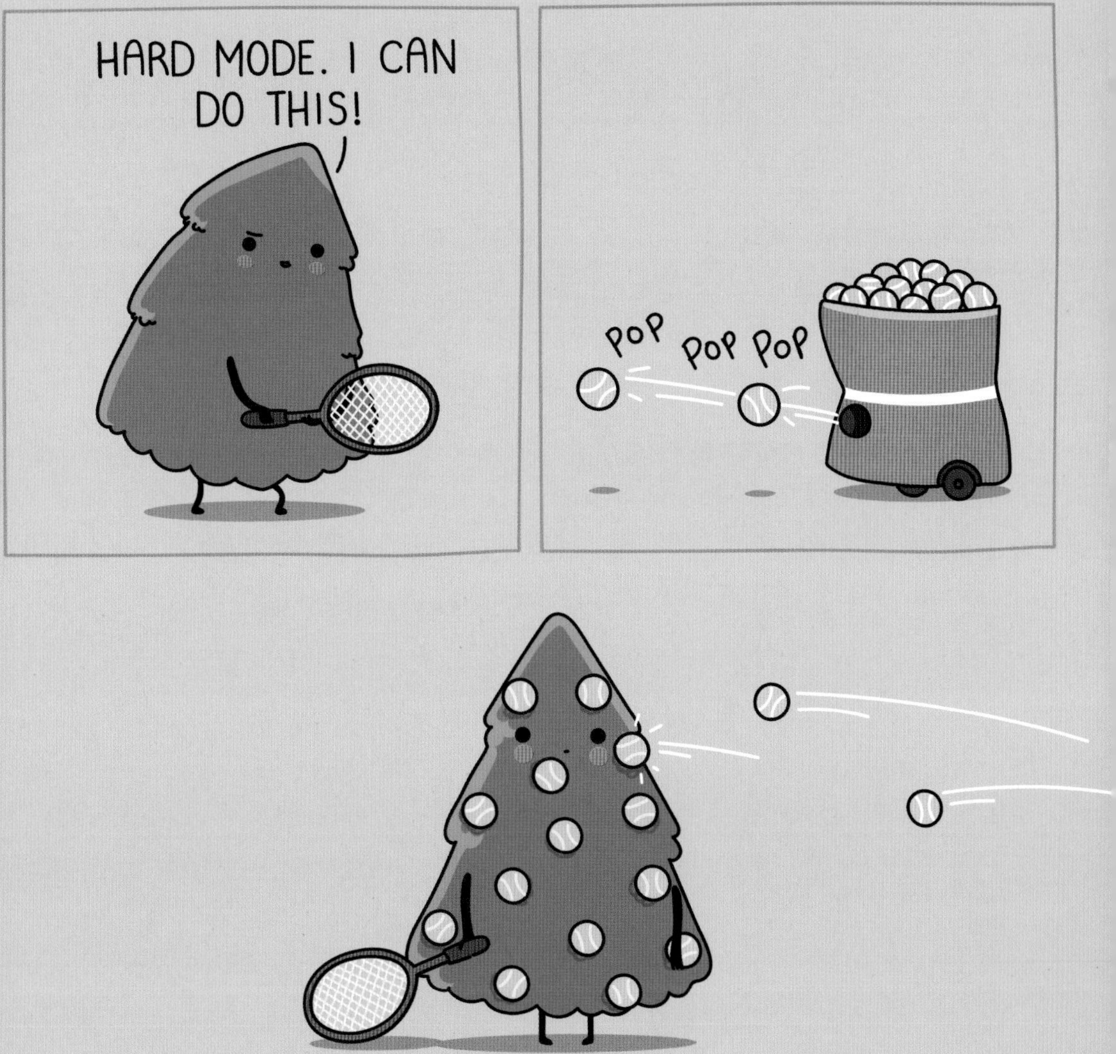
HARD MODE. I CAN DO THIS!
POP
POP POP

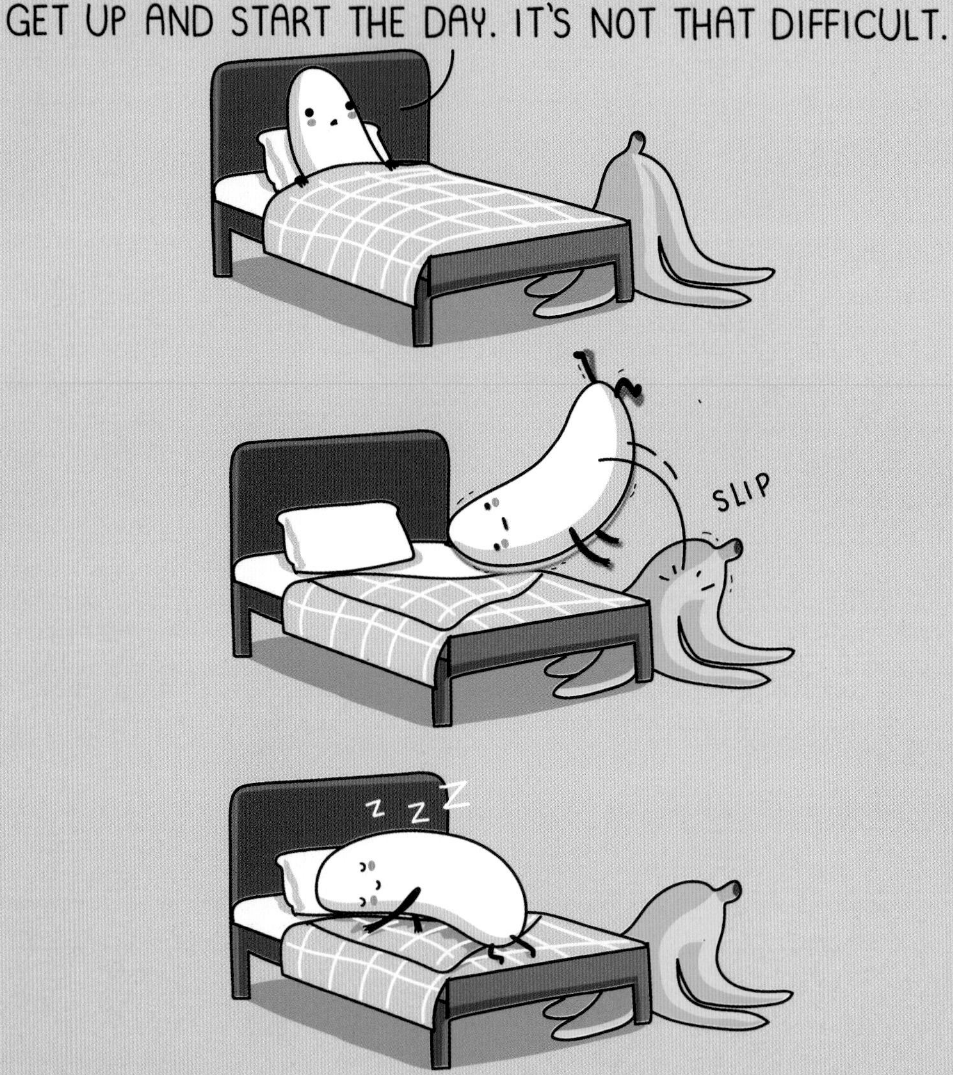
GET UP AND START THE DAY. IT'S NOT THAT DIFFICULT.
SLIP
Z Z Z

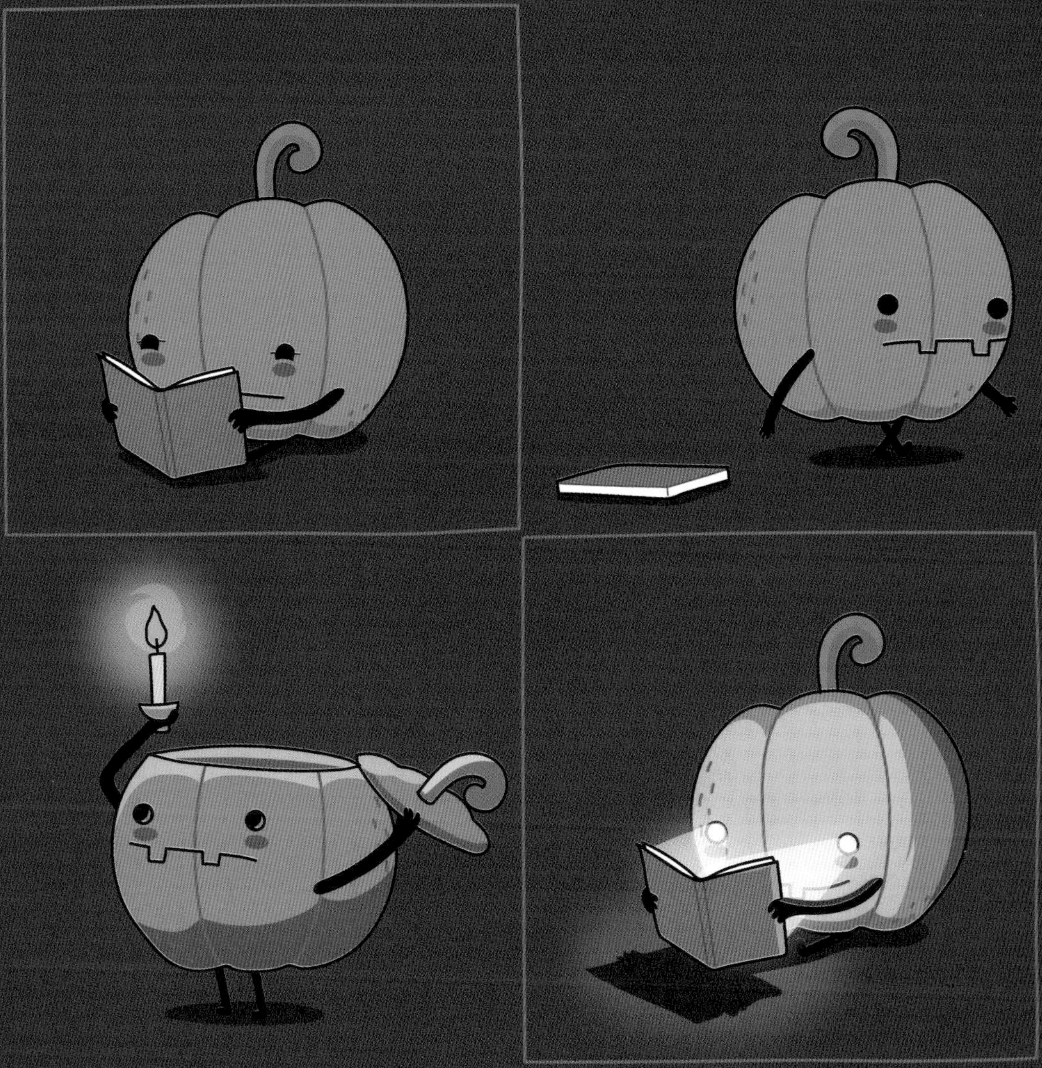

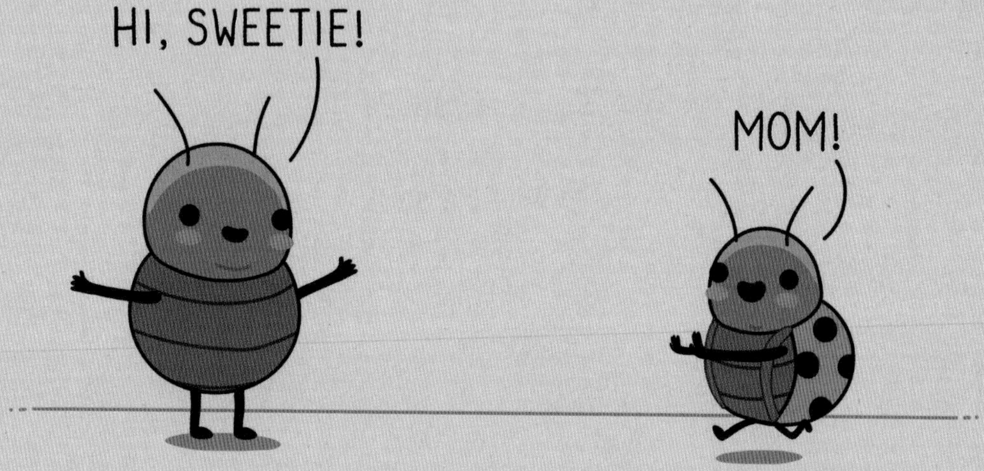
HI, SWEETIE!
MOM!

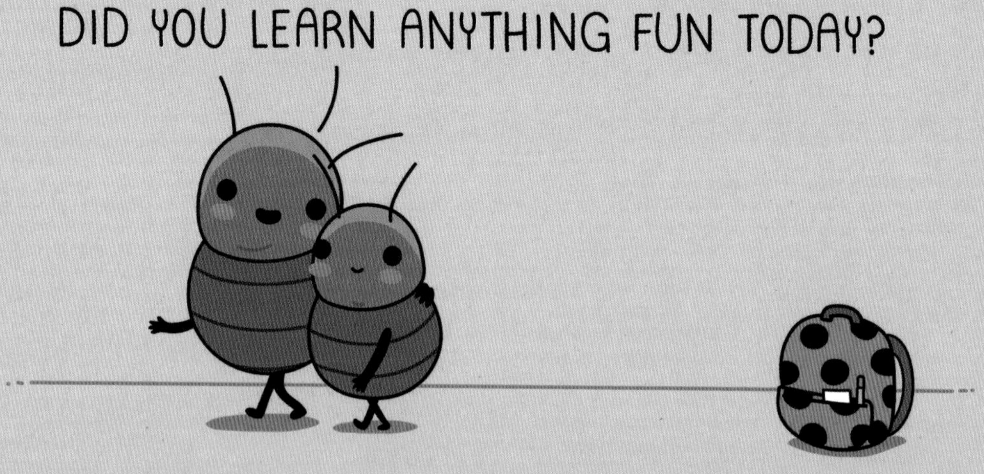
DID YOU LEARN ANYTHING FUN TODAY?

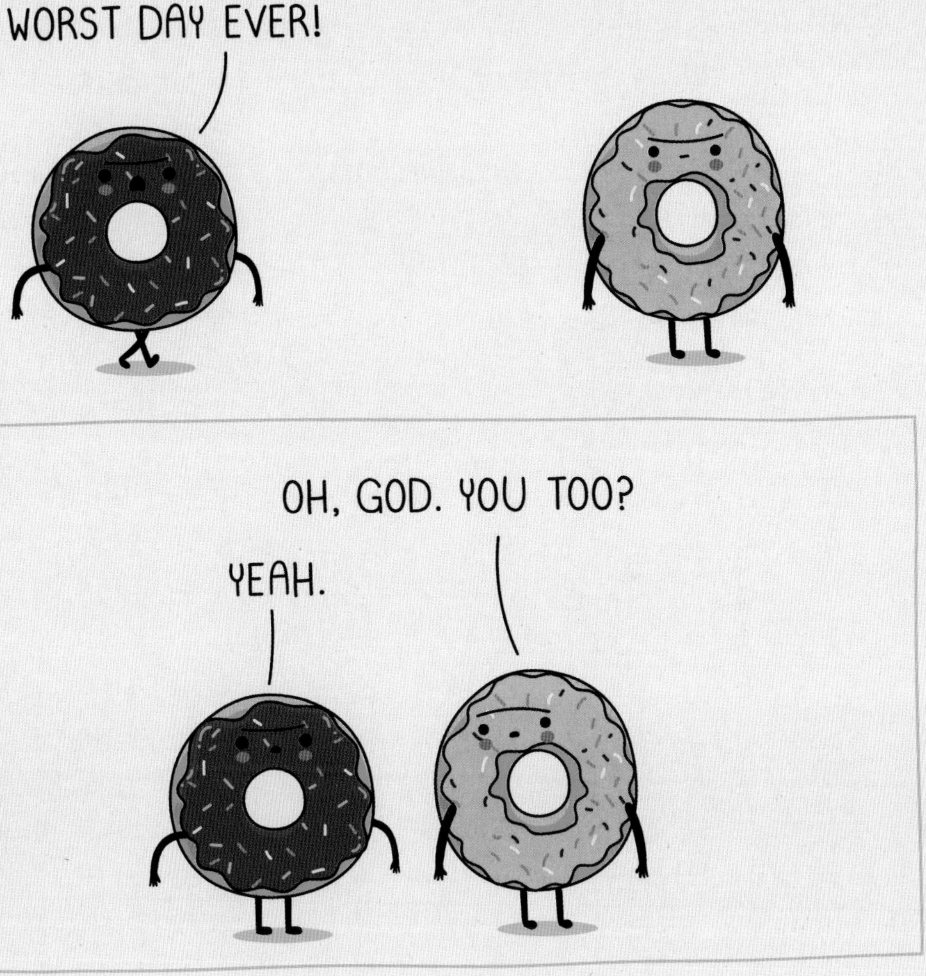
WORST DAY EVER!
OH, GOD. YOU TOO?
YEAH.

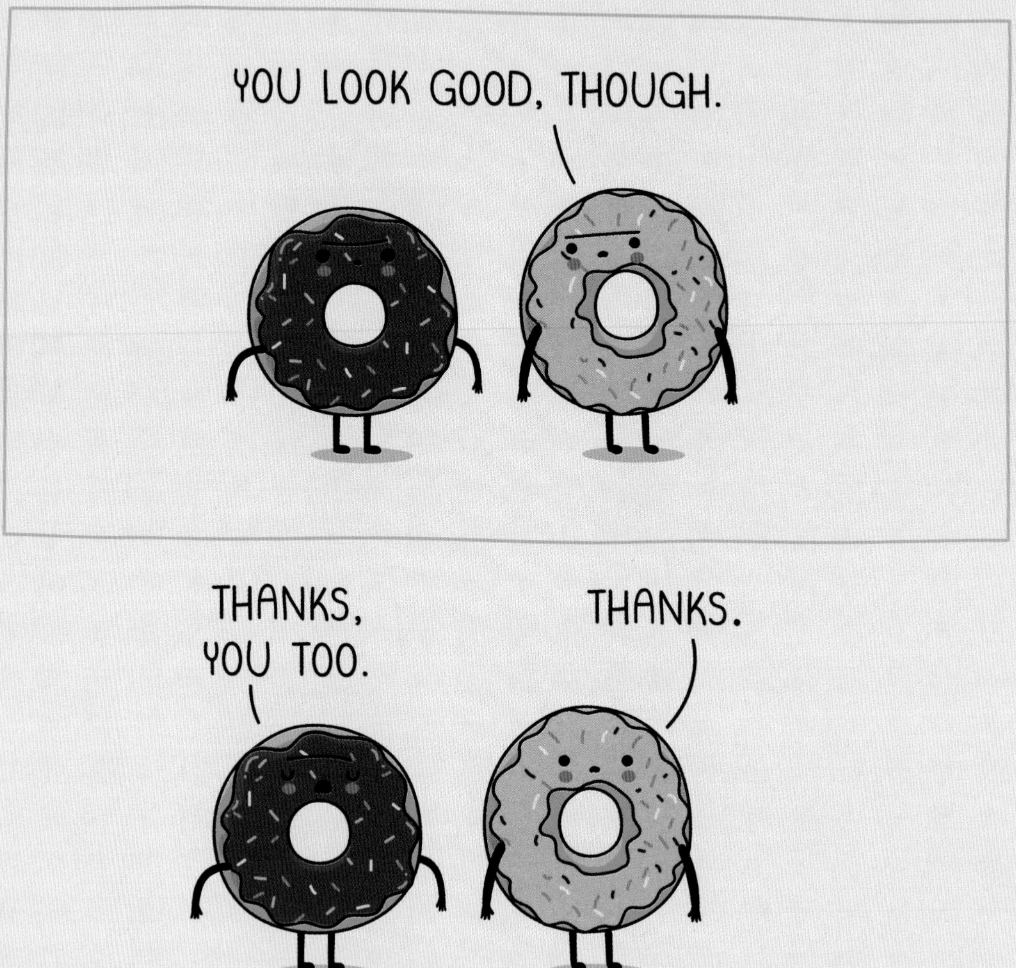
YOU LOOK GOOD, THOUGH.
THANKS, YOU TOO.
THANKS.

About the Author

Andrés J. Colmenares is a Colombian
self-taught illustrator and the creator of
Wawawiwa Comics, which he describes as
being like a "visual hug" for his millions of
readers around the world. He lives in Bogotá,
Colombia, with his wife, Viviana Navas,
and their two children.

You can follow his work at
wawawiwacomics.com.